A UNIFIED APPROACH TO SUBCHAPTERS K & S

By

George Mundstock

Dorsey & Whitney
Professor of Law
University of Minnesota

AMERICAN CASEBOOK SERIES®

WEST GROUP

A THOMSON COMPANY

ST. PAUL, MINN., 2002

American Casebook Series, and the West Group symbol
are registered trademarks used herein under license.

COPYRIGHT © 2002 By WEST GROUP
           610 Opperman Drive
           P.O. Box 64526
           St. Paul, MN 55164–0526
           1–800–328–9352

ISBN 0–314–24499–9

 *TEXT IS PRINTED ON 10% POST CONSUMER RECYCLED PAPER*

It's not my fault!
— Han Solo

*

Preface

For over a decade, I refused to teach partnership taxation because I though it to be unteachable. Then, the University of Miami Tax LL.M. class of 1999 talked me back into the fray of Subchapter K. Separation had made the heart grow fonder. It was suggested that I should do a casebook. Douglas Powell of West Group was interested. I thank you all.

This book would not have been possible without having as a reference William S. McKee, William F. Nelson & Robert L. Whitmire, *Federal Taxation of Partnerships and Partners* (3d ed. 1996 & Supp.). I learned a great deal from teaching materials that William Andrews was kind enough to share with me and let me use. Teaching from Jeffrey L. Kwall, *The Federal Income Taxation of Corporations, Partnerships, Limited Liability Companies, and Their Owners* (2d ed. 2000), and Stephen A. Lind, Stephen Schwarz, Daniel J. Lathrope, and Joshua D. Rosenberg, *Fundamentals of Partnership Taxation* (5th ed. 1998), provided very useful insights.

My work on this book was supported by The University of Minnesota Law School and The University of Miami School of Law. The Deloitte & Touche Scholarship Fund at the University of Minnesota made it possible for John Seiner, JD 2003, to provide me valuable help in completing the manuscript.

Finally, thanks to all of the lawyers over the years who have trusted me with their clients' Subchapter K problems. To them, I say: I do not care how much you scream, there is a 751(b) problem with your transaction!

As is customary, in the longer excerpts, omissions, including footnotes, are not clearly indicated.

George Mundstock

January 2002

*

Summary of Contents

*

Table of Contents

Table of Cases

The principal cases are in bold type. Cases cited or discussed in the text
are roman type. References are to pages. Cases cited in principal
cases and within other quoted materials are not included.

*

Table of Statutes

*

Table of Internal Revenue Code Sections

Table of Treasury Regulations

*

Table of Revenue Procedures

*

Table of Revenue Rulings

*

A UNIFIED APPROACH
TO SUBCHAPTERS
K & S

*

Chapter I

INTRODUCTION

A. PARTNERSHIPS AND TAXES

1. Subchapter K

This text is about Subchapter K of the Internal Revenue Code, the federal income tax rules that apply to partnerships and other partnership-like state-law forms of business organization (like LLCs) and their partners or other equity owners (like members of LLCs).[1] Subchapter S, which taxes certain corporations much like partnerships, is reviewed as well.[2] Students familiar with Subchapter C, the corporate rules, will find Subchapter K to be similar.[3] Subchapter K, like Subchapter C, focuses on business transactions, such as distributions to the (equity) owners of the business and changes in the form or structure of the business organization

Subchapter K is extraordinarily complicated—even more involved than Subchapter C. Under Subchapter C, most of the complexity arises from applying fairly simple rules to intricate transactions. In contrast, Subchapter K provides complicated rules for even the most straightforward transactions. This complexity is due (i) to Congress adopting a hybrid approach to taxing partnerships and (ii) to Congress and the Treasury providing detailed rules for many of the remarkable variety of economic arrangements that can be effected using partnerships.[4] In order to avoid becoming lost in the legal mechanism, this text, rather than examining specific rules in isolation, instead looks at how various rules work together to tax entire transactions. It is hoped that this exposition, by putting the complexity in context, will be the most helpful to students trying to come to grips with Subchapter K.

---

1. Subchapter K contains Code Sections 701 through 777.

2. Sections 1361 through 1378 constitute Subchapter S of the Code.

3. These corporate rules are in Sections 301 through 385.

4. What is now Subchapter C developed early in the 20th Century, when Congress generally adopted more broad-brush rules; while Subchapter K first appeared in 1954 and has been extensively supplemented starting in 1976, an era of more detailed tax legislation and regulation.

1

2. How State Business Organization Law Impacts Tax Rules

Partnership transactions are controlled by substantive state partnership (or similar) law. This law, in turn, influenced the tax law considerably, as will be seen throughout this text. Thus, some background in state partnership law is important in understanding Subchapter K, and will be set out later in this chapter. Before looking at this state law, however, a brief consideration of how state law influences tax law is in order. Corporations provide an handy and straightforward case study.

Originally, corporations were an extension of the power of the sovereign—entities created by the state (or, earlier, the church). In the U.S., at first, each corporation was created by a legislature individually, in order to implement a specific public or quasi-public project. Then, corporations with a private, for-profit purpose were authorized by legislatures on a case-by-case basis. Finally, the progenitors of the modern general corporate statutes were enacted. Thus, the modern private corporation is a thing created by sovereign power: Modern corporations are children of their authorizing statutes, only come into existence when filed with the state (at the office of the Secretary of State or of the Corporations Commissioner), and so on.

The tax law applicable to corporations reflects this state-law heritage. Corporations are taxed as entities: They have their own taxable incomes. Shareholders are viewed as separate from their corporations. For example, corporate earnings are not taxable to shareholders until distributed to them by their corporation in cash or as other non-stock property. Similarly, the sale of corporate stock is viewed as the disposition of an interest in the corporate entity, not as a sale of interests in the corporation's assets.[5]

Corporate tax rules that treat corporations as entities seem natural. This demonstrates how much our—and Congress'—view of corporations has been framed by the entity character of corporations under state law. There are other views of the corporation, however, which lead to different tax rules. For example, under the Civil War income taxes, private corporations were not taxed as entities. Rather, corporations' incomes were taxed directly to their shareholders (which was similar to how partnerships are taxed today).[6]

---

5. Sections 336(e) and 338 can provide an election for asset-sale treatment in stock sale transactions.

6. The current corporate tax regime creates a "double tax" on corporate income. Earnings are taxed as earned to the corporation, and taxed again to its shareholders when the earnings are distributed as dividends (and, perhaps, a third time, if the earnings increase stock value and stock is sold so as to trigger capital gains tax on this increased value). Many are troubled by this extra tax on doing business in corporate form. They would integrate the corporate tax into the individual tax, much like current Subchapter K. Any analysis of the economics of the double tax requires a sense of who bears the extra tax, however. Currently, the economic evidence is inconclusive. Moreover, as this text demonstrates, entity taxation has powerful simplicity advantages over pass-through treatment. Thus, the trend is toward an entity tax. *See generally* George Mundstock, *Taxation of Intercorporate Dividends under an Unintegrated Regime*, 44 TAX L. REV. 1 (1988).

The key point here is that corporate taxation evolved in line with state corporate law. State partnership law developed quite differently from state corporate law. It is not surprising, therefore, that partnership taxation grew quite differently from corporate taxation.

3. State Partnership Law

In the US, substantive partnership law arose as the courts, and then legislatures, worked to respect private business arrangements—as compared to the public arrangements that motivated the earliest corporations. The basic form of these private arrangements had developed on the European continent under the law commercial. In these arrangements, individuals pooled resources—capital and services—to conduct business. For the common law to respect these established continental arrangements, a form of joint ownership and mutual accountability not available theretofore at common law was created.

Two key features of the common-law partnership developed: First, partners were co-owners of property with a right of survivorship and a duty of accountability to the others with regard to partnership property. Second, a partnership involved a consensual mutual agency between the partners. Partners acted on each other's behalf with regard to the partnership's business. As a consequence, partners were jointly and severally liable for partnership debts.

In other words, from the beginning, a state-law partnership was not an independent entity, like a corporation, but merely an aggregate of relationships between the partners with respect to both the partnership's business and the partnership's property. For example, since a partnership was only an aggregate of relationships, persons could enter into a partnership without specifically agreeing that their arrangement was to be treated as a "partnership," as long as the requisite relationships were established. (In contrast, a corporation, as a thing, must be intentionally created as such.) Similarly, admission of a new partner, withdrawal of a partner, or transfer of a partnership interest technically created a new partnership, as the identity of the members in the partnership arrangement had changed. (Transfer of corporate stock has no effect on the entity or its property.) Finally, because a partnership is a private arrangement (rather than a one-size-fits-all entity, like the early corporations), state law affords considerable flexibility in crafting the particulars of a given partnership.

As state partnership law developed, the aggregate approach proved increasingly unwieldy. For example, title to partnership property was held in the name of the partners. Mutual agency helped deal with the associated problems in transferring title (buying and selling partnership property), but, particularly with property as to which title must be recorded (primarily real estate), considerable problems persisted. (As to recorded property, any change in the identity of the partners could have required a re-recording of title to the property, as its legal owners had changed.) Thus, as partnership law became increasingly statutory, legislatures (following the guidance of the Conference of Commissioners on

Uniform State Laws) added more and more entity features to the state-law partnership.

Now, partnerships are entities.[7] They own property in their own name.[8] The transfer of an interest in a partnership does not transfer an interest in the partnership's property, but transfers only the transferor's rights to profits, losses, and distributions.[9] The transfer of a partnership interest and the admission or withdrawal of a partner do not terminate the partnership's existence automatically.[10] Lawsuits are brought in the name of the partnership (rather than in the name of the partners).[11]

B. THE DEVELOPMENT OF THE TAX LAW

1. Overview

The development of the tax law applicable to partnerships parallels the development of state partnership law. Subchapter K's basic ideas derive from the aggregate approach, but entity features were added as appropriate, with the result being the current hybrid regime. This development is the subject of the next section.

Before looking at the historical development of the taxation of partnerships, it is helpful to step outside of the complexities of history and reflect briefly on the tax regime for partnerships that, in the abstract, flows from an aggregate view: Partnerships would not be taxed as such. Their incomes would be taxed to the partners as if earned directly. Distributions by a partnership to a partner of her share of partnership property would have no tax effect, as the distribution would be viewed as giving the partner what already was hers—in effect moving the property from one of the partner's pockets (the share of partnership property pocket) to another (the property owned directly pocket). A sale of a partnership interest would be treated as a sale of the partner's interests in the underlying partnership properties.

2. 1913 to 1976: A Vehicle for Small Business

There were few rules specifically for partnerships in the early revenue acts. The 1913 Act did provide:

> That any persons carrying on business in partnership shall be liable for income tax only in their individual capacity, and the share of the profits of a partnership to which any taxable partner would be entitled if the same were divided, whether divided or otherwise, shall be returned for taxation and the tax paid, under the provisions of this section, and any such firm, when requested by the Commissioner of Internal Revenue, or any district collector, shall forward to him a correct statement of such profits and the names of the

---

7. Revised Uniform Partnership Act § 201 (1997) (" '97 UPA").

8. '97 UPA § 203.

9. '97 UPA §§ 501, 502.

10. '97 UPA § 801.

11. '97 UPA § 307.

individuals who would be entitled to the same, if distributed.[12]

This early statute set the stage for the current regime for the taxation of partnerships: A partnership pays no tax itself.[13] Rather, partners pay tax on their share of the partnership's income, regardless of whether or when the income is withdrawn or made available to the partners. In other words, with regard to the taxation of income arising from partnership operations, the partnership is viewed as an aggregate of the partners with no separate tax identity.

As to other aspects of the taxation of partnerships, however, the 1913 Act, like current law, adopted entity-like features: An individual partner did not calculate her income from partnership operations independently. This would be burdensome on the partner—and on the IRS— if the partners' calculations differ from each other. Thus, the law provided that the IRS looks to a single return, by the partnership as an entity, for the determinations (i) of the taxable income arising from the partnership's operations and (ii) of the partners' respective shares of this income. Even in 1913, the tax law applicable to partnerships was an hybrid of aggregate and entity rules.

As the law developed, further hybrid features were adopted. Most importantly, the law never adopted a pure aggregate or entity approach either (i) to contributions of property by a partner to her partnership or (ii) to non-pro-rata distributions of partnership property to the partners.

Consider the tax treatment of A and B, who form a 50–50 partnership: A contributes Whiteacre. B contributes machinery and equipment. The respective contributions are of equal value.[14] Under an aggregate view, A is exchanging a half interest in Whiteacre for a half interest in the machinery and equipment. This would result in tax to both A and B on half of the gain in their respective properties.

A pure entity approach also would result in tax. A and B would be viewed as exchanging their respective properties for partnership interests. This would result in a full tax to both, rather than the half tax under the aggregate approach.[15]

12. Tariff Act of 1913, Pub. L. No. 63–16, § II.D, 38 Stat. 114, 169 (1913)

13. Partnerships pay no income tax or minimum tax, but do pay other taxes, such as payroll tax, Social Security tax, Medicare tax, and the like.

14. The question arises as to whether to use the after-tax or pre-tax values of assets in pricing transactions. In the real world, the parties would negotiate based on after-tax values. High basis property is worth more after tax than low basis property in situations were the property's basis remains unchanged after the transaction (e.g., with transferred basis property, see Section 7701(a)(43)). The parties would reflect this in pricing the transaction. Reflecting this reality in a basic text presents pedagogical problems, however. If the examples depend on the tax result they are trying to explain, circularity results. Thus, this text, as is customary, uses pre-tax, rather than after-tax, values in its examples.

Similarly, assets can have a different tax basis in the hands of a partner (say, if distributed from a liquidating partnership) than to the partnership. This means that the same asset can have a different after-tax value depending upon how and who owns the asset. This also is ignored in this text in the interests of simplicity.

15. Even as to the retained half economic interests in their respective properties, there is an exchange of a fee simple for an interest in partnership.

The Commissioner never pursued either the pure aggregate approach or the pure entity approach, however. Rather, she allowed tax-free treatment on contributions to a partnership. The transfer from A and B is viewed as a transfer to an entity, but to a transparent "pass-through" entity, so that it is not appropriate to tax the exchange of property for an interest in the entity. Basis rules that assured that no gain escaped tax permanently as a result of a tax-free contribution were in force.[16]

Similarly, under either pure approach, a non-pro-rata distribution of property by a partnership to a partner would result in tax, but the law never required it. Consider the 50–50 partnership between C and D: The partnership owns 4 parcels of real estate of equal value. Then, the partnership distributes one parcel to D in exchange for a reduction of his interest in the partnership from 1/2 to a 1/3d pro-rata interest. Under an aggregate view, D is exchanging a 1/6th interest in the three parcels retained by the partnership (as a consequence of the reduction in his share of the partnership from 1/2 to 1/3d) for the 1/2 of the distributed property previously owned by C (through the partnership).[17] Both C and D would be taxed on this exchange. Under the pure entity approach, the distribution would be treated as a redemption by the partnership of a 1/6th partnership interest from D in exchange for the one parcel.[18] This would result in tax to both D and the partnership.

Early administrative pronouncements rejected both pure approaches—again adopting a pass-through entity approach—and provided that distributions of (non-cash) property by a partnership to a partner were tax-free, with appropriate basis rules to assure that such treatment did not effect permanent tax avoidance.[19]

Things had not evolved much by 1954. The 1939 Code's core partnership provisions consisted of 11 short sections and dealt primarily with the computation of partnership tax items and their treatment to the partners.[20] The taxation of partnership transactions, like contributions, distributions, liquidations, and sales of partnership interests was left to regulations or simply unresolved.[21] In 1942, Jacob Rabkin & Mark Johnson, prominent New York tax practitioners, noted in an influential Harvard Law Review article that:

16. G.C.M. 10092, XI–1 C.B. 114 (1932). This ruling taxed the partners on pre-contribution gain when the partnership disposed of contributed property. This feature was rejected by the courts, but finally blessed by Congress. *Helvering v. Walbridge*, 70 F.2d 683 (2d Cir.1934)(Learned Hand concludes that precontribution gain is taxed only when distributed in cash.); Revenue Act of 1934, Pub. L. No. 73–216, § 113(a)(13), 48 Stat. 680 (1934).

17. The student should think about the pricing of this transaction, as understanding such is required later.

18. This is the corporate rule under Sections 302 and 311(b).

19. Reg. No. 45, Art. 1570, T.D. 2831, 21 Treas. Dec. Int. Rev. 170, 396 (1919) (1918 Revenue Act)(liquidating distributions); G.C.M 10092, *supra* note 16.

20. I.R.C. 1939, §§ 181–191.

21. Section 113(a)(13), *supra* note 16, did address the basis consequences of contributions and distributions of property.

Basically, the tax law adopts the common-law concept of the partnership as an aggregate of individuals operating the properties of the partnership enterprise as coowners. ... Yet, time after time the regulations and decisions waiver between the "entity" and "coownership" concepts. If it were a matter of redrafting the partnership tax law, perhaps as good a case could be made out for one theory as the other. One of them, however, must be consistently applied—and under the present statute there is scarcely a choice. The partnership "entity" is to be accepted insofar as it serves accounting expediency, but the complex issues of partner-partnership relation may be resolved only in terms of "coownership." If the essential "non-entity" of the partnership is recognized, most of the partnership problems will ultimately crystallize into an intelligible tax pattern.[22]

As this quotation suggests, the state of affairs in 1942 was troubling.

The Section of Taxation of the American Bar Association created the Committee on Partnerships, chaired initially by Mark Johnson, to study partnerships. Then, the American Law Institute's Income Tax Project turned to partnerships, again under the leadership of Mark Johnson. The resulting 1954 ALI report (with proposed new legislation) noted that:

Most of the problems encountered in the partnership area are concerned with the distribution of the burden of taxation among the members of the group. Since the Treasury from the standpoint of tax policy is not greatly concerned about this allocation, the issues are essentially not between Treasury and taxpayer partner but between partner and partner. Consequently, tax technicians should be able to agree on the formulation of rules to govern the complex partnership relationship, and this formulation should not raise issues that pass beyond technical tax policy. ...

As a general proposition the standard rules ... proposed ... treat the partners as co-owners of the partnership property, on the assumption that this approach most nearly conforms to the understanding of the parties in the usual small business. In the interest of flexibility, however, a series of elective rules based upon the entity theory are provided to take care of those partnerships which have numerous partners or a complex variety of assets.[23]

22. Jacob Rabkin & Mark H. Johnson, *The Partnership under the Federal Tax Laws,* 55 HARV. L. REV. 909, 949 (1942).

23. J. Paul Jackson, Mark H. Johnson, Stanley S. Surrey & William C. Warren, *A Proposed Revision of the Federal Income Tax Treatment of Partnerships and Partners—American Law Institute Draft* 9 TAX L. REV. 109, 112–13 (1954) (hereinafter 1954 ALI). In hindsight, as will be clear to the student as she becomes more familiar with partnership taxation, the analysis in the quotation is remarkably naive. This naivete is characteristic of the times. Also, the apparent tacit assumption that most partnerships were small businesses—primarily service businesses—contributed to the oversimple analysis. One suspects, however, that the authors may have effected this naivete so as to appear uncontroversial, and thereby increase the likelihood of legislative success.

Small business was the focus in 1954. The ALI's major partnership proposals involved (i) partners' shares of profit and loss, (ii) transactions between partners and their partnership, (iii) treatment of death or retirement of a partner, (iv) sales of partnership interests, and (v) partnership liquidation. Also, attention was paid to preventing the conversion of ordinary income into more favorably taxed capital gain.

In 1954, Congress—working with the ALI, the ABA, and the American Institute of Certified Public Accountants—adopted rules that followed the basic emphasis and approach of the ALI's partnership proposals as Subchapter K of the Code. With amendments, this regime continues in force today and is the focus of this text. As the student proceeds through these materials, she will note that the ALI's—and Congress'—failure to consistently apply either the aggregate approach or the entity approach, as recommend by Rabkin and Johnson in 1942,[24] resulted in a confused statute and opened the door to later abuses, which, in turn, forced the statutory and regulatory responses that are responsible for much of the current complexity.

3. 1976 to 1987: Individual Tax Shelters

After 1954, there were few important developments for over 20 years. Subchapter K worked adequately with regard to the small businesses to which it applied.[25]

The seed of change had been planted, however. A form of partnership other than the general partnership, existed. "Limited partnerships" have been authorized by state statutes since the New York statute of 1822. A limited partnership, as the name implies, has, in addition to one or more unlimitedly liable "general" partners, "limited" partners with limited liability and no agency authority. Limited partners are more like corporate shareholders than general partners.

Initially, limited partnerships were not popular, in part because of uncertainties in their taxation. 1960 tax regulations based on the 1935 Supreme Court opinion in *Morrissey*[26] made cautious tax counsel concerned that limited partnerships would be taxed as corporations because of their practical resemblance to corporations. In fact, at one time, the

---

24. The ALI proposals had a more aggregate flavor than Subchapter K as ultimately enacted, however. Also, the ALI proposals contained a rule that provided that, when the law otherwise was unclear, a tax issue was to be resolved by viewing a partnership as an aggregate. Congress did not follow this recommendation, but contemplated that aggregate treatment could be appropriate in many circumstances. H.R. Conf. Rep. No. 83–2543, at 59 (1954).

25. There were good business reasons for not forming larger businesses as partnerships. Back then, most partnerships were general partnerships (or treated as general partnerships by all states other than the states of their formation). (Many

states did not respect limited liability of out-of-state limited partnerships.) The only equity interests in a general partnership are general partner interests. A general partner is jointly and severally liable for partnership obligations (regardless of whether incurred with her consent), including tort liabilities. Large firms customarily involve equity investors who do not participate in the firm's business and, thus, who are unwilling to so expose themselves to liability. Under these circumstances, a corporation had to be used to get outside equity capital.

26. *Morrissey v. Commissioner*, 296 U.S. 344, 56 S.Ct. 289, 80 L.Ed. 263 (1935).

SEC insisted on an IRS private ruling that a limited partnership would be taxed as a partnership under Subchapter K before limited partnership interests could be sold as such to the public. The IRS ruling requirements were quite strict.[27]

Notwithstanding the tax risks, the use of limited partnerships, particularly for tax shelters, grew. Partnership tax treatment has a particular advantage in tax shelter transactions: Partners can claim partnership tax losses on their returns so as to shelter the partner's non-partnership income from taxation. Thus, a tax shelter promoter (syndicator) could sell limited partner interests, claiming that the buyers would be entitled to tax benefits—like accelerated depreciation, R & D deductions, and expensing of intangible (oil and gas well) drilling costs—without the buyers risking personal liability.[28]

The dam broke in 1976: In its 1976 opinion in *Larson*,[29] the Tax Court blessed a syndicated limited partnership tax shelter. The IRS acquiesced in 1979.[30] Investment bankers and other promoters began marketing limited partnership tax shelters at retail.

By the mid–1980s, there was considerable public concern about the proliferation of tax shelters. Shelters were viewed as unfairly helping the wealthy escape taxation. Congress responded. The Tax Reform Act of 1986 enacted the Passive Activity Loss (PAL) rules contained in Section 469. These rules provide that individual passive investors in active businesses, including, specifically, limited partners, cannot take losses from the underlying active businesses against earned or investment income. The PAL rules essentially eliminated the forms of individual tax shelter common in the mid–1980s.

Congress took a final shot at limited partnerships in 1987 by enacting Section 7704. It provides that most partnerships whose interests are publicly traded are taxed as corporations rather than as partnerships.

C.   CURRENT AFFAIRS AND THE FUTURE

1.   LLCs, Similar Beasts, and Check-the-Box

Another part of the recent saga of Subchapter K began in 1977 in, of all places, Wyoming. In an attempt to be the Delaware of small business, Wyoming enacted a statute creating a new form of business organization: the Limited Liability Company (LLC). The LLC is a flexible vehicle for conducting a business that resembles a partnership except that no member of the LLC (equity owner, like a partner or corporate stockholder) is liable for LLC obligations automatically. In other words, all

---

27. *See* Rev. Proc. 72–13, 1972–1 C.B. 735; Rev. Proc. 74–17, 1974–1 C.B. 438; Rev. Proc. 75–16, 1975 C.B. 676.

28. In 1976, Congress enacted the At-Risk Rules of Section 465 as an early shot at tax shelters.

29. *Larson v. Commissioner*, 66 T.C. 159 (1976).

30. Rev. Rul. 79–106, 1979–1 C.B. 448.

members of an LLC have limited liability similar to that enjoyed by limited partners of a limited partnership.[31] Cleverly, Wyoming drafted its statute with an eye toward qualifying the LLC for partnership tax treatment under the *Morrissey* regulations. Other states quickly imitated Wyoming with similar statutes. Treasury at first threatened to tax LLCs as corporations. Then, the IRS granted most LLCs partnership tax status.[32]

Thus, the LLC now is a very attractive vehicle for small business. The LLC provides the single-tax and tax loss pass-through benefits of Subchapter K with limited state-law liability.[33]

After the multistate success of the LLC, many states created even newer forms of business organization by enacting Limited Liability Partnership (LLP) or Limited Liability Limited Partnership (LLLP) statutes. LLPs and LLLPs are similar to LLCs.[34]

Confronted with all of the new state-law forms of business organization (as well as with all of the different forms under the laws of foreign countries), Treasury had a hard time drawing meaningful distinctions under the *Morrissey* regulations. Treasury felt that they were spending an inordinate amount of time on issues regarding the tax classification of the different forms of business organization. Finally, the Treasury adopted regulations, which took effect on January 1, 1997, that changed the basic approach to determining which business organizations are taxed under Subchapter K. The *Morrissey* regulations had looked at the underlying state-law relationships involved with a form of business organization (limited liability of members, continuity of life of the organization, free transferability of interests, and centralized management) to determine whether the organization more closely resembled a

31. Under then state limited partnership law, a limited partner who participated in the partnership's business was treated as a general partner. Members of an LLC can participate in its business while maintaining limited liability.

32. In 1988, the Wyoming statute was the first blessed. Rev. Rul. 88–76, 1988–2 C.B. 360.

33. Of course, as to be discussed in Chapter III of this text, the PAL rules of Section 469 may limit utilization of these losses by outside investors.

34. In a regular limited partnership, the general partners are unlimitedly liable and, under older statutes, limited partners can be held liable if they exercise control over the business (i.e., if they act inconsistently with being limited partners). In contrast, an LLLP can fully protect general and limited partners from partnership liabilities. There are still two classes of owners with an LLLP, however. The limited partners cannot participate in management. An LLP resembles a general partnership with limited liability for all partners. Finally, with an LLC, all members have equal management rights and limited liability.

partnership or a corporation. The 1997 regulations provide that a business organization (i) that is called a "corporation" under the creating state law is taxed as a corporation, but (ii) that, otherwise (i.e., if the organization is not called a "corporation" under the applicable state law) Subchapter K applies unless the organization elects to be taxed as a corporation.[35] Because of this elective feature, the current regulations are referred to as the "check-the-box" regulations. As a consequence, most newly-formed small businesses are LLCs or LLPs that are taxed under Subchapter K.[36] This has made the subject of this text that much more important.

35. Treas. Reg. §§ 301.7701–2, –3. These rules only apply if there are at least 2 equity owners. One-equity-owner entities not called "corporations" in the organizing state law that do not check the box to be taxed as corporations for tax purposes are ignored—treated as "nothings"—so that the owner is treated as conducting the underlying business directly.

The check-the-box election is available freely for new business organizations. As to existing firms, tax status may be changed once every 60 months or, with IRS permission, after an over 50% change in the ownership of the entity. Treas. Reg. § 301.7701–3(c)(1)(iv).

It is not clear that these regulations are valid, since they are inconsistent with *Morrissey*. *Bankers Trust N.Y. Corp. v. U.S.*, 225 F.3d 1368 (Fed.Cir.2000)(Properly promulgated regulations cannot interpret statute differently from prior judicial decision.). Practitioners generally assume, however, that the IRS will not challenge Treasury regulations, and, therefore, rely on the new regulations when favorable to the taxpayer. A "partner" not interested in bearing tax on her entity's current operating income could challenge the regulations, however.

36. Most pre–1997 small businesses taxed as corporations did not change their status because the associated actual or deemed liquidation of the corporation would have triggered a double tax under Sections 331 and 336. *See* Treas. Reg. §§ 301.7701–3(g)(ii), (iii).

The check-the-box form looks as follows:

Form **8832** (December 1996) Department of the Treasury Internal Revenue Service	**Entity Classification Election**	OMB No. 1545-1516

Please Type or Print	Name of entity	Employer identification number (EIN)
	Number, street, and room or suite no. If a P.O. box, see instructions.	
	City or town, state, and ZIP code. If a foreign address, enter city, province or state, postal code and country.	

1 **Type of election** (see instructions):

a ☐ Initial classification by a newly-formed entity (or change in current classification of an existing entity to take effect on January 1, 1997)

b ☐ Change in current classification (to take effect later than January 1, 1997)

2 **Form of entity** (see instructions):

a ☐ A domestic eligible entity electing to be classified as an association taxable as a corporation.

b ☐ A domestic eligible entity electing to be classified as a partnership.

c ☐ A domestic eligible entity with a single owner electing to be disregarded as a separate entity.

d ☐ A foreign eligible entity electing to be classified as an association taxable as a corporation.

e ☐ A foreign eligible entity electing to be classified as a partnership.

f ☐ A foreign eligible entity with a single owner electing to be disregarded as a separate entity.

3 Election is to be effective beginning (month, day, year) (see instructions) . . . . ▶ ___/___/___

4 Name and title of person whom the IRS may call for more information | **5** That person's telephone number

Consent Statement and Signature(s) (see instructions)

Under penalties of perjury, I (we) declare that I (we) consent to the election of the above-named entity to be classified as indicated above, and that I (we) have examined this consent statement, and to the best of my (our) knowledge and belief, it is true, correct, and complete. If I am an officer, manager, or member signing for all members of the entity, I further declare that I am authorized to execute this consent statement on their behalf.

Signature(s)	Date	Title

For Paperwork Reduction Act Notice, see page 2.   Cat. No. 22598R   Form **8832** (12-96)

2. Check-the-Box and Foreign Entities

To the apparent surprise of the Treasury, the check-the-box regulations' biggest impact has been in international tax planning. The regulations make it easy to create foreign entities that are treated inconsistently under U.S. and applicable foreign law—treated as corporations for US purposes and partnerships for foreign purposes, or vice versa. The inconsistent treatment of these "hybrid" entities, including under tax treaties, presents remarkable opportunities to reduce the worldwide tax of a business (although not necessarily the US tax).

Consider an example: A foreign corporation has a US corporate subsidiary. The foreign corporation forms an wholly-owned US LLC that does not check the box (so it is a tax nothing for US tax purposes but a corporation for purposes of the foreign tax). The foreign parent contributes money to the LLC, which then lends the money to the US corporation. The deduction for the interest paid by the US corporation reduces US income tax. The foreign parent is taxed on the interest paid by the US subsidiary (because the LLC is a nothing for US tax purposes). But, as interest paid to a foreign corporation, that interest bears a reduced rate of tax under the US tax treaty with the foreign country. Under the foreign tax, the LLC is treated a U.S. corporation, so that its income is not taxed. Payments from the US LLC to its parent are treated as tax-free dividends (on the false assumption that the LLC already has been taxed as a corporation on its income in the US.) Thus, this structure reduces the foreign tax (by converting taxable interest to tax-free dividends) at no US tax cost (as the results to the US corporation would have been the same if the parent had simply lent the money directly to its US subsidiary). After US corporations complained that this structure gave unfair advantage to their foreign competitors, in 1997 Congress outlawed this use of certain tax treaties.[37]

On one level, the US should not care about foreign tax avoidance. On another, particularly when bilateral tax treaties aimed at limiting tax avoidance are impacted, the US should be quite concerned. Treasury, and then Congress, tried to deal with the first problems that arose by changing the relevant substantive tax rules, rather than changing the check-the-box regulations. Finally, in 1999, the IRS proposed regulations that would limit US taxpayers' use of check-the-box in certain foreign transactions involving artful changes of elections so as to treat stock sales as asset sales that are more favorably taxed under Subpart F.[38] While of limited impact if adopted, this proposal may be significant, as it may show that the Treasury now is willing to acknowledge that the check-the-box regulations themselves are the problem in the foreign context.

3. Corporate Shelters and the Anti–Abuse Regulations

The 1986 Act's PAL rules apply only to individuals, including in their roles as partners. It was hoped that the corporate alternative minimum tax, as expanded in 1986 to be tougher than the individual alternative minimum tax, would be adequate to deal with corporate abuses. The hope was not realized. Corporate tax shelters[39] grew to become the most prominent issue in contemporary domestic tax policy. Many of these shelters involve creative and aggressive use of technical provisions in Subchapter K. Treasury responded to these uses of partnerships in 1994 with the Anti–Abuse Regulations, Section 1.701–2. They apply beyond corporate tax shelters.

37. I.R.C. § 894(c).

38. Prop. Treas. Reg. § 301.7701–3(h) (1999).

39. Some of the transactions are marketed to wealthy individuals engaging in private business (so as to avoid the PAL rules and Section 7704), but nevertheless are referred to as "corporate" shelters.

The details of the Anti–Abuse Regulations are best left until Chapter XI. At this point, however, it is interesting to note that the regulations basically attack transactions that involve use of more entity-like rules of Subchapter K and provide a general preference for aggregate-like treatment. As the ALI noted almost half a century ago, "this [aggregate] approach most nearly conforms to the understanding of the parties."[40]

Congress also has responded to tax shelters by modifying a few of the structural aspects of Subchapter K that enabled these transactions. Specifically, a variety of legislation was enacted at various times in the 1990s that provides, in certain circumstances, more aggregate-like treatment with regard to both contributions of property by partners to partnerships and partnership distributions. These rules are discussed below in Chapters VI through VIII.

40.   1954 ALI, *supra* note 23, at 113.

Chapter II

PARTNERSHIP FORMATION

A. INTRODUCTION: PEELING AN ONION

Chapter I introduced the policies and problems that shaped Subchapter K by summarizing its historical development. Now, it is time to begin the detailed examination of current law. Unfortunately, Subchapter K is not organized into discrete, separate portions. Multiple statutory provisions apply simultaneously, even with simple transactions. Moreover, earlier transactions can impact the taxation of a current transaction. It is not possible to scrutinize any rule of Subchapter K or any one type of partnership transaction carefully in isolation. For this reason, the discussion of partnership taxation is organized best by starting with transactions that are simple from a tax point of view and then looking at increasingly tax-complicated matters. This chapter provides an overview of the formation of a simple partnership.[1] The analysis must begin with the birth of a partnership, because the details of formation impact the taxation of the partners throughout their partnership's life. Next, in Chapter III, this text will look at the basic taxation of a very simple partnership throughout its life. With this foundation, the text can then scrutinize more involved matters.

B. BASICS

READ: Code §§ 721(a), 723, and 724

The rules that control the taxation of partnership formations reflect an hybrid approach, as suggested in Chapter I. Consider the basic problem of the taxation of a partnership formation with regard to the example already examined in Chapter I: A and B form a 50–50 partnership. They make property contributions of equal value, A contributing Whiteacre and B contributing machinery and equipment. There are a variety of ways to look at this partnership formation. Under a pure

---

1. Note that, in general, this text refers to LLCs that are taxed under Subchapter K as "partnerships," to the members of these LLCs as "partners," and to the organizing instruments of these LLCs as "partnership agreements." Also, no partnership checks the box to be taxed as a corporation, unless stated otherwise.

aggregate approach, A is exchanging a 1/2 interest in Whiteacre for a 1/2 interest in the machinery and equipment. Under a pure entity approach, A is exchanging Whiteacre for a partnership interest that gives no direct interest in the underlying partnership assets. Consider the tax regimes that flow from these 2 pure views. The taxation under the first, pure aggregate, view is 1/2 as if nothing happened and 1/2 as an exchange. The taxation under the second, pure entity, view would be a full exchange.

Current law adopts neither of these approaches. Rather, a partnership formation is viewed as a mere change in form of an investment in an ongoing enterprise such that no current tax is appropriate.

Given current law's approach, the student may ask: who cares about the entity and aggregate views? The views are quite important. Failure to follow a consistent view of partnership formation opened the door to tax avoidance through transfers of property to partnerships by partners. The student will have to suffer through the considerable complexity that resulted as Congress and the Treasury tried to limit this avoidance. This complexity is somewhat tolerable, however, when one realizes that it follows from the decision not to tax partnership formations. Moreover, an understanding of the pure treatments, particularly that under the aggregate approach, informs a richer understanding both of the problems to which the current complexity is directed and of the their solutions.

Current law's tax-free treatment of partnership formations, to both the partners and the partnership,[2] is contained in Section 721(a). It applies to all contributions of property to a partnership by a partner, not just to formation transactions. Section 721 does not apply to the contribution of services by a partner to her partnership, however, which can be taxable, as discussed below.

Section 721 is intended to effect tax deferral, not permanent tax avoidance. The most important rule that assures that Section 721 operates merely as a deferral provision is Section 723. It provides the partnership with a transferred basis in contributed property. Thus, for example, when the partnership sells contributed property, all gain or loss arising from the time the property was acquired by the transferee partner until sold by the partnership is recognized. No gain or loss escapes tax.

Other applicable tax rules operate so that the partnership steps into the contributing partner's shoes with regard to the contributed property. For example, the contributed property gets a tacked holding period under Section 1223(2). Section 724 protects ordinary income treatment on certain assets. Under Section 168(i)(7), the partnership steps into the partners' shoes with regard to depreciation. Under Sections 1245 and 1250, depreciation recapture is not triggered when property is contributed to a partnership, but any built-in recapture follows the contributed

---

2. Section 721(a) thus serves the same functions in the partnership formation con-text that Sections 351 and 1032 serve in the corporate formation context.

property.[3] Section 704(c), which is discussed in detail in Chapter VI, taxes the contributing partner with regard to precontribution unrealized gain or loss as that gain or loss is realized by the partnership.

REVIEW: Code §§ 168(i)(7), 704(c)(1)(A), 721(a), 723, 724, 1223(2), 1245(a)(2)(A) and (b)(3), and 1250(b)(5) and (d)(3)

C. PARTNERSHIP INTERESTS: OUTSIDE BASIS

READ: Code §§ 705, 722, 741, 742, 743(a), and 1223(1)

Once the partnership has been formed, the tax law must have a view as to the nature of the partners' interests in their partnership. Under a pure aggregate view, a partner has a separate interest in each partnership asset. Accordingly, under this view, if the partnership were to sell an asset, each partner would be taxed on the difference between her share of the amount realized and her basis in her interest in the sold asset. If a partner were to sell her partnership interest, she would be treated as selling her respective shares of the partnership's assets, recognizing a variety of items of gain and loss. Such an aggregate approach obviously would be quite involved in practice.

As usual, an entity approach is simpler. Under the entity approach, a partnership interest is treated as separate from the underlying partnership assets, so that a partnership interest is a separate, whole, tax asset with its own basis in the hands of the partner, like corporate stock is to a corporate shareholder. The partnership (i) has a basis in each of its assets, and (ii) calculates its gain or loss using this basis. This is the approach reflected in Subchapter K. A partner's basis in her partnership interest sometimes is referred to as the "outside" basis, as compared to the partnership's "inside" bases in its assets.[4]

Accordingly, Subchapter K provides rules for determining outside basis directly, but, in many cases, the rules have the same effect as under the pure aggregate approach.[5] There are numerous circumstances, however, where a partner's outside basis differs from her share of inside basis, as discussed throughout this text. The most common situation where this occurs is when a new partner buys an existing partnership interest from a departing partner, so that the new partner's cost basis in the interest purchased is different from the selling partner's basis, which was her share of partnership inside basis. Read Section 743(a).

Subchapter K's rules for determining a given partner's outside basis follow the general tax principal that a taxpayer's basis in an asset is her after-tax investment in the asset. Thus, a partner has no basis in her

---

3. I.R.C. §§ 1245(a)(2)(A), 1245(b)(3), 1250(b)(5), 1250(d)(3).

4. This text also refers to a partner's share of the partnership's inside basis as the partner's "inside" basis.

5. In fact, Section 705(b) allows a partner to use her share of inside basis as her outside basis in certain circumstances, but these rules are used in practice rarely. *See* Treas. Reg. § 1.705–1(b).

partnership interest merely upon signing the partnership agreement. Then, Section 722 comes into play. Cash contributions increase outside basis. Similarly, the partner's basis in her interest is increased by the basis (the after-tax investment, not the value) of non-cash property contributed. Section 1223(1) gives a tacked holding period in the portion of the interest attributable to the contributed property. The numerous other adjustments to outside basis are discussed throughout this text.

Outside basis then is used for important partner tax calculations. For example, under Section 741, when a partnership interest is sold, the selling partner is taxed on the difference between the amount realized and her basis in the sold interest.[6] Similarly, the purchaser of a partnership interest gets an initial cost basis by operation of Section 742. Transfers of partnership interests are examined in more detail later in Chapters III and VI.

The mechanics of Subchapter K's rules regarding outside basis work to assure that a partner is taxed once and only once with regard to her economic profit or loss realized from participation in the partnership. They do not assure that profit and loss are taxed at the proper time and with the proper character (capital vs. ordinary gain or loss) in every instance, however. This will be examined in considerable detail in later chapters.

A partner can own more than one state-law partnership interest in a given partnership. For example, a partner can own both an interest as a general partner and a limited partnership interest. These multiple interests may be acquired at different times from different persons. For example, an original general partner may buy out one of her limited partners years after the formation of the partnership. Nevertheless, Subchapter K treats a partner as owning one unified interest for most purposes, including for purposes of determining outside basis.[7] There seems to be a trend away from this unified interest approach, however. For example, Section 1.1223–3 of the regulations, promulgated in 2000, provides that a partner can have different holding periods in portions of a unified partnership interest.

REVIEW: Code §§ 705, 722, 741, 742, 743(a), and 1223(1) and Reg. § 1.1223–3

Problem Set II.C

Ethyl owns an undeveloped parcel of investment real estate, Blackacre, with a value of $100,000 and a tax basis of $10,000. Fred owns

---

6. Since, under a simple analysis, the value of a partnership interest should equal the total value of the associated shares of the underlying partnership assets, and since, at this juncture, the outside basis should equal the partner's share of inside basis, the total outside gain taxed by Section 741 should equal the partner's share of total unrealized inside gain and loss. The character of such gain is reviewed later in this chapter.

7. Rev. Rul. 84–53, 1984–1 C.B. 159. Under Section 1.704–1(b)(2)(iv)(*b*) of the regulations a partner has only one capital account in a partnership regardless of the number of and the character of the interests in the partnership that she owns. (The significance of capital accounts is discussed below in Chapter IV.)

Greenacre, which has the same character, value, and basis. Both parcels have been owned for years. Ethyl and Fred form a partnership, contributing their respective parcels. The partnership holds the parcels for investment.

1. How are Ethyl, Fred, and the partnership taxed on the formation of the partnership?

2. If Ethyl were to sell her interest six months later for $150,000, how much would she be taxed?

3. If the partnership were to sell Blackacre six months after the formation of the partnership for $150,000, how would the partnership measure and characterize any recognized gain or loss? (While somewhat premature, the student may wish to speculate as to how this gain should be allocated between Ethyl and Fred.)

D. BOOT

READ: Code §§ 707(a)(2)(B) and 752 and Reg. §§ 1.707–3(a)(1), (a)(2), and (b)(1), –5(a)(1), (5)(i)(first sentence), (6), and (7)

Frequently boot is received by a partner when she contributes noncash property to a partnership. For example, Allison may have property worth $1.5 million, while Greta has property worth $1 million. If they want a 50–50 partnership,[8] Greta can contribute an additional $250,000 in cash, which is immediately distributed to Allison, and then their interests are 50–50. The question then arises as to how Allison is taxed on the receipt of the $250,000 from the partnership. Those familiar with the rules applicable in the analogous corporate context, Section 351(b), might expect that Allison is taxed on the $250,000 up to the gain that she otherwise realized. Old-guard Subchapter K lawyers would view the $250,000 as a partnership distribution, which, as to be studied in Chapter VII,[9] under Section 731, would reduce Allison's outside basis before she recognizes any gain.[10] In 1984, Congress adopted a third view. Section 707(a)(2)(B), as interpreted by Sections 1.707–3(a) and 1.707–3(b)(1) of the regulations, views Allison as selling 1/6th ($250,000/$1,500,000) of the property **to the partnership**, triggering 1/6th of the gain.[11]

This result is best understood from an aggregate perspective. After the formation of a 50–50 partnership, Allison and Greta each effectively own 1/2 of each property. In effect, they are swapping 1/2 interests in their respective properties. The $250,000 payment is needed to make the numbers work out: Greta must buy 1/6th of Allison's property in order

---

8. Modern partnership law and the associated flexibility provides an infinite variety of ways of dealing with their disparate contributions, as well.

9. As noted at the beginning of this chapter, in Subchapter K, everything is connected to everything.

10. This treatment is analogous to that provided under Sections 301(c)(2) and (3) for corporate distributions not out of earnings and profits.

11. Treas. Reg. § 1.61–6.

for their swap to be even. Thus, under an aggregate view, Greta is buying 1/6th of Allison's property. Section 707(a)(2)(B), as interpreted by the current regulations, instead treats the transaction as involving a sale to the partnership, but otherwise is consistent with the aggregate view. This treatment avoids (i) the need to trace cash received from a partnership by a partner to another partner and (ii) the need to give Greta a special basis adjustment with respect to the purchased interest. Presumably, if a transaction were structured to abuse this result, the IRS could treat the sale as occurring between partners.

The basis consequences of the boot transaction follow from its characterization under Section 707(a)(2)(B): Assume that the basis of Allison's property is $900,000, while Greta's is $100,000. Section 1.707–3(a)(2) of the regulations, as explained in Example 1 of Section 1.707–3(f), provides that Allison recognizes $100,000 of gain (1/6th of [$1.5 million less $900,000]) on the 1/6th of the property deemed sold. She has an outside basis in her partnership interest attributable to the 5/6ths of the property deemed contributed of $750,000. Greta has an outside basis of $350,000 ($100,000 property basis plus $250,000 cash). The partnership has a transferred basis of $750,000 in the 5/6ths of Allison's property that was treated as received as a contribution (under Section 723) and a cost basis of $250,000 in the remaining 1/6th, which was deemed purchased. Greta's property has a $100,000 transferred basis to the partnership. The total inside basis is $1.1 million, which mirrors the total outside basis of $1.1 million.[12] The student just got her first taste of how Subchapter K taxes simple transactions in a complicated fashion. Unfortunately, many more examples are reviewed in later chapters.

The partnership taking property subject to debt presents a related boot issue. Under the broad reading of the *Crane* rule in Sections 752(b) and (c), taking property subject to debt would be treated as involving a payment of cash by the partnership to the contributing partner, which would trigger a tax under Section 707(a)(2)(B). This result is troubling. Any ongoing business has debt. Thus, automatic application of the *Crane* rule would mean that any transfer of an ongoing business to a partnership would trigger a tax. But, Congress does not want a mere change in form of a business to be taxable. So, the Section 707(a)(2)(B) regulations provide a general rule of no tax on the transfer of debts in Section 1.707–5(a). An apparent mere change in form should not disguise a transaction that really is a sale, however. Borrowing against property that quickly is contributed to a partnership should be taxable. Sections 1.707–5(a)(6) and 1.707–5(a)(7) draw the line between debt transfers that are nontaxable because they are part of a mere change in form of an ongoing investment and those taxable because they represent a withdrawal of cash from the continuing enterprise. Basically, the closer the contribution and the borrowing are in time, the more likely that the borrowing had a tax-avoidance motive. Under Section 1.707–5(a)(1), in a tax avoid-

---

12. To fully understand how the inside basis is allocated between the partners when non-cash property is contributed to a partnership requires familiarity with Section 704(c), which is not discussed until Chapter VI.

ance transaction, a partner is taxed; but, since a partner can remain at least partially liable on partnership debt, a contributing partner treats contributed non-qualified debt as boot only to the extent that her share of the liability is reduced (as determined under Section 752, discussed later in Chapter V). For example, if debt-laden property is contributed by a partner to a 50–50 partnership, and the effect under state law is that thereafter the partners are jointly and severally liable on the debt, the potential boot is only 1/2 the debt, as the transferee partner remains liable on 1/2 the debt in her capacity as a partner.

REVIEW: Code §§ 707(a)(2)(B) and 752 and Reg. §§ 1.707–3(a)(1), (a)(2), (b)(1), and (f)(Example 1) and –5(a)(1), (5)(i)(first sentence), (6), and (7)

Problem Set II.D

John has a piece of undeveloped investment real estate worth $1.5 million that is subject to $500,000 of debt and that has a tax basis of $750,000. Sally has a piece of undeveloped debt-free investment real estate worth $1 million with a basis of $100,000. John and Sally form a 50–50 partnership by contributing their respective properties. As a consequence, Sally becomes jointly and severally liable on the $500,000 debt, with a right against John if she has to pay more than her half. What are the consequences to Sally and John upon the formation of their partnership?

E. SERVICES

READ: Code §§ 83(a) and (h) and 707(a)(2)(A) and Reg. § 1.721–1(b)(1)

Many partners contribute their services to their partnership. In the ordinary case, these partners are compensated for their services through their share of partnership profits. Under these circumstances, the partner's partnership interest should have little value that is independent from the partner's future services.[13] On occasion, however, a partner receives a valuable interest for services. This usually makes sense to the partnership only when the partner is being paid for services performed prior to payment of the partnership interest (for example, in forming the partnership), as it can difficult to assure performance after payment.[14]

Because of these economics, many thought that the law was that (i) a service partner who received a partnership interest in partnership

---

13. Service partnerships frequently assure that a partner's share of profits is related to her performance by determining profit shares after the close of the year, as authorized by Section 761(c).

14. One way of assuring performance is by restricting the service partner's ownership in the partnership interest so that the service partner loses the interest if she does not perform the contemplated services. In this case, Section 1.83–1(a)(1) of the regulations provides that the service partner is not treated as owning the partnership interest for tax purposes until her ownership is free of the restriction, at which point the interest is transferred for services that already have been provided.

profits for her services was not taxed at that time (but, rather, was taxed on the allocated profits), but that (ii) a partner who received an interest in partnership capital (presumably for prior services) was taxed. The idea was that a taxpayer receiving a profits interest probably was not receiving compensation at such time. Any partnership interest was merely the legal foundation for the performance of future services, which would be taxed as the services are provided under Section 702. But, this analysis ignores the fact that an interest in partnership profits may be in profits that are independent from the partner's performance of future services, so that the profits interest, while an interest in profits in an accounting sense, really is an interest in economic capital with a current value. For example, consider a corporate bond. An interest in future interest payments has present value. The right to a future payment itself can be viewed as a zero-coupon (no stated interest) bond. Thus, a partnership interest in the likely regular return on property, while not accounted for until some time in the future, can have a present value. Section 83 taxes the value of any property received in connection with the performance of services. Consequently, receipt of a partnership interest in the future regular return on capital can be viewed as the receipt of property with a fair market value, which, if for services, is taxed under Section 83. Not surprisingly, the IRS has adopted this position, as reflected in the following Revenue Procedure:

REVENUE PROCEDURE 93–27
1993–2 C.B. 343.

SECTION 1. PURPOSE

This revenue procedure provides guidance on the treatment of the receipt of a partnership profits interest for services provided to or for the benefit of the partnership.

SEC. 2. DEFINITIONS

The following definitions apply for purposes of this revenue procedure.

.01 A capital interest is an interest that would give the holder a share of the proceeds if the partnership's assets were sold at fair market value and then the proceeds were distributed in a complete liquidation of the partnership. This determination generally is made at the time of receipt of the partnership interest.

.02 A profits interest is a partnership interest other than a capital interest.

SEC. 3. BACKGROUND

Under section 1.721–1(b)(1) of the Income Tax Regulations, the receipt of a partnership capital interest for services provided to or for the benefit of the partnership is taxable as compensation. On the other hand, the issue of whether the receipt of a partnership profits interest for services is taxable has been the subject of litigation. Most recently, in

Campbell v. Commissioner, 943 F.2d 815 (8th Cir.1991), the Eighth Circuit in dictum suggested that the taxpayer's receipt of a partnership profits interest received for services was not taxable, but decided the case on valuation. Other courts have determined that in certain circumstances the receipt of a partnership profits interest for services is a taxable event under section 83 of the Internal Revenue Code. *See, e.g., Campbell v. Commissioner,* T.C.M. 1990–236, *rev'd,* 943 F.2d 815 (8th Cir.1991); *St. John v. United States,* No. 82–1134 (C.D.Ill. Nov.16, 1983). The courts have also found that typically the profits interest received has speculative or no determinable value at the time of receipt. *See Campbell,* 943 F.2d at 823; *St. John.* In *Diamond v. Commissioner,* 56 T.C. 530 (1971), *aff'd,* 492 F.2d 286 (7th Cir.1974), however, the court assumed that the interest received by the taxpayer was a partnership profits interest and found the value of the interest was readily determinable. In that case, the interest was sold soon after receipt.

SEC. 4. APPLICATION

.01 Other than as provided below, if a person receives a profits interest for the provision of services to or for the benefit of a partnership in a partner capacity or in anticipation of being a partner, the Internal Revenue Service will not treat the receipt of such an interest as a taxable event for the partner or the partnership.

.02 This revenue procedure does not apply:

(1) If the profits interest relates to a substantially certain and predictable stream of income from partnership assets, such as income from high-quality debt securities or a high-quality net lease;

(2) If within two years of receipt, the partner disposes of the profits interest; or

(3) If the profits interest is a limited partnership interest in a "publicly traded partnership" within the meaning of section 7704(b) of the Internal Revenue Code.

————

When a partnership interest is received for both property and services, the transaction is bifurcated based on the respective (net) values of the property and services involved, so that the portion received for services is potentially taxable under Revenue Procedure 93–27.

When a partnership transfers an interest in itself in connection with the performance of services for it, the question arises as to how the partnership is taxed. Section 83(h) allows a deduction at the time the transferee is taxed if a cash payment would not be capitalized or otherwise disallowed. This does not end the inquiry, however. Under an aggregate view, the other partners would be viewed as exchanging a portion of their shares of partnership property (including, if applicable, an interest in future profits) with the service-providing transferee. This would be taxable to the other partners, resulting in capital gain, Section

1231 gain, and ordinary income, depending on the nature of the underlying partnership assets. For corporations, Section 1032 prevents this tax. There is no analogous provision in Subchapter K, however. For this reason, many believe that the partnership has such a taxable exchange. It is significant, however, that the IRS never has taken a public position on this issue.

The final rule that applies to partners who contribute services to their partnerships is contained in Section 707(a)(2)(A). It deals with a taxpayer abuse of the capitalization requirements. The basic abuse involved a partnership that, rather than paying a fee that would be capitalized (say, to an architect), admitted the payee as a partner, specially allocated her income, and, then, effectively redeemed her out of the partnership with a special distribution.[15] If this transaction were respected, the allocation of income to the payee would take the income off the returns of the other partners, so that the allocation would have the same effect as a deduction. Yet, the economics do not differ materially from the partnership simply paying a fee. As a consequence, Section 707(a)(2)(A) provides that, to the extent there is a matching between the allocation and the distribution, the transaction will be treated, not by its form, but as a payment to a non-partner, so as to be subject to the capitalization rules.[16]

REVIEW: Code §§ 83(a) and (h) and 707(a)(2)(A) and Reg. § 1.721–1(b)(1)

Problem Set II.E

1. Daryl, Darrell, and David form a 1/3d–1/3d–1/3d partnership. Darryl contributes land worth $100,000 with a basis of $10,000. Darrell contributes supplies worth $100,000 with a basis of $90,000. David receives his 1/3d interest for his services in putting the deal together and for future services. Thus, if the partnership were to liquidate, David would get 1/3d of the partnership's assets. Does the deal make sense? How is the partnership formation taxed? (Note that Section 709 requires 60–month amortization for costs incurred in organizing a partnership, analogously to Section 248's rule for corporations, and disallows any deduction—ever—for costs of selling interests in a partnership.)

2. What if David gets only 1/3d of future profits, which are speculative, but gets no interest in the partnership's existing assets?

3. What if David gets only 1/3d of future profits, but Daryl and Darrell also contributed high quality corporate bonds to the partnership?

15. The new partner does not have a significant interest in future partnership affairs after the distribution.

16. Notwithstanding the "under regulations" language at the beginning of Section 707(a)(2), Section 707(a)(2)(A) is viewed generally as effective even though there are no regulations implementing it yet. This presents problems, as the scope of the statute is anything but clear. For example, it can be read to apply to any service partner, since, in the long run, all allocations are matched with distributions.

F. DE FACTO TAX PARTNERSHIPS

READ: Code §§ 761(a) and 7701(a)(2) and Reg. § 301.7701–1

The discussion up to this point has looked at partnerships created as such by a formal partnership agreement or other state-law organizing instrument, such as an LLC's articles of organization. At common law, a partnership could be created without any agreement by the parties to form a partnership if the underlying relationships constituted a partnership de facto. The usual consequence of the finding of a de facto state-law partnership was to hold somebody liable for debts to which she was not a formal party. This law was a child of agency, particularly the law of apparent authority.

The Code also contains de facto tax partnership law. Since a partnership is a separate, if non-taxable, entity, there can be numerous untoward tax consequences of inadvertently forming a tax partnership, as illustrated by the following case:

MADISON GAS AND ELECTRIC COMPANY
v. COMMISSIONER

United States Court of Appeals, Seventh Circuit, 1980.
633 F.2d 512.

The question is whether certain training and related expenses incurred by a public utility in the expansion of its generating capacity through the joint construction and operation of a nuclear plant with two other utilities are deductible as ordinary and necessary expenses in the years of payment or are non-deductible pre-operating capital expenditures of a new partnership venture. The Tax Court held that they are non-deductible capital expenditures. We affirm.

Taxpayer Madison Gas and Electric Co. (MGE) is an operating public utility which has been engaged since 1896 in the production, purchase, transmission and distribution of electricity and the purchase and distribution of natural gas.

MGE has over the years kept pace with the increasing demand for electrical power and provided it at reasonable rates by expanding the generating capacity of its facilities, contracting for the purchase and sale of excess electrical power, interconnecting transmission facilities with those of other Wisconsin utilities, and finally by building and operating additional facilities in conjunction with other utilities. Expenses incurred in connection with one of these joint ventures is the subject of the present suit.

On February 2, 1967, MGE entered into an agreement, entitled "Joint Power Supply Agreement" (Agreement), with Wisconsin Public Service Corporation (WPS) and Wisconsin Power and Light Co. (WPL) under which the three utilities agreed, inter alia, to construct and own together a nuclear generating plant now known as the Kewaunee Nuclear Power Plant (Plant). Under the Agreement, the Plant is owned by MGE, WPS and WPL as tenants-in-common. Electricity produced by the Plant is distributed to each of the utilities in proportion to their ownership interests. Each utility sells or uses its share of the power as it does power produced by its own individually owned facilities, and the profits thereby earned by MGE contribute only to MGE's individual profits. No portion of the power generated at the Plant is offered for sale by the utilities collectively, and the Plant is not recognized by the relevant regulatory bodies as a separate utility licensed to sell electricity. Each utility also pays a portion of all expenditures for operation, maintenance and repair of the Plant corresponding exactly to its respective share of ownership. Under utility accounting procedures mandated by the PSC and the FERC [the Wisconsin Public Services Commission and the U.S. Federal Energy Regulatory Commission, which regulate MGE's rates], these expenses are combined with and treated in the same manner by MGE as expenses from its individually owned facilities. The ownership and operation of the Plant by MGE, WPS and WPL is regarded by the PSC and the FERC as a tenancy-in-common. It was the intention of the utilities to create only a co-tenancy and not a partnership and to be taxed as co-tenants and not as partners.

In its 1969 and 1970 taxable years, MGE incurred certain expenses relating to the nuclear training of WPS employees, the establishment of internal procedures and guidelines for plant operation and maintenance, employee hiring activities, nuclear field management, environmental activities and the purchase of certain spare parts. MGE had to incur these expenses in order to carry out its Plant activities.

MGE's position was, and is, that the claimed expenses were currently deductible under Section 162(a) as ordinary and necessary business expenses. The Commissioner's position was, and is, that the claimed expenses were non-deductible capital expenditures. The Tax Court agreed with the Commissioner, holding that the operation of the Plant by MGE, WPS and WPL is a partnership within the meaning of Section 7701(a)(2) of the Code, that the expenses in question were incurred not in the carrying out of an existing business but as part of the start-up costs of the new partnership venture, and that the expenses were therefore not currently deductible. MGE appeals from this judgment, arguing that its arrangement with WPS and WPL is not a partnership within the meaning of the Code and, alternatively, that even if it is a partnership the expenses are currently deductible.

The threshold issue is whether MGE's joint venture with WPS and WPL is a tax partnership. The Commissioner concedes that if it is not, the expenses are currently deductible under Section 162(a). A partnership for federal tax purposes is defined by the Code in Section 7701(a)(2), which provides in pertinent part:

"The term 'partnership' includes a syndicate, group, pool, joint venture, or other unincorporated organization, through or by means of which any business, financial operation, or venture is carried on, and which is not, within the meaning of this title, a trust estate or a corporation.''

MGE's arrangement with WPS and WPL in connection with the Plant clearly establishes an unincorporated organization carrying on a ''business, financial operation, or venture'' and therefore falls within the literal statutory definition of a partnership. The arrangement is, of course, not taken out of this classification simply because the three utilities intended to be taxed only as a co-tenancy and not as a partnership. While it is well-settled that mere co-ownership of property does not create a tax partnership, co-owners may also be partners if they or their agents carry on the requisite ''degree of business activities.''

MGE's argument is that a co-tenancy does not meet the business activities test of partnership status unless the co-tenants anticipate the earning and sharing of a single joint cash profit from their joint activity. Because its common venture with WPS and WPL does not result in the division of cash profits from joint marketing, MGE contends that the venture constitutes only a co-tenancy coupled with an expense-sharing arrangement and not a tax partnership. The Tax Court held that the Code definition of partnership does not require joint venturers to share in a single joint cash profit and that to the extent that a profit motive is required by the Code it is met here by the distribution of profits in kind. We agree.

MGE cites to us case law referring to a joint profit motive as a characteristic of partnerships.[17] Neither the above-quoted Treasury Regulation Sections nor the case law distinguish between the division of cash profits and the division of in-kind profits, and none of the cited cases involved in-kind profits. Moreover, while distribution of profits in-kind may be an uncommon business arrangement, recognition of such arrangements as tax partnerships is not novel.

The practical reality of the venture in issue here is that jointly produced electricity is distributed to MGE and the other two utilities in direct proportion to their ownership interest for resale to consumers in their service areas or to other utilities. The difference between the market value of MGE's share of that electricity and MGE's share of the cost of production obviously represents a profit. Just as obviously, the three utilities joined together in the construction and operation of the Plant with the anticipation of realizing these profits. The fact that the profits are not realized in cash until after the electricity has been channeled through the individual facilities of each participant does not negate their joint profit motive nor make the venture a mere expense-sharing arrangement.[18] We hold therefore that MGE's joint venture with

---

17. [Court's Note 3:] The Commissioner takes the position that the presence of a joint profit motive is merely one factor to be considered in determining partnership status, while MGE argues that it is a necessary element. Because we find a joint profit mo- tive here, albeit for in-kind profits, we need not resolve this dispute.

18. [Court's Note 5:] Treasury Regulation Sections 301.7701–3 and 1.761–1(a) state that a ''joint undertaking merely to share expenses is not a partnership,'' and

WPS and WPL constitutes a partnership within the meaning of Sections 7701(a)(2) and 761(a) of the Code.

[The court then determined that the expenditures under examination were non-deductible start-up costs of the tax partnership as an entity, which is separate and distinct from it partners for tax purposes.]

Under the Internal Revenue Code the joint venture here is a partnership and the expenses were non-deductible, pre-operational start-up costs of the partnership venture. Accordingly, the judgment of the Tax Court is affirmed.

REVIEW: Code §§ 761(a) and 7701(a)(2) and Reg. § 301.7701–1

Problem Set II.F

The Big Corporation and Mega, Inc. have executed an "alliance agreement." Big manufactures computers. Mega develops software. Under the alliance agreement, each will bundle their respective products with those of the other. Big will sell the bundled product through its retail stores. Mega will sell through its online retail facility. They will pay each other the customary wholesale price for the respective products. All advertising expenses for the bundled product, which must be jointly agreed to, will be shared equally. Big and Mega will work together on the technology required to fully integrate their respective products, bearing their respective costs. Big wants to expense its Section 174 expenditures in this activity, while Mega wants to amortize its Section 174 expenditures over 60 months. Under Section 703, discussed in the next chapter of this text, if the alliance agreement is treated as creating a partnership for tax purposes, the deemed partners, Big and Mega, must use the same accounting method for Section 174 expenses. Accordingly, the question arises as to whether Big and Mega can chose different treatments of these items?

go on to give the example of neighboring landowners who jointly construct a ditch "merely to drain surface water from their properties." We agree with the Tax Court that the venture here is "in no way comparable to the joint construction of a drainage ditch".

Chapter III

LIFE OF A SIMPLE PARTNERSHIP

A. INTRODUCTION

Chapter II described the basic taxation of partnership formation. This chapter looks at the life of a simple partnership—one where (i) the partners share everything pro-rata, (ii) the only distributions by the partnership to its partners are cash, and (iii) all taxpayers' tax years are the calendar year. Such discussion should familiarize the student with the core tax rules that apply over the life of a partnership as well as further inform her understanding of how everything connects with everything in Subchapter K.

B. THE BASIC HYBRID APPROACH TO PARTNERSHIP OPERATIONS

READ: Code §§ 701, 702, 703, 704(a), 706(a), and 6031 and Reg. § 1.702–1(a)(8)

Current law's basic approach to the taxation of partnership operations is unchanged from 1913: Under current Section 701, a partnership is not a taxpayer. It determines its income as if it were a taxpayer under Section 703, however. The partners pay tax on their respective shares of the partnership's income under Section 702.

As contemplated by Section 703 and required by Section 6031(a), the partnership files a return, Form 1065, with the IRS, which makes preliminary determinations of tax items and allocates them among the partners. The partnership provides each partner a personal Schedule K–1 (to the Partnership's Form 1065) that shows her specific share of partnership items, as required by Section 6031(b):[1]

---

1. Section 6103(e)(1)(C) gives all partners the right to see their partnership's Form 1065, including the attached Schedules K–1 of all the partners, as filed with the IRS. This is particularly useful for partners in partnerships, say, law or accounting firms, that try to keep the partners' respective shares secret.

SCHEDULE K-1	**Partner's Share of Income, Credits, Deductions, etc.**	OMB No. 1545-0099
(Form 1065)	▶ See separate instructions.	
Department of the Treasury Internal Revenue Service	For calendar year 2000 or tax year beginning _____ , 2000, and ending _____ , 20 ___	**2000**

Partner's identifying number ▶	Partnership's identifying number ▶
Partner's name, address, and ZIP code	Partnership's name, address, and ZIP code

A This partner is a ☐ general partner   ☐ limited partner
☐ limited liability company member

B What type of entity is this partner? ▶ ....

C Is this partner a ☐ domestic or a ☐ foreign partner?

D Enter partner's percentage of:
(i) Before change or termination   (ii) End of year

Profit sharing . . . . % .... %
Loss sharing . . . . % .... %
Ownership of capital . . . . % .... %

E IRS Center where partnership filed return:

F Partner's share of liabilities (see instructions):
Nonrecourse . . . . $ ....
Qualified nonrecourse financing . . $ ....
Other . . . . $ ....

G Tax shelter registration number. . ▶ ....

H Check here if this partnership is a publicly traded partnership as defined in section 469(k)(2) . . . . . . ☐

I Check applicable boxes: (1) ☐ Final K-1   (2) ☐ Amended K-1

J   Analysis of partner's capital account:

(a) Capital account at beginning of year	(b) Capital contributed during year	(c) Partner's share of lines 3, 4, and 7, Form 1065, Schedule M-2	(d) Withdrawals and distributions	(e) Capital account at end of year (combine columns (a) through (d))
			( )	

	(a) Distributive share item		(b) Amount	(c) 1040 filers enter the amount in column (b) on:
Income (Loss)	1 Ordinary income (loss) from trade or business activities . .	1		See page 6 of Partner's Instructions for Schedule K-1 (Form 1065).
	2 Net income (loss) from rental real estate activities	2		
	3 Net income (loss) from other rental activities.	3		
	4 Portfolio income (loss):			
	a Interest	4a		Sch. B, Part I, line 1
	b Ordinary dividends	4b		Sch. B, Part II, line 5
	c Royalties	4c		Sch. E, Part I, line 4
	d Net short-term capital gain (loss)	4d		Sch. D, line 5, col. (f)
	e Net long-term capital gain (loss):			
	(1) 28% rate gain (loss)	4e(1)		Sch. D, line 12, col. (g)
	(2) Total for year.	4e(2)		Sch. D, line 12, col. (f)
	f Other portfolio income (loss) (attach schedule)	4f		Enter on applicable line of your return.
	5 Guaranteed payments to partner	5		See page 6 of Partner's Instructions for Schedule K-1 (Form 1065).
	6 Net section 1231 gain (loss) (other than due to casualty or theft) .	6		
	7 Other income (loss) (attach schedule)	7		Enter on applicable line of your return.
Deductions	8 Charitable contributions (see instructions) (attach schedule) . .	8		Sch. A, line 15 or 16
	9 Section 179 expense deduction.	9		See pages 7 and 8 of Partner's Instructions for Schedule K-1 (Form 1065).
	10 Deductions related to portfolio income (attach schedule) . . .	10		
	11 Other deductions (attach schedule).	11		
Credits	12a Low-income housing credit:			
	(1) From section 42(j)(5) partnerships for property placed in service before 1990	12a(1)		
	(2) Other than on line 12a(1) for property placed in service before 1990	12a(2)		Form 8586, line 5
	(3) From section 42(j)(5) partnerships for property placed in service after 1989	12a(3)		
	(4) Other than on line 12a(3) for property placed in service after 1989	12a(4)		
	b Qualified rehabilitation expenditures related to rental real estate activities	12b		
	c Credits (other than credits shown on lines 12a and 12b) related to rental real estate activities.	12c		See page 8 of Partner's Instructions for Schedule K-1 (Form 1065).
	d Credits related to other rental activities	12d		
	13 Other credits.	13		

For Paperwork Reduction Act Notice, see Instructions for Form 1065.   Cat. No. 11394R   **Schedule K-1 (Form 1065) 2000**

Schedule K-1 (Form 1065) 2000   Page **2**

	(a) Distributive share item		(b) Amount	(c) 1040 filers enter the amount in column (b) on:
Investment Interest	**14a** Interest expense on investment debts.	**14a**		Form 4952, line 1
	b (1) Investment income included on lines 4a, 4b, 4c, and 4f .	**14b(1)**		See page 9 of Partner's instructions for Schedule K-1 (Form 1065).
	(2) Investment expenses included on line 10.	**14b(2)**		
Self-employment	**15a** Net earnings (loss) from self-employment.	**15a**		Sch. SE, Section A or B
	b Gross farming or fishing income.	**15b**		See page 9 of Partner's Instructions for Schedule K-1 (Form 1065).
	c Gross nonfarm income.	**15c**		
Adjustments and Tax Preference Items	**16a** Depreciation adjustment on property placed in service after 1986	**16a**		See page 9 of Partner's Instructions for Schedule K-1 (Form 1065) and Instructions for Form 6251.
	b Adjusted gain or loss	**16b**		
	c Depletion (other than oil and gas)	**16c**		
	d (1) Gross income from oil, gas, and geothermal properties . .	**16d(1)**		
	(2) Deductions allocable to oil, gas, and geothermal properties	**16d(2)**		
	e Other adjustments and tax preference items(attach schedule)	**16e**		
Foreign Taxes	**17a** Name of foreign country or U.S. possession ▶			
	b Gross income sourced at partner level	**17b**		Form 1116, Part I
	c Foreign gross income sourced at partnership level:			
	(1) Passive	**17c(1)**		
	(2) Listed categories (attach schedule)	**17c(2)**		
	(3) General limitation	**17c(3)**		
	d Deductions allocated and apportioned at partner level:			
	(1) Interest expense	**17d(1)**		
	(2) Other	**17d(2)**		
	e Deductions allocated and apportioned at partnership level to foreign source income:			
	(1) Passive	**17e(1)**		
	(2) Listed categories (attach schedule)	**17e(2)**		
	(3) General limitation	**17e(3)**		
	f Total foreign taxes (check one): ▶ ☐ Paid ☐ Accrued . . .	**17f**		Form 1116, Part II
	g Reduction in taxes available for credit and gross income from all sources (attach schedule)	**17g**		See Instructions for Form 1116.
Other	**18** Section 59(e)(2) expenditures: **a** Type ▶			See page 9 of Partner's Instructions for Schedule K-1 (Form 1065).
	b Amount	**18b**		
	19 Tax-exempt interest income	**19**		Form 1040, line 8b
	20 Other tax-exempt income.	**20**		See pages 9 and 10 of Partner's Instructions for Schedule K-1 (Form 1065).
	21 Nondeductible expenses	**21**		
	22 Distributions of money (cash and marketable securities) . . .	**22**		
	23 Distributions of property other than money	**23**		
	24 Recapture of low-income housing credit:			
	a From section 42(j)(5) partnerships	**24a**		Form 8611, line 8
	b Other than on line 24a.	**24b**		
Supplemental Information	**25** Supplemental information required to be reported separately to each partner(attach additional schedules if more space is needed):			

Schedule K-1 (Form 1065) 2000

One might think that this long-established regime would work simply. This is not the case. Difficulties arise because income and deductions come in flavors and different taxpayers have different tastes.

For an example of income with a special flavor, consider interest on municipal bonds that is tax-exempt under Section 103. If a partnership determined one taxable income number that included the muni bond interest and that partnership income was allocated among the partners, the effect would be that the muni bond interest would be taxable to the partners. After all, corporate dividends paid out of tax-exempt income are taxable dividends.[2] Taxing Section 103 interest earned through a partnership seems wrong, however. Thus, Section 703(a) provides that a partnership determines its income as if an individual, so that the partnership applies Section 103 and does not include the muni bond interest in its taxable income. Then, Section 702(b) respects this treatment in taxing the partners, with the result that the interest is not taxable to the partners. As this example illustrates, flavor matters. Section 103 interest tastes differently from other income, and therefore must be treated separately. This seems simple enough.

Unfortunately, matters are more complicated, because different taxpayers have different tastes in income and deductions. To continue with our example, not only does muni bond interest taste differently from taxable interest, there are different flavors of muni bond interest income, which different taxpayers have different preferences for. Under Section 57(a)(5), interest on some private activity muni bonds is subject to the alternative minimum tax. Thus, this interest may or may not have been taxable if earned directly by the partners, depending upon whether they would have been subject to the alternative minimum tax thereon. In other words, different partners have different tastes.

The first sentence of Section 1.702–1(a)(8)(ii) of the regulations deals with this. It provides a catch-all rule, authorized by Section 702(a)(7), that each partner must reflect the special character of any partnership income, deduction, or loss item when that special character affects her tax liability. Then, Section 703(a)(1) requires the partnership to account for these items separately. Look at the sample Schedule K–1 above. Line 25 breaks out all Section 702(a)(7) items.

This aggregate approach is complicated. A partnership must take into account the tax positions of **all** of its partners in characterizing tax items. Congress has reduced this complexity, by adopting a more entity-like rule, in certain circumstances, however. Partnerships with 100 or more partners can elect a simplified regime that provides (i) that only a limited list of items' character passes through from the partnership to the partners and (ii) that some calculations, like capital gains netting, are done at the partnership level.[3]

The basic aggregate approach does not apply to all aspects of the determination of partnership income and loss, however, even of a partnership that does or cannot elect the simplified rules. For example, Section 703(b) requires most tax elections to be made by the partnership rather than by the partners. This simplifies matters considerably, but at the cost of precluding partners from making inconsistent elections in their respective tax self-interests.[4]

---

2. Treas. Reg. § 1.312–6(b).

3. I.R.C. §§ 771–777.

4. For example, in *Demirjian v. Commissioner*, 54 T.C. 1691 (1970), *aff'd*, 457 F.2d 1 (3d Cir.1972), partnership property was involuntarily converted into cash. The partnership liquidated, distributing the cash to the partners. In order to qualify the conversion for tax-free treatment under Section 1033, each partner purchased separate qualifying replacement property and made a timely Section 1033 election. The court held that the Section 1033 election

In the following case, the Tax Court describes in more detail some of the problems presented by current law's hybrid regime:

COGGIN AUTOMOTIVE CORPORATION v. COMMISSIONER

United States Tax Court.

115 T.C. 349 (2000).

JACOBS, *Judge*:

[Section 1363(d) imposes a recapture tax with regard to inventory that has been accounted for under the LIFO (last-in-first-out) method that is held by a corporation that converts from C to S (partnership-like) status. In this case, a C corporation contributed its LIFO inventory to a partnership and then elected S status. The Tax Court determined that the contribution transaction was valid, so that, under general tax rules, the partnership was the owner of the property at the time that the corporate partner elected S status. Then, the court had to decide whether the corporation was treated as owning the inventory held by the partnership for purposes of applying the Section 1363(d) tax.]

For tax purposes, a partnership may be viewed either (1) as an aggregation of its partners, each of whom directly owns an interest in the partnership's assets and operations, or (2) as a separate entity, in which separate interests are owned by each of the partners. Subchapter K of the Internal Revenue Code blends both approaches. In certain areas, the aggregate approach predominates. See sec. 701 (Partners, Not Partnership, Subject to Tax), sec. 702 (Income and Credits of Partner). In other areas, the entity approach predominates. See sec. 742 (Basis of Transferee Partner's Interest), sec. 743 (Optional Adjustment to Basis of Partnership Property). Outside of subchapter K, whether the aggregate or the entity approach is to be applied depends upon which approach more appropriately serves the Code provision at issue. See *Holiday Village Shopping Ctr. v. United States*, 773 F.2d 276, 279 (Fed.Cir.1985); *Casel v. Commissioner*, 79 T.C. 424, 433 (1982); Conf. Rept. 2543, 83d Cong., 2d Sess. 59 (1954).

Respondent argues that the legislative intent underlying the enactment of section 1363(d) requires the application of the aggregate theory. Respondent asserts that Congress enacted section 1363(d) in order to ensure that the corporate level of taxation be preserved on built-in gain assets (such as LIFO reserves) that fall outside the ambit of section 1374. In this regard, respondent contends that failure to apply the

and acquisition of replacement property with regard to partnership property must be done by the partnership so that the reinvestments did not support nonrecognition under Section 1033.

The student may now be beginning to understand why partnership agreements provide rules regarding tax matters. For example, it is customary to provide in a partnership agreement that the managing partners make tax elections at their sole discretion, so that they are not liable to partners who would benefit from a different partnership position. In contrast, corporate documents rarely address tax matters, as corporate tax determinations do not have differing effects on the shareholders in most cases.

aggregate theory to section 1363(d) would allow the gain deferred under the LIFO method to completely escape the corporate level of taxation upon a C corporation's election of S corporation status and would eviscerate Congress' supersession of *General Utils. & Operating Co. v. Helvering*, 296 U.S. 200, 80 L.Ed. 154, 56 S.Ct. 185 (1935).

Petitioner maintains that although there are no cases that apply the aggregate or entity approach to inventory items, the focus with respect to accounting for inventory is done at the partnership level. In essence, petitioner asserts that the LIFO recapture amount under section 1363(d) is a component of a partnership's taxable income that must be computed at the partnership level. Petitioner posits that it would be incongruent to treat the calculation of the LIFO recapture amount as an item of income under the entity approach while applying the aggregate approach to attribute the ownership of inventory to the partners.

In 1986, Congress enacted the Tax Reform Act of 1986 (TRA), Pub. L. 99–514, secs. 631–633, 100 Stat. 2085, 2269–2282, which did away with the General Utilities doctrine. Under the General Utilities doctrine, corporations generally had not been taxed on the distribution of assets whose fair market values exceeded their tax bases. In TRA section 632(a), section 1374 (Tax Imposed on Certain Built–In Gains) was amended to prevent the potential circumvention of the corporate level of tax on the distribution of appreciated (built-in gain) assets by a former C corporation that held such assets at the time of its conversion to an S corporation.[5] See *Rondy, Inc. v. Commissioner*, T.C. Memo 1995–372 ("the original purpose of section 1374 was to support Congress' repeal of the *General Utilities* doctrine"); H. Conf. Rept. 99–841 (Vol. II), at II–198 to II–199, II–203 (1986), 1986–3 C.B. (Vol. 4), 1, 198–199, 203.

It became apparent that the goal of section 1374 was not being achieved with respect to former C corporations that used the LIFO method of accounting because a taxpayer that experienced rising acquisition costs would seldom, if ever, experience a decrement of its LIFO reserves. Congress thus recognized that the deferred built-in gain resulting from using the LIFO method might escape taxation at the corporate level. In light of this potential for abuse, section 1363(d) was enacted. See H. Rept. 100–391 (Vol. II), at 1098 (1987).

After considering the legislative histories of sections 1374 and 1363(d), we conclude that the application of the aggregate approach (as opposed to the entity approach) of partnerships in this case better serves Congress' intent. By enacting sections 1374 and 1363(d), Congress evinced an intent to prevent corporations from avoiding a second level of taxation on built-in gain assets by converting to S corporations. Application of the aggregate approach to section 1363(d) is consistent with Congress' rationale for enacting this section and operates to prevent a corporate taxpayer from using the LIFO method of accounting to perma-

---

5. [Court's Note 6:] In general, sec. 1374 requires an S corporation to pay a corporate-level tax on any net recognized built-in gains recognized within 10 years following the effective date of the S election.

nently avoid gain recognition on appreciated assets. In contrast, applying the entity approach to section 1363(d) would potentially allow a corporate partner to permanently avoid paying a second level of tax on appreciated property by encouraging transfers of inventory between related entities. This result clearly would be inconsistent with the legislative history of sections 1363(d) and 1374 and the supersession of the *General Utilities* doctrine.

Courts have, in some instances, used the aggregate approach for purposes of applying nonsubchapter K provisions. For instance, in *Casel v. Commissioner*, 79 T.C. at 433, we upheld the Commissioner's use of the aggregate approach for purposes of applying section 267 (disallowance of losses between related parties). In *Holiday Village Shopping Ctr. v. United States*, 773 F.2d at 279, the Court of Appeals for the Federal Circuit applied the aggregate approach for purposes of determining the extent of depreciation recapture to each shareholder. Similarly, the Court of Appeals in *Unger v. Commissioner*, [290 U.S.App.D.C. 259,] 936 F.2d 1316 (D.C.Cir.1991), affg. T.C. Memo 1990–15, used the aggregate approach in determining a taxpayer's permanent establishment. In each of these instances, the court analyzed the relevant legislative history and statutory scheme in determining whether the aggregate or entity approach was more appropriate. Moreover, we are mindful that the aggregate approach is generally applied to various subchapter K provisions dealing with inventory and other built-in gain assets (i.e., receivables). See, e.g., secs. 704(c), 731, 734(b), 743(b), 751.

We recognize that in several instances courts have found the entity approach better than the aggregate approach. For example, in *P.D.B. Sports, Ltd. v. Commissioner*, 109 T.C. 423 (1997), this Court used the entity approach for purposes of applying section 1056. Similarly, in *Madison Gas & Elec. Co. v. Commissioner*, 72 T.C. 521, 564 (1979), affd. 633 F.2d 512 (7th Cir.1980), this Court and the Court of Appeals for the Seventh Circuit applied the entity approach in determining whether expenses were ordinary and necessary under section 162. Likewise, in *Brown Group, Inc. & Subs. v. Commissioner*, 77 F.3d 217 (8th Cir.1996), revg. 104 T.C. 105 (1995), the Court of Appeals for the Eighth Circuit concluded that the entity approach, rather than the aggregate approach, should be used in characterizing income (subpart F income) earned by the partnership. We do not believe the holdings in those cases to be dispositive here. The outcomes in those cases were based upon the specific legislative histories and statutory schemes of the respective Code provisions at issue. Each court viewed the respective statute in the context in which it was enacted and concluded that the entity approach was more appropriate than the aggregate approach to carry out Congress' intent. Here, as stated, both the legislative history and the statutory scheme of section 1363(d) mandate the application of the aggregate approach

To conclude, we hold that the aggregate approach (as opposed to the entity approach) better serves the underlying purpose and scope of section 1363(d) in the circumstances of this case. Consequently, petitioner is deemed to own a pro rata share of the dealerships' inventories. Accordingly, we hold that upon its election of S corporation status, petitioner was required to include in its gross income the LIFO recapture amount.

The Anti–Abuse Regulations, already mentioned in Section I.C.3 of this text, also apply aggregate treatment in certain circumstances. This feature of these regulations is discussed below in Section XI.D of this text.

REVIEW: Code §§ 701, 702, 703, 704(a), 706(a), and 6031 and Reg. § 1.702–1(a)(8)

SKIM: Code §§ 771–777 and Reg. § 1.701–2(e)

Problem Set III.B

A and B, unmarried individuals, form the AB general partnership. All partnership items are shared equally. The partnership has a $50,000 Section 1231 gain and no Section 1231 losses.[6] The partnership has no other relevant tax items. B has a $30,000 Section 1231 loss incurred directly. A and B also have large amounts of long-term capital gains from stock trading and no other items that are relevant to determining the impact of the special tax rules applicable to gains and losses. What is the tax effect on A and B of their participation in AB?

C. BORROWING AND DISTRIBUTIONS

READ: Code §§ 705(a), 731(a)(1), 733, and 752

As a partnership engages in business, it generates taxable income. That income is taxed to the partners, not the partnership. What happens when that income is cashed out by the partners withdrawing cash from the partnership in the form of cash distributions? Since that income has been taxed already, the partners should be able to withdraw their share without further taxation. After all, under an aggregate view, the money already belongs to the partners. Partnership distribution is a mere change in form that should have no tax consequences.

Current law achieves this result. When profit (taxable **and tax-free**) is allocated to a partner, she increases her outside basis under Section 705(a)(1). She is treated as if she earned the money directly and then contributed the money to the partnership, with a corresponding positive adjustment to her outside basis. Then, Section 731(a)(1) allows her to withdraw cash tax-free in an amount equal to her outside basis. As a consequence, the Section 705(a)(1) basis adjustment guarantees that the partner has sufficient outside basis to withdraw all profits

---

6. This text measures Section 1231 gains after taking out any amount taxed   specially under either Section 1245 or Section 1250.

previously allocated to her (plus her original investment) without tax. Finally, to reflect the withdrawal, the outside basis is reduced by the amount distributed under Section 733. Note that this regime has the effect that tax-free items earned by a partnership can be pulled out of the partnership tax-free.

It is common for service partnerships, like law firms, to allow partners to withdraw some portion of their share of the current year's profits as a "draw" prior to the underlying income being allocated among the partners on the partnership's books. Under these circumstances, a partner may not have sufficient outside basis at the time of a distribution so as not to be taxed on it under Section 731. Sympathetically, Section 1.731–1(a)(1)(ii) of the regulations provides that such a draw is treated as an interest-free loan from the partnership to the partner that is paid off with cash received in a deemed distribution on the last day of the partnership's tax year (after the year's income allocation, so that the partner has sufficient basis to receive the distribution tax-free).[7]

Section 731 applies to all partnership distributions. Only cash distributions are considered here. Later chapters look at the other types of distributions. Cash distributions first are tax-free to the distributee partner and reduce her outside basis under Section 733. Then, to the extent that a cash distribution exceeds the partner's remaining outside basis, gain is recognized. A loss is allowed only with regard to a distribution in complete liquidation of a partner's entire interest in the partnership. As to non-liquidating distributions, the partner's investment transaction is not over, so that any loss has yet to be realized by a closed transaction for which it is appropriate to allow the loss for tax purposes. The partner still owns a partnership interest with a positive basis so that the loss can be allowed later, if necessary, when the interest is liquidated.

Partnership borrowing requires further rules. Under state law, unless the loan documents provide otherwise, a general partner is jointly and severally liable for partnership obligations. In effect, the partners are the borrowers. For sound reasons, Subchapter K reflects this state-law reality.

Consider a partnership that owns highly appreciated (high value and low basis) land. Rather than sell the land, the partners use the land's value by using it as security for a cash borrowing (giving the lender a first mortgage). The partnership then distributes the borrowed cash to the partners. What is the tax treatment? The partnership has no income for Section 703(a) purposes, as borrowing, per se, is not a taxable event. The distribution presents more difficulty. If the partnership has a low (inside) basis in the property, the partners probably have low (outside) bases in their partnership interests. Thus, without some basis adjustment to respect the new borrowing, Section 731 could trigger a tax on

---

7. Presumably, interest is not imputed on this loan, as it is not a tax avoidance   loan or otherwise described in Section 7872.

the distribution of the proceeds of the borrowing. However, when an individual borrows cash directly, she gets a basis in the borrowed cash even though the borrowing is tax-free. Thus, under an aggregate approach, a partner would get free basis when the partnership borrows. Section 752(a) achieves this result, but using entity-approach formalism. Partnership borrowing is taxed as if the partners borrowed directly and then contributed the borrowed cash to their partnership.[8] Then, to be consistent, Section 752(b) provides that partnership payments on debt are treated as if the partnership distributed cash to the partner to pay the debt.[9]

An example illustrates how this mechanism effects sound results: A partnership formed just for this purpose borrows $100,000. The partnership uses this $100,000 plus $50,000 contributed by the partners to buy a piece of land. After applying Section 752(a), the total outside basis is $150,000, the same as the inside basis of the land. The land is leased for a rent stream that exactly matches the payments (principal and interest) required on the debt. After 20 years, the debt is paid off and the partnership owns the land (which still has its cost basis of $150,000) without owing a dime. Thus, after 20 years, the total outside basis also should still be $150,000; which it is, but the mechanics are involved: Each year, to the extent that the rent pays interest, the interest deduction shelters the rent income, so that no income is allocated to partners so as to impact their outside bases. Similarly, to the extent that the rent is used to pay principal on the debt, outside basis increases for the associated unsheltered taxable income and decreases in the exact same amount to reflect that the debt has been reduced.[10] Thus, outside basis stays unchanged at $150,000 every year. Over 20 years, the partners earned the additional $100,000 of debt-free outside basis by being taxed on the $100,000 of rent applied toward the principal of the

8. At this juncture, a student with a background in financial accounting may be puzzled by the notion of an outside basis. Up until the application of Section 752, the total outside basis resembles the total partners' equity. After application of Section 752, however, outside basis looks more like the entire right-hand side of the balance sheet. In fact, for a simple partnership with all the original partners, the best way to view outside basis is as the right-hand side of the balance sheet. Under Generally Accepted Accounting Principles, all forms of business organization (corporation, partnership, proprietorship, and so on) are viewed the same and as separate from their owners. Thus, in financial accounting, creditors are viewed like corporate creditors, as having a direct claim to the business' assets that does not go through the entity to the equity owners (shareholders, partners, or proprietor). In contrast, under the tax law's partially aggregate approach to partnerships, debt is viewed as flowing through to the partners, so that the partners own the

gross assets subject to debt rather than only owning the (net-of-debt) equity. (For this purpose, liabilities are determined under the partnership's accounting method, so that accrued but unpaid expense obligations are not tax liabilities. Rev. Rul. 88–77, 1988–2 C. B. 128.)

9. Partnership resources have been consumed to reduce the indirect burden on the partners. In contrast, if the partners pay the debt with their own funds, there is no net effect on basis.

10. To assure that the deemed distribution that results from the debt payment does not occur prior to the outside basis increase associated with the income used to pay the debt, which timing mismatch could trigger gain inappropriately, the deemed distribution so related is taken into account at year end, after the outside basis is adjusted for income, regardless of when the debt is paid during the year. Rev. Rul. 94–4, 1994–1 C.B 196.

debt. The multiple outside basis adjustments in this example may seem much ado about nothing, since they have no net effect. It is comforting, however, to see that the Section 752 formalism achieves common sense results. Also, in more complicated examples, Section 752's rules can have a net effect.

REVIEW: Code §§ 705(a), 731(a)(1), 733, and 752 and Reg. §§ 1.705–1(a)(1) and 1.731–1(a)(1)(ii)

Problem Set III.C

Sally and Ann form a 50–50 partnership, each contributing $75,000. The partnership buys as an investment a portfolio of non-dividend-paying corporate stock. After 10 years, during which the partnership has continued the original portfolio, the portfolio is worth $1 million. The partnership sells the portfolio (assume no commissions) and liquidates, distributing the sales proceeds, which are the partnership's only assets. How are Sally and Ann taxed over the years with regards to their involvement in this partnership?

D. LOSS LIMITATIONS

READ: Code §§ 469(a)–(d), (g), and (h)(1)–(2) and 704(d)

Perhaps the most important impact of outside basis is through Section 704(d). It provides that the total partnership loss that may be claimed by a partner cannot exceed her basis in her partnership interest. In other words, since her outside basis is her after-tax investment in the partnership, she cannot claim losses in excess of her investment—cannot claim losses paid with another partner's money.[11]

The Section 704(d) limit does not necessarily disallow a loss altogether. A loss not allowed to a partner in the current year because it is in excess of the partner's outside basis carries forward indefinitely to be used when and if the partner gets outside basis. For example, if the partner contributes cash to the partnership in a later year (say, to pay her share of the partnership's loss for the earlier year), the contribution gives the contributing partner basis that triggers the deferred loss. Similarly, if the partnership later turns a profit, that profit increases the partner's outside basis, which frees up the deferred loss so that it can be used against the later income.

Congress, in 1976, 1978, and 1986, felt that section 704(d) was inadequate to deal with individual tax shelters. In a typical limited partnership tax shelter, a wealthy individual buys a limited partnership interest that will pass through losses that the investor limited partner

---

11. In the pro-rata partnerships considered up to now, a partner cannot be allocated losses in excess of her share of partnership capital and borrowing, as the partnership cannot lose more money than it has or borrows. Section 704(d), a 1954 provision, is so fundamental, however, that it is important to introduce it as soon as possible.

uses to shelter other—service or investment—income. The At–Risk Rules of Section 465, enacted in 1976 and toughened in 1978, provide a limit on partnership loss pass-throughs in addition to Section 704(d). They deal with problems presented by nonrecourse and related-party debt and is discussed in Chapter V.

Section 465 was inadequate to stem the tax shelter tide. Practitioners found ways, many questionable, to skirt the At–Risk Rules. The Passive Activity Loss (PAL) rules, Section 469, reflect a broad legislative edict that "individuals shalt not shelter!" Under these 1986 rules, an individual cannot use losses from her "passive activities" against active or investment income.[12] Activities are evaluated with regard to the specific taxpayer's participation therein.[13] These passive losses are somewhat misnamed, as they arise from activities that are more active than truly passive investing, although less active than a real business.[14] In applying Section 469, all of an individual's passive activities are thrown together. If that big ball shows a net loss, that loss is limited.[15] Thus, passive losses from one passive activity can shelter income from another passive activity.[16] There is the customary indefinite carryforward of any disallowed loss under Section 469(b). The loss carried forward can be used against future passive income, and, under Section 469(g), when a passive activity is disposed of.[17]

Section 469(h)(2) provides that an interest as limited partner alone is a passive investment, presumably because historically, under most states' laws, a partner could not participate in the partnership's business and be treated as a limited partner. Temporary regulations, however, provide that the interest of a limited partner or of an LLC member is not treated as passive if the partner or member satisfies a fairly high standard of participation in the business specified in the regulation.[18]

12. I.R.C. § 469(a)(1)(A).

13. I.R.C. § 469(c)(1)(B).

14. I.R.C. §§ 469(c)(1), (e)(1).

15. I.R.C. § 469(d)(1).

16. This cross-deducting between passive activities has no analogy under either Section 465 or 704(d). Losses not at risk with regard to one activity cannot be used when the taxpayer has an excess amount at risk in another activity. Similarly, losses from a partnership in which the taxpayer has insufficient basis cannot be used when the taxpayer has excess basis in another partnership.

17. This loss allowance makes sense. The PAL Rules are intended to disallow artificial losses only. In this light, consider a partnership that owns a building subject to non-economic accelerated ACRS depreciation for tax purposes. Because of the de-

preciation, the partnership will show a non-economic tax loss in the early years. That loss will be reversed either (i) by paper net taxable income in later years when depreciation is understated or, (ii) if the machinery is disposed of, by paper gain. The PAL rules allow the early paper loss to offset the paper gain in the later years so that the activity is not overtaxed. If there is any tax loss left after the activity has been disposed of, the unused carried-over loss is not a paper loss (to be offset by future paper gain), but an economic loss that should be allowed at such time.

18. Treas. Reg. § 1.469–5T(e). Section 469(e) provides a special grant of authority to write regulations under the PAL Rules, which presumably is the basis for this regulation.

REVIEW: Code §§ 469(a)–(d), (g), and (h)(1)–(2) and 704(d)

SKIM: Reg. § 1.469–5T(e)

Problem Set III.D

Beth is a partner in 2 partnerships. She is a capital (general) partner in a law firm. For 2000, her share of this partnership's profits is $450,000. Also, Beth has invested as a limited partner in a debt-free limited partnership that owns and operates an office building. At the beginning 2000, her outside basis was $25,000. Her 2000 share of the partnership's loss (attributable to accelerated depreciation) is $30,000. How does Beth's participation in these 2 partnerships affect her 2000 taxable income?

E.   TRANSFERS OF PARTNERSHIP INTERESTS

READ: Code §§ 1(h)(11) and (12), 741, 742, 743, 751(a), 754, and 755 and Reg. §§ 1.751–1(a)(1) and (2)

SKIM: Reg. § 1.1(h)–1

Current law's basic entity approach to the sale of partnership interests already was noted in Chapter II's discussion of the importance of outside basis: The selling partner has gain or loss equal to the difference between the amount realized and the outside basis. This gain generally is capital gain under Section 741. The buyer has a cost basis in her partnership interest under Section 742.

With transfers of partnership interests, as with most things partnership, an entity approach has not been adequate to deal with all concerns, and aggregate rules have been adopted to supplement the entity rules when needed. As to the transferor of a partnership interest, the basic concern is a partner selling her partnership interest being taxed on any gain recognized only at capital gain rates when that gain is attributable to appreciated partnership assets that, if sold by the partnership, would generate ordinary income, Section 1250 recapture, or collectibles gain to the partner.[19]

Congress has taken two passes at this problem, with (i) 1954's collapsible partnership rules[20] contained in Section 751(a), which protect ordinary income (and loss), and with (ii) 1997's Section 1(h)(11), which protects Section 1250 recapture and collectibles gain (but not collectibles loss). Basically, when an interest is sold, the selling partner is taxed on the net Section 751 ordinary income (which is discussed in the next paragraph), Section 1250 recapture, and collectibles gain as if the partnership had sold all of its assets for their respective fair market values and the selling partner had been allocated her share of this gain. For this

---

19. Note 26, below, explains why this can cause permanent tax savings, even taking the future taxes on the partnership's assets into account.

20. So called due to their similarity to the collapsible corporation rules that are contained in Section 341.

purpose, the net Section 751(a) amount is determined by offsetting gains and losses of the same character. Any net Section 751(a) gain is backed out of the gain or loss otherwise realized on the interest sale. Then, any Section 1250 or collectibles gain is similarly backed out of this post-Section 751(a) residual gain or loss.[21] This adjusted amount is the gain or loss on the interest, which usually is capital gain or loss.[22] If the partnership would realize a net loss on Section 751 property if it were sold for its fair market value, that loss also passes through to the selling partner, increasing capital gain or reducing capital loss.[23] There is no analogous rule for collectibles loss.[24]

The 2 types of "hot" assets that trigger ordinary income treatment under Section 751(a) are unrealized receivables and inventory. One might think that unrealized receivables for this purposes would consist solely of the receivables of cash basis partnerships. After all, the focus of the 1954 legislation that enacted Section 751 was small business. In fact, Section 751(c) defines unrealized receivables remarkably broadly. Read Section 751(c). For example, gain attributable to recapture is an unrealized receivable, with, in effect, a zero basis (under the assumptions of this chapter). Read the first sentence of Section 1.751–1(c)(6)(ii) of the regulations. Moreover, the courts have interpreted Section 751(c) to include valuable contracts to provide goods and services even when those contracts have yet to give rise to a receivable under financial accounting. For example, a real estate partnership that has a valuable contract to provide management services to a third party owns a Section 751(c) unrealized receivable. Similarly, the definition of inventory in Section 751(d) is broader than one would expect, as it treats as inventory most types of ordinary income property, not just property subject to inventory accounting. Read Section 751(d).

An example helps illustrate the operation of these rules. Mary and Norm are 50–50 partners in a cash basis partnership. For simplicity, assume that the partnership has no liabilities. The partnership's assets are as follows:

	FMV	Basis
Cash	$100,000	$100,000
Receivables	200,000	–0–
Real Estate Held for Sale	1,000,000	250,000
Investment Real Estate	400,000	900,000
Goodwill	300,000	–0–
	2,000,000	1,250,000

Mary sells her interest, which has a basis of $625,000, for $1 million. Under Section 741, she has $375,000 of gain. Section 751(a) bifurcates

---

21.   Treas. Reg. § 1.1(h)–1(c).

22.   The partnership interest could be held for sale to customers so as not to be a capital asset.

23.   Treas. Reg. §§ 1.751–1(a)(1), (2).

24.   Treas. Reg. § 1.1(h)–1(b)(2)(ii). There can be no negative Section 1250 recapture.

the transaction, however. The ordinary income part relates to her share of the partnership's hot assets, the receivables (under Section 751(c)) and the real estate held for sale (under Section 751(d)(1)). If the partnership sold these assets for their fair market values, it would have $950,000 of ordinary income. Her half of this is $475,000. Thus, Section 751(a) converts her $375,000 of capital gain into $475,000 of ordinary income and a $100,000 capital loss.

Analogous problems are involved with the transferee of a partnership interest. A buyer of a partnership interest gets a cost basis in the purchased interest under Section 742. Section 743(a), however, prevents the partnership from making the corresponding adjustment in the bases of its assets. This destroys the identity between inside and outside basis. Under the aggregate approach, the buyer would be treated as buying a pro-rata share of the partnership's assets, getting a new cost basis in these shares, so that she would not be taxed on her share of any unrealized gain in the partnership's assets that accrued economically prior to her purchase. The seller paid tax on the gain, so that it should not be taxed again to the buyer. For example, if the partnership sells an asset that had a high value and low basis when the buying partner bought her interest, that extra value would have been reflected in the purchase price paid for the interest, yet she would be taxed on her share of any gain over the old, before her entry, historical basis.[25]

A partnership willing to take on extra recordkeeping can avoid many of the problems associated with a new partner buying an interest, however. An election is available to a partnership under Section 754 when a partnership interest is transferred. If the election is made, Section 743(b) gives the purchasing partner a special inside basis adjustment in the partnership's assets. Then, Section 755, as interpreted in Section 1.755–1(b) of the regulations, allocates this special inside basis adjustment among the partnership's assets so as to achieve tax results that approximate giving the purchasing partner cost bases in her shares of the partnership's assets. Basically, the purchasing partner has a positive (negative) special adjustment with regard to assets with unrealized appreciation (depreciation) at the time of her purchase.[26]

25. She would get outside basis for this extra gain, so that she would get a loss, probably capital, at some distant point in the future to compensate her for the current overtaxation, but this future benefit may provide little relief in present value terms.

26. Just as the mechanics of Section 751(a) drive rules implementing Section 743(b), Section 743(b) impacts the policies underlying Section 751(a): If there were no Section 743(b) adjustment, the Section 751(a) problem would not be that troubling, as the less tax-favored gain would be preserved at the partnership level. But, when a Section 754 election is in place, the buyer gets a special inside basis adjustment that eliminates this gain, so that the gain must be taxed to the seller of a partnership interest if at all.

Compare this situation to the analogous corporate situation. When a shareholder of a corporation sells her stock, she has capital gain, regardless of the composition and character of the corporation's assets. The future corporate tax is not affected by the stock sale, so giving the shareholder capital gain treatment is not troubling. In those cases where the corporate tax may be avoided, Section 341 comes in and creates an ordinary income tax on the stock sale.

Consider an example: Faith, Fran, and Fred are equal partners. The partnership's sole material asset is a piece of investment real estate with a basis of $270,000 and a value of $1.5 million. Fred sells his interest to Freda for $500,000. The partnership makes a timely election under Section 754. As a consequence, Freda gets a special Section 743(b) basis adjustment with regard to the real estate of $410,000 (under Section 1.755–1(b)(3)(ii)(A)[27] of the regulations, this is the gain that Freda would have been taxed on if the partnership had sold the property for its fair market value on the day that she bought her interest.) Thus, if the partnership were to sell the property for $1.5 million, each partner would be allocated $410,000 of gain, but Freda would then offset that by her $410,000 of special basis. This makes sense, as, in effect, she paid $500,000 for 1/3d of the property, so that she realizes no economic gain when her 1/3d is sold for $500,000. More complicated examples are considered in Chapter VI.

REVIEW: Code §§ 1(h)(11) and (12), 741, 742, 743, 751(a), 754, and 755 and Reg. §§ 1.1(h)–1, 1.751–1(c)(6)(ii), and 1.751–1(a)(1) and (2)

SKIM: Reg. §§ 1.743–1(a)–(e) and 1.755–1(b)

Problem Set III.E

1. Olivia, Paula, and Quincy are 1/3d–1/3d–1/3d partners. Their partnership net leases equipment. Its assets are as follows:

	FMV	Basis
Cash	10,000	10,000
Equipment	1,550,000	650,000
Leases[28]	240,000	–0–
	1,800,000	660,000

Olivia sells her interest, which has a basis of $220,000, to Roberta for $600,000. All gain on the equipment would be subject to Section 1245. How is Olivia taxed?

2. If the partnership above makes a timely Section 754 election with respect to Olivia's sale, how does that effect the partnership and the partners in the future?

F. PARTNERSHIP AUDIT

SKIM: Code §§ 6221, 6222(a) and (b)(1), 6223(a), 6224(a), 6226(a) and (b), 6229(a), and 6231(a)(3) and (a)(7)

The discussion thus far has not looked at procedural concerns. One is worth noting at this juncture: partnership audits.

---

27. For this purpose, the "hypothetical sale" is described in Section 1.755–1(b)(1)(ii) of the regulations.

28. The leases have value because they require above-market rent for the remaining lease terms.

A little history informs the discussion of the current law controlling partnership audits. As partnerships with numerous partners began to flourish in the late 1970s and early 1980s, problems with the then-applicable law became apparent. Under old law, the partnership was not audited, per se. Each partner presented a potential separate controversy. This required duplication of IRS efforts, particularly when partners of one partnership were scattered throughout the country. Also, partners took inconsistent positions—say, each saying income should be taxable to another—whipsawing the IRS. In this environment, the IRS had little incentive to settle with just one partner.

The current partnership audit rules were enacted in 1982. Under these rules, a partner generally is required to report consistently with her Schedule K–1 as received from the partnership. The partnership is audited. Determinations at the partnership level, including extensions of the statute of limitations, settlements, and litigation, bind the partners. All of the partners may participate in discussions with the IRS. If the matter goes to court, there is only one proceeding, usually managed by the "tax matters partner" specified in the partnership agreement.

In practice, these partnership audit rules have worked well, except when a group of partners has had a falling out with the tax matters partner. There has been considerable litigation as to who may act as the tax matters partner. Also, since the partnership audit rules only apply to a partner with regard to partnership items, there have been numerous cases addressing issues as to which tax items constitute partnership items determined at the partnership level.

G. CONCLUDING COMMENTS

The student now has been exposed to the basics of Subchapter K. Hopefully, the student now has a better idea of what it means to say that Subchapter K is an hybrid of aggregate and entity rules. At this time, a review of the discussion of the development of Subchapter K above in Section I.B.1 should be helpful.

Chapter IV

ALLOCATIONS IN A DEBT–FREE PARTNERSHIP

A. INTRODUCTION

Chapter III assumed a pro-rata partnership that uses the calendar year in order that the discussion did not need to consider the difficult issues of **when** tax items are attributed to the partners and **how** tax items are allocated between the partners in non-pro-rata partnerships. This chapter addresses these hard issues with regard to a partnership that has no debt and that has not received any non-cash property contributions from a partner. **When** items pass through to the partners is considered first. The next section looks at the partnership's tax year and its significance when either new partners are admitted or old partners leave. Then, the remainder of this chapter deals with **how** items are allocated among the partners. Basically, the tax law tries to respect the partners' agreement as to allocations. For this reason, the bulk of the discussion in this chapter reviews (i) how the tax law interprets the partners' agreement and, (ii) once so interpreted, when the tax law respects the agreement. Later chapters then look at debt-laden partnerships and the other contexts that present allocation issues that are not considered here.

B. TAX YEAR AND OTHER TIMING ISSUES

READ: Code § 706

SKIM: Reg. §§ 1.706–1(c)(2) and 1.706–1T(a)

Section 706(a) is the key provision controlling when a partner is taxed on partnership tax items. The provision provides that a partner is taxed on her share of her partnership's income for a partnership tax year in her tax year that includes the last day of the partnership's tax year.[1] Under this rule, if a partnership were free to chose any tax year, there

---

1. For estimated tax purposes, some of this is deemed to have been earned earlier in the year. Treas. Reg. § 1.6654–2(d)(2).

would be considerable opportunities for deferral. Consider the classic example: Ernest, a calendar-year taxpayer, has been an associate employed by a law firm that is organized as a general partnership and that has a tax year that ends January 31. He is admitted as a partner on February 1, 2000. Under Section 706(a), he is first taxed as a partner on January 31, 2001, the end of the first partnership tax year in which he is a partner. Thus, in 2000, his only taxable income from being a lawyer is one month's (January's) wages.

Because of the possibilities for deferring partners' taxes by the artful choice of partnership taxable years, Section 706(b) substantially limits the ability of partnerships to chose their tax years. Congress realized that timing abuse is least likely when the tax year of the partnership tracks those of the partnership's partners. Thus, under Section 706(b)(1)(B)(i), if partners owning 50% or more of the partnership (profits **and** capital) have the same tax year, the partnership must use that year. In a partnership of individuals, who almost always have calendar-year tax years, this rule virtually guarantees a calendar-year tax year. Corporate partners frequently have tax years other than the calendar year, however. To reflect this, Section 706(b)(1)(B) has rules that determine a partnership's tax year when no group of its partners that own more than 50% have the same tax year. If all partners with 5% or more interests (in profits **or** capital) have the same tax year, the partnership must use that year. In default of the 2 preceding rules, Section 1.706–1T(a) of the regulations, which is authorized by Section 706(b)(1)(B)(iii), overrides Section 706(b)'s presumption of a calendar year and requires a partnership to use the tax year that results in its partners deferring the least income.

There are 2 exceptions to the rules of Section 706(b)(1)(B). First, under Section 706(b)(1)(C), the IRS may allow a partnership to use a tax year that makes business sense. For example, retailers may use a year that ends January 31 in order that Christmas sales and returns are included in the same tax year.[2] Second, Section 444 permits a partnership to use a tax year that otherwise is not allowed, but, in order to do so, the partnership must pay interest to the IRS (under Section 7519) for the privilege of the associated deferral, so that Section 444 provides few, if any, opportunities to reduce taxes in present value terms.

A related problem is so-called "retroactive" allocations with regard to partners admitted after the beginning of the partnership's tax year. Retroactive allocations were a standard feature of the old individual tax shelters: All initial partners admitted would be allocated their proportionate shares of the partnership's losses incurred during the year, including, as to later-admitted partners, a portion of losses incurred prior to their being admitted as partners. This simplified the marketing of the partnership interests, as a salesman could promise a fixed amount

---

2. The rules are contained in Rev. Rul. 87–57, 1987–2 C.B. 117, and Rev. Proc. 87–32, 1987–2 C.B. 396. Basically, a partnership may use a "natural business year," one in which 25% of the gross receipts are earned in the last 2 months. Beyond that, little satisfies the business purpose exception.

of losses regardless of when the investor bought her interest during the year. Section 706(d)(1) generally prevents such retroactive allocations, however. Under this rule, a partner can be allocated only those tax items that are booked by the partnership (i.e., taken into account by the partnership under its tax accounting method) while she was a partner.

One strategy beat what is now Section 706(d)(1), however. Under this strategy, a cash basis partnership would not pay expenses incurred during a year until all of the new partners were admitted and then would allocate the expenses among the partners pro-rata. This strategy allocated to a new partner expenses that were incurred prior to, but accounted for after, her admission to the partnership. The Tax Court held in 1981 that this was not an impermissible retroactive allocation.[3] In response, Section 706(d)(2) was enacted in 1984. This provision assigns certain cash basis income and deduction items only to partners who were partners at the time that the income was earned or the expenses were incurred. Deduction items so attributable to persons who were not partners during the tax year are treated as capital expenditures.

The obvious mirror case to admitting a new partner is an historic partner leaving the partnership. Under Sections 706(c)(1) and 706(c)(2)(B), adjustments to a partner's share of profits, including adjustments made as a consequence of a partial redemption of a partnership interest, are controlled by the rules of Section 704(b), the topic of the remainder of this chapter. When a partner sells her entire interest or is completely liquidated by the partnership, however, Section 706(c)(2)(A) applies.[4] As to the departing partner, the partnership's tax year closes on her last day. Her final share of partnership income or loss is taxable then rather than at the end of the partnership's tax year. For purposes of determining this share, the partnership closes the partnership books on such day, determines a pro-forma taxable income for the short tax year through such day, and taxes the departing partner only with respect to her share of income and loss for that short year (leaving the remaining profit and loss for the full tax year to the ongoing partners). Alternatively, the partnership can simply apportion income to the period prior to the partner's departure using a simple pro-ration and tax the departing partner upon her share of this income. Read Section 1.706–1(c)(2) of the regulations.

---

3. *Richardson v. Commissioner*, 76 T.C. 512 (1981), *aff'd*, 693 F.2d 1189 (5th Cir. 1982).

4. Of course, the departing partner also may be taxed on gain or loss triggered by the departure. Taxation of interest sales was considered in Chapter II. Chapter VI further explores how to calculate a buyer of a partnership interest's share of profit and loss so as to reflect the buyer's cost and the seller's gain or loss. Chapter VIII of this text explores the taxation of distributions made in liquidation of a partnership interest and their effect on subsequent determinations and allocations of partnership profit and loss.

LIPKE v. COMMISSIONER
United States Tax Court, 1983.
81 T.C. 689.

OPINION

FAY, *Judge*:

[T]he issues are (1) whether a certain partnership's retroactive reallocation of losses in 1975 to both new and existing partners was allowable under the "varying interest" rules of section 706[(d)(1)], and if not, (2) [omitted].

In 1972 and 1973, the [relevant] partnership acquired several apartment buildings. At all relevant times, these apartment buildings were subject to mortgages. In 1974 and 1975, the partnership experienced severe financial problems and defaulted on the mortgages. After the mortgagee foreclosed on one of the apartment buildings, the partnership obtained additional capital of $300,000 in order to avoid losing its remaining apartment buildings. Of the $300,000, $84,000 was contributed by 6 of the 14 original limited partners who together held interests in the partnership totaling 28 percent. The remaining $216,000 was contributed by [then general and limited partners], in return for new limited partnership interests. All of these capital contributions were made on October 1, 1975.

In connection with these additional capital contributions, the general and limited partners executed an amendment to the partnership agreement (herein the amendment). The amendment created two classes of limited partners. All of the original limited partners were designated as class A limited partners. Together with the new partners, the original partners who made new capital contributions also became class B partners.

The amendment also provided that the partnership was to be owned 49 percent by the class A limited partners, 49 percent by the class B limited partners, and 2 percent by the general partners.

The amendment reallocated 98 percent of all the partnership's 1975 losses to the class B limited partners. This reallocation was made expressly in consideration of the new capital contributions made to the partnership. The amendment also reallocated 2 percent of all the partnership's 1975 losses to the general partners.

The primary issue is whether the partnership properly allocated its 1975 losses among its partners. Respondent contends that section 706[(d)(1)] prevents the partnership from reallocating losses accrued before October 1, 1975, to either the class B limited partners or to the general partners. For the following reasons, we hold that the partnership's retroactive reallocation of losses to the class B limited partners was not permitted by section 706[(d)(1)] because it was made as a result of additional capital contributions. It makes no difference that the additional capital was contributed by, and the resulting retroactive reallocation was made to, both new and existing partners. However, we also hold that the partnership's retroactive reallocation of losses to the general partners was permissible since it did not result from additional capital contributions and, therefore, constituted nothing more than a readjustment of partnership items among existing partners.

In *Richardson v. Commissioner*, 76 T.C. 512 (1981), affd. 693 F.2d 1189 (5th Cir.1982), this Court ruled that section 706[(d)(1)] was applicable to situations involving the admission of new partners. Therein, we held that the reduction in the capital interests of the original partners resulting from the admission of the new partners constituted a reduction of interests within the meaning of section 706[(d)(1)]. The fact that the original partners' equity interests in the partnership remained the same was deemed to be irrelevant. Accordingly, under section 706[(d)(1)], the original partners and the new partners were required to determine their distributive shares of partnership items by taking into account their varying interests in the partnership during the taxable year.

For purposes of section 706[(d)(1)], we find no difference between a reduction in partners' interests resulting from the admission of new partners, and, as here, the reduction in partners' interests resulting from additional capital contributions made by existing partners. In both situations, partners' interests were reduced and retroactive reallocations were made as a result of the additional capital contributions. [Different rules in the 2 contexts] would create an illusory distinction which the language of section 706[(d)(1)] simply does not require us to make.

With respect to the partnership's retroactive reallocation of losses to the general partners [who did not make additional capital contributions], however, we find that it did not contravene the varying interest rules of section 706[(d)(1)]. Prior to October 1, 1975, the general partners held only a residual interest in gains arising from "major capital events." Pursuant to the October 1, 1975, amendment to the partnership agreement, however, the general partners were granted a 2 percent interest in the partnership's 1975 profits and losses including the losses accrued by the partnership during the preceding nine months. In contrast to the retroactive reallocation of losses to the class B limited partners, this reallocation to the general partners was not made in consideration for additional capital contributions. Accordingly, this reallocation of losses to the general partners was not directly accompanied by a reduction in any other partner's capital. It constituted nothing more than a readjustment of partnership items among existing partners which, by itself, is permissible.

REVIEW: Code §§ 444, 706, and 7519 and Reg. §§ 1.706–1(c)(2) and 1.706–1T(a)

Problem Set IV.B

1. All of the 5 equal members of an LLC that is taxed as a partnership are individuals. The LLC uses a June 30 fiscal year for financial accounting purposes. When may it use that year for tax purposes?

2. A general partnership has 2 equal partners: Alex and ALEXCO, Inc. ALEXCO is owned 100% by Alex and uses a June 30 Fiscal year for

financial accounting purposes. What tax years are available to the partnership?

3. ABLE, Inc. and The CAPITAL Corporation form a general partnership. CAPITAL provides 90% of the cash. ABLE provides 100% of the partnership's management. Their deal is that all profits and losses are allocated 10% to ABLE and 90% to CAPITAL until the partnership has earned a 10% cumulative annual return on original capital. Thereafter, all profits and losses are shared 50–50. ABLE uses a calendar-year tax year. CAPITAL has a June 30 tax year. What tax years are available to the partnership?

4. The REALTY Partnership rents realty profitably. Thus, it earns profit pretty evenly throughout the year. It has a calendar-year tax year. The partnership has had 9 partners for years. Now, on July 1, it admits Barnie as a 10% partner. How much of the partnership's income is Barnie taxed on this year? Does it matter whether the partnership is cash or accrual basis?

5. The FUEL Partnership does wildcat oil exploration. It has a calendar-year tax year and uses the cash method of accounting. This year, it pays all of its deductible drilling costs (under Section 263(c) of the Code) on December 15. Mary is admitted as a 10% partner on December 1. How much of the deduction for drilling costs may be allocated to Mary?

6. Larry, Mo, and Curly were equal partners in a calendar-year partnership. On September 30, 2001, Curly sold his entire interest to Larry. The partnership' only tax item for 2001 was a $120,000 long-term capital gain from a sale of real property on June 30, 2001. How are the partners taxed on the partnership's 2001 taxable income?

C. SPECIAL ALLOCATIONS: CAPITAL ACCOUNTING

READ: Code §§ 704(a) and (b) and 761(c)

Section 704(b) is the key provision controlling how a partnership's tax items are allocated among the partners at a given time. The discussion thus far has assumed that all partners in a given partnership share items pro-rata, so allocation has not been an issue. Frequently, partnerships are not pro-rata, however. State partnership law affords partners virtually unlimited flexibility in crafting their economic arrangement. The partners can agree to specially allocate certain kinds or amounts of income among the partners in different ways. For example, a law firm may give its partners larger shares of the profits of the office in which they are situated than of other offices. These "special allocations" became more common as partnerships became used as the vehicle of choice for syndicated tax shelters.

Special allocations of tax items present the most challenging problem for Subchapter K. The tax law, because of its hybrid approach to partnerships, must allocate the partnership's tax items among the partners.[5] Unfortunately, when a partnership has a complex (equity) capital structure, there is no simple, right way to allocate income under a hybrid approach. Breathtaking complexity is required to accommodate the various tax concerns. In contrast, for example, Subchapter C, because of its entity approach, usually does not have to deal with complex capital structures in taxing operating profit and loss, as all tax items are taxed to the corporation itself. A corporation may have classes of stock, but that does not impact the tax on the corporation's income.

Section 704(a) provides the general rule that a partner's share of a partnership's tax items is determined in accordance with the partnership agreement. This rule alone would be adequate to deal with a partnership that gives a partner a bigger share of the profits of her home office than of other offices. Moreover, recognizing that many partnerships, like law firms, negotiate the partners' respective shares after the year is over and its results evaluated, Section 761(c) allows the partners to set their deal after the fact.[6]

Unfortunately, often it is difficult to translate the partners' deal into tax terms. For example, consider the following deal between Earl and John: The partnership is going to use $100,000 of John's cash. Earl is making no investment other than services. Their deal is that all cash distributions from the partnership go first to John until he gets his money back, with all later distributions going 50–50.[7] In the partnership's first year, its profit is $20,000 and it distributes $40,000,[8] all to John. One is tempted to say that, since John got all the cash, he should be taxed on all the profits.

A more careful analysis of the economics suggests otherwise. Let us look at how things play out if the partnership runs for 5 years with the same $20,000 of income and $40,000 of cash in each year, and then, at the end of Year 5, the partnership goes out of business with no assets (after it makes the 5th $40,000 distribution).[9] By the middle of Year 3, John has received back his initial $100,000, so that all further distributions are 50–50. Thus, John gets all $40,000 of cash distributed in each of the first 2 years, $30,000 in the 3d, and $20,000 in each of the last 2 years. Earl gets nothing in the first 2 years, $10,000 in the 3d, and $20,000 in Years 4 and 5. In total, over the 5–year life of the partnership,

---

5. Subchapter S avoids this problem by requiring an electing corporation to have only one class of stock.

6. This is not a retroactive allocation to a late-admitted partner to which Section 706(d) is directed. Section 761(c) lets a partnership whose membership has not changed determine the partners' shares retroactively.

7. Oil and gas lawyers call this standard deal, when done using interests in minerals in place, as a "carried interest" since John is carrying Earl by providing all the cash. *See generally U.S. v. Cocke,* 399 F.2d 433 (5th Cir.1968). In *Hamilton v. U.S.,* 687 F.2d 408 (Ct.Cl.1982), which is the basis for the example in the text, the taxpayer tricked the old Court of Claims into letting it do under pre–1976 Section 704(b), discussed in Note 11, below, what could not be done under the oil and gas tax cases like *Cocke.*

8. Some of the cash receipts have been sheltered by depreciation, so that taxable income is less than unneeded cash flow.

9. Say, the partnership buys a 5–year leasehold which is subleased for 5 years.

John receives back his original $100,000 plus an additional $50,000. Earl receives $50,000. They each have made a $50,000 profit taking all 5 years into account. Yet, allocating a given year's income to the partners in the same proportion as cash distributions were made in that year would allocate John $75,000 of income, and Earl only $25,000, which is inconsistent with the true economics over the life of the partnership. Each year, a better handle on the economics than yearly cash flow is required.

To deal with this problem, Subchapter K looks to a standard feature of partnership agreements. The trick is to view the partnership as an entity. Each partner's interest in the partnership is treated as analogous to a bank account. A partner's contributions to her partnership are viewed as being like deposits into a bank account, increasing the balance in her partnership account. Distributions are treated like withdrawals, reducing the distributee partners' accounts accordingly. Profits allocated to a partner but not distributed are accounted for like interest earned and credited to a bank account but not withdrawn.[10] In RUPA, these accounts are referred to as "partner accounts." The tax Section 704(b) regulations call these accounts "capital accounts," which is the more standard usage.

The partnership accounts provide a very helpful tool for analyzing the John and Earl deal: Earl's account opens at zero, since he makes no investment. John's opens with his $100,000 investment. At the end of the first year, John has withdrawn $40,000, so his account should be reduced by $40,000. But, what about the $20,000 profit? The obvious accounting, already noted, would allocate profit proportionately to distributions so that the $20,000 is treated as a further deposit to John's account. The $40,000 distribution reduces his account to a Year 1 closing balance of $80,000. Earl's account opens and stays at zero throughout Year 1. Year 2 is much the same. In Year 3, after $20,000 of cash has been distributed to John, he has received his initial $100,000 back, so that the remaining $20,000 of cash is distributed equally, $10,000 to each partner. Since the cash goes 3/4 to John and 1/4 to Earl, it makes sense to allocate the partnership's $20,000 profit similarly, $15,000 to John and $5,000 to Earl. Finally, in Years 4 and 5, everything is 50–50.

---

10. A student with a financial accounting background may wish to note that the sum of the capital accounts is the total partnership equity, with each capital account reflecting the associated partner's share of the total partnership equity.

The following table summarizes the capital accounting:

	Earl	John
Year 1		
Open	–0–	$100,000
Income	–0–	20,000
Distribution	–0–	–40,000
Close	–0–	80,000
Year 2		
Open	–0–	80,000
Income	–0–	20,000
Distribution	–0–	–40,000
Close	–0–	60,000
Year 3		
Open	–0–	60,000
Income	5,000	15,000
Distribution	–10,000	–30,000
Close	–5,000	45,000
Year 4		
Open	–5,000	45,000
Income	10,000	10,000
Distribution	–20,000	–20,000
Close	–15,000	35,000
Year 5		
Open	–15,000	35,000
Income	10,000	10,000
Distribution	–20,000	–20,000
Close	–25,000	25,000

This table confirms that something is wrong with allocating a year's income proportionately to the year's cash distributions. John gets total cash distributions that are $25,000 less cash than his capital plus profits. Earl gets $25,000 more.

Thinking about the John and Earl deal over multiple years suggests a second take on the overall economics: John puts up cash. He gets his cash back first. Thereafter, Earl gets 1/2 of the deal even though he put up no cash. Earl is a 50% partner in all cash distributions in excess of John's original cash contribution. In other words, over the life of the partnership, Earl gets 50% of the partnership's profits. Allocating profits 50–50 each year, results in the following capital accounting:

	Earl	John
Year 1		
Open	–0–	$100,000
Income	10,000	10,000
Distribution	–0–	–40,000
Close	10,000	70,000
Year 2		
Open	10,000	70,000
Income	10,000	10,000
Distribution	–0–	–40,000
Close	20,000	40,000
Year 3		
Open	20,000	40,000
Income	10,000	10,000
Distribution	–10,000	–30,000
Close	20,000	20,000
Year 4		
Open	20,000	20,000
Income	10,000	10,000
Distribution	–20,000	–20,000
Close	10,000	10,000
Year 5		
Open	10,000	10,000
Income	10,000	10,000
Distribution	–20,000	–20,000
Close	–0–	–0–

Now, things work out. When the partnership is done, Earl has pulled out $50,000—representing the profit that was allocated to his capital account. John has pulled out $150,000—his original $100,000 plus the $50,000 of profit allocated to him. By looking at capital accounts, which are common in partnership agreements, it is possible to better understand the economics of a deal, in order to restate the deal into tax terms. This notion—capital accounting—forms the basis for the most important tax rules regarding special allocations.

The capital accounting notion is read into Subchapter K through Section 704(b). It provides that the allocation of tax items in a partnership agreement is respected for tax purposes only if that allocation has "substantial economic effect."[11] Otherwise, tax items are allocated in accordance with the partners' "interests in the partnership." There are very extensive regulations interpreting "substantial economic effect."

Read Section 1.704–1(b)(2)(ii)(*b*)(1) of the regulations. It provides that a deal, in order to be respected for tax purposes, i.e., in order to have "economic effect," must be drafted in capital accounting terms. Thus, most partnership agreements contain lengthy provisions providing for capital accounting that were designed to comply with the Section 704(b) regulations.

The basic rules regarding how capital accounts must be kept to satisfy the tax standard are in Section 1.704–1(b)(2)(iv). Read Sections 1.704–1(b)(2)(iv)(*a*), (*b*), and (*q*). Basically, a partner's tax capital account is kept as described above: increased for contributions to the partnership by the partner, increased for income allocated to the partner, decreased for losses allocated to the partner, and decreased for distributions to the partner. The only wrinkle is that the tax capital accounts generally must be kept using its tax accounting method rather than under the partnership's accounting method for financial accounting purposes. A partner has one, unified capital account for all partnership interests held under Section 1.704–1(b)(2)(iv)(*b*). Note that, under the regulations, as to an original partner in a partnership (i) that has no debt, (ii) that has all of, and only, the original partners, (iii) that received only cash contributions, and (iv) that made only cash distributions, the partner's tax capital account will be the same as her outside basis. The situations where a partner's capital account balance differs from her outside basis are analyzed in later chapters.

All this accounting seems rather virtual at first. The regulations, however, make the accounting real. Read Section 1.704–1(b)(2)(ii)(*b*), particularly –1(b)(2)(ii)(*b*)(2). The capital accounts must have state-law legal, and, therefore, economic, consequences. Specifically, the partnership agreement must provide that, when the partnership liquidates, cash is to be distributed in accordance with the partners' respective positive capital account balances. In other words, an allocation of $1 income to a partner's capital account must mean that the partner will receive $1 of cash at some point. An allocation of $1 of loss must mean $1 less cash at some point. Moreover, under this general rule, if a partner has a negative capital account balance at the end of the partnership,[12] she

---

11. Prior to 1976, Section 704(b) only looked askance at a partnership agreement if "the principal purpose of any provision in the partnership agreement with respect to the partner's distributive share of such item is the avoidance or evasion of any tax imposed by this subtitle." Courts read a simple capital accounts analysis into this language, however. *See, e.g., Orrisch v.* *Commissioner*, 55 T.C. 395 (1971), *aff'd per curiam*, (9th Cir. 1973).

12. In a debt-free partnership, the subject of this chapter, the sum of the partners' capital account balances cannot be less than zero, as negative total equity implies insolvency. Thus, with a debt-free partnership, if one partner's capital account is negative,

must be required to repay that amount to the partnership (so that the partnership can pay creditors or make distributions to other partners with unpaid capital account balances). For example, if (i) the John and Earl partnership's capital accounts were kept under the first method of profit allocation described above (a year's income allocated between the partners' proportionately to the respective cash distributions received) and (ii) the partnership were liquidated at the end of Year 5, Earl would have to repay his negative $25,000 capital account balance to fund Earl's $25,000 positive balance. Such an obligation is referred to as a "deficit makeup."

Which presents one the most difficult problems presented when advising partnerships with special allocations: Much of the time, the tax lawyer can draft complicated capital accounting the gives the desired tax results, but that presents the possibility of economic surprises. The following case (from before RUPA and the current Section 704(b) regulations) shows how a special tax allocation can cost somebody a lot of money:

PARK CITIES CORPORATION v. BYRD

Supreme Court of Texas, 1976.
534 S.W.2d 668.

This suit was brought by the executors of the estate of Mattie Caruth Byrd against Park Cities Corporation. Mrs. Byrd and Park Cities Corporation entered into a limited partnership agreement for the purpose of building, owning and operating a large apartment complex in Dallas, Texas. It was agreed that Mrs. Byrd was to be the managing general partner and Park Cities was to be a limited partner. No additional partners ever existed. On February 12, 1972 Mrs. Byrd died, which effectively dissolved the limited partnership as of that date pursuant to their agreement. Thereafter, a dispute arose between the executors of Mrs. Byrd's estate and Park Cities Corporation. The only problem to be resolved [on this appeal] is whether or not the $1,987,344 deficit in Mrs. Byrd's capital account, created mainly by annual allocation of depreciation losses, is to be treated as an asset of the partnership, and as a liability of Mrs. Byrd.

[G]overning articles of agreement signed by the parties which are crucial and controlling of our ultimate decision, reveal the following:

V. The parties hereby agree to divide the net income of the partnership at least annually and to share same in the percentages set forth opposite their names below:

Mattie Caruth Byrd, General
Partner   50%

one or more other partners must have positive balances that entitle them to the negative partner's cash.

Park Cities Corporation, Limited
Partner   50%

    The parties further agree that for tax purposes they will share all net losses of the partnership according to the actual losses suffered by each party, and it is further expressly agreed that Park Cities Corporation shall not be financially responsible for any of the losses of the partnership in excess of its capital contribution as herein elsewhere set forth.

    X.   The Limited Partner shall not be responsible for the debts of the partnership in excess of a capital contribution as herein provided and any losses shall be borne entirely by the General Partner, Mattie Caruth Byrd.

    VIII.   In the event it is desired and the parties enter into an agreement to sell the property, or on the retirement, death or insanity of the General Partner, the partnership shall terminate and a final accounting and distribution be made as provided by law;

As per article VIII, upon the death of Mrs. Byrd the partnership was dissolved and under article IX the assets of the partnership were to be distributed in the following manner and in the priority set forth:

    1.   All charges, debts and obligations of the partnership shall be paid.

    2.   The contribution of the Limited Partner shall be returned to it.

    3.   The parties hereto shall each own and hold and be entitled to receive the percentages of the remaining partnership assets set out opposite their names below:

Mattie Caruth Byrd, General
Partner   50%

Park Cities Corporation, Limited
Partner   50%

The key to the present dispute involves the $1,987,344 capital deficit evident in Mrs. Byrd's capital account as substantially created by depreciation. The partnership computed depreciation upon its buildings on an accelerated basis. The controversial deficit of nearly $2,000,000 came into existence in the following manner. As the articles of agreement earlier set out reveal, the parties agreed that "for tax purposes they will share all net losses of the partnership according to the actual losses suffered by each party." In order to clarify the amount of loss each party was intended to suffer, the agreement further provided, "Park Cities Corporation shall not be financially responsible for any of the losses of the partnership in excess of its capital contribution" which was set at $100. Thus, it seems clear that when taken together, these two provisions reveal that Mrs. Byrd as the general partner was to be financially responsible for all losses incurred by the partnership in excess of the initial capital contribution of $100 made by Park Cities. It was this allocation of 100 percent of the depreciation losses to Mrs. Byrd's capital account that created the controversy now before us. Each of the accountant's reports showed clearly that Mrs. Byrd had used the depreciation allowance upon the partnership properties as a credit upon her personal income tax obligations to the extent allowed by law.

The dispute before us has resolved itself into two central points that Park Cities as petitioner has urged throughout the litigation. Park Cities maintains that the debit balance or deficit in Mrs. Byrd's capital account is an asset of the partnership. Further, Park Cities urges as error the failure of the courts below to declare that Mrs. Byrd was liable to the partnership for this $1,987,344 ultimate debit balance or deficit in her capital account. Cumulative losses on the books of the partnership in the amount of $2,076,177 were debited to Mrs. Byrd's capital account. She had made capital contributions of $88,833 in 1964 and 1965. This left Mrs. Byrd with the capital deficit in controversy totaling $1,987,344. Both parties' arguments are based upon the theory that the final accumulated depreciation charged to Mrs. Byrd's capital account exceeded $1,987,344 and thus depreciation alone fully accounts for the controversial deficit. The depreciation allocation is the major concern of the parties here since the court of civil appeals has apparently held that the debit balance in a partner's capital account is to be disregarded if an approximately corresponding amount of depreciation has been charged against the partnership assets and income.

If the deficit created by the allocation of all of the depreciation charges to Mrs. Byrd's capital account is to be treated as an asset, her estate will presently be liable to the partnership for the $1,987,344 deficit. If under the law, and more particularly under the agreement between the partners, this capital deficit is held not to be an asset of the partnership, the estate of Mrs. Byrd will not be subjected to liability for payment of that amount into the limited partnership now being wound up. Park Cities contends that the capital deficit is definitely an asset under their agreement with Mrs. Byrd, and consequently, she should be required to suffer the actual present financial loss for the entire sum. Under their theory, Mrs. Byrd's estate would be liable to contribute to the capital of the partnership an amount sufficient to bring the debit balance of her capital account to zero.

It is also evident that the agreement provides for an equal division of the partnership assets upon dissolution. Thus, throughout this controversy the executors of Mrs. Byrd's estate have argued that Park Cities by its attempt to have Mrs. Byrd's capital deficit declared an asset, has simply been trying to maximize its final distributive share by increasing the scope of the assets available for distribution.

It has been held that upon dissolution, a partner whose capital account evidences a deficit is required to make a contribution to the capital of the partnership in an amount equal to the deficit. The executors of Mrs. Byrd's estate, as respondents, argue that this principle can have no application to the present situation in which depreciation charges fully account for Mrs. Byrd's capital deficit. They argue that the general partner's capital account was merely a "receptacle or repository" to which such items as "non-cash depreciation" were to be allocated for "bookkeeping purposes." They maintain that unlike a cash withdrawal situation, the present factual pattern reveals that Mrs. Byrd never "withdrew" anything from the partnership. They argue that none of the capital deficit involved in this suit reflects any "withdrawal" by Mrs. Byrd.

Park Cities, as petitioner, contends that Mrs. Byrd indeed received a valuable benefit in the form of this non-cash depreciation allocation and that she should be required to repay this amount into the partnership as it constituted an asset of the partnership. One portion of their argument is that due to the taxation benefits Mrs. Byrd realized by having all of the depreciation losses allocated to her capital account, that as between partners, this non-cash depreciation figure represents an item of clear economic value. They maintain that their interests were affected by such a loss allocation agreement and the deficit is not simply evidence of a mere bookkeeping item. Thus, they contend that Mrs. Byrd fully intended to bear all these annual depreciation losses as is clearly evident under article X of their agreement and that it was to her distinct advantage to do so. Park Cities further argues that as the limited partner they gave up the right to utilize their one-half of these depreciation losses, and therefore surrendered the right to realization of the annual tax benefits such losses would allow. This was allegedly done in sole reliance upon Mrs. Byrd's agreement to suffer an equivalent dollar financial loss upon dissolution of the partnership in the future, which presently amounts to almost $2,000,000.

We believe that under the agreement, this capital deficiency created a valid claim of the partnership against Mrs. Byrd. This is because a capital deficit may be created by the charging of losses against a partner's capital account as well as by the withdrawal of funds by a partner. Mrs. Byrd's capital account was not merely a receptacle or a repository to which such items as non-cash depreciation were to be allocated for bookkeeping purposes as the respondents contend. It is obvious from a practical standpoint that the allocation of all of the partnership losses to the capital account of Mrs. Byrd was intended to have, and did result in, beneficial financial consequences to her.

It seems that these parties would not intend that Mrs. Byrd should receive the entire tax benefit from the nearly $2,000,000 in partnership losses and never be required to suffer any actual financial loss as a result of those allocations. Park Cities could have made use of some of these losses to offset its taxation burden had they not agreed to allow Mrs. Byrd to make full use of this benefit. Mrs. Byrd made use of a potentially deductible loss which was an economic benefit to the partner to whom it was allocated. Due to the nature of the agreement entered into in this particular case, the liability of Mrs. Byrd because of her capital deficit is founded upon the fact that the deficit exists and not upon what created this particular deficit.

What is made clear in this case is the fact that Park Cities was to receive a potentially substantial benefit from a seemingly meager investment. As the limited partner, Park Cities was not liable for any of the partnership's debts beyond its $100 capital contribution and further, it was not required to bear any of the partnership's losses. Indeed, Park Cities did not at any time make any further contribution to the capital of Limited. Nevertheless, Park Cities was to receive 50 percent of the income as well as 50 percent of the assets remaining after final distribution. Obviously, it was intended that Park Cities benefit materially from this limited partnership arrangement. Though the specific intent of the parties is not clear, the articles of agreement signed by these partners are clear and concise and will admit of only one interpretation:

> The Limited Partner shall not be responsible for the debts of the partnership in excess of a capital contribution as herein provided and any losses shall be borne entirely by the General Partner, Mattie Caruth Byrd.

As agreed, the cumulative net loss of Mattie Caruth Byrd Limited was reflected in Mrs. Byrd's capital account. The agreement does not even attempt to exclude depreciation from the scope of the term "losses." "Loss is a generic relative term, it is not a word of limited, hard and fast meaning." Black's Law Dictionary, 1094 (4th Ed. 1968). As depreciation is normally viewed as being a loss, though not always entirely a real economic loss to the partnership, we may not construe the above agreement in any fashion other than as is generally set out. In the absence of anything indicating a contrary intent, we must view the broad phrase, "any losses," as it is normally viewed. If the parties had intended to allocate only certain types of losses, they should have set this out in their agreement. Finally, aside from the fact that such loss allocation gave rise to economic benefits favoring Mrs. Byrd, the parties expressly agreed that she was to bear the total financial burden of all losses. Having agreed to bear the losses and agreeing to the method of accounting for such losses, and having accepted those charges and using them as an income tax deduction, we will not now allow the agreement and its intended consequences to be subverted.

The terms of the agreement indicate that the general partner was to receive the partnership losses, including those caused by depreciation, so long as the general partner actually bore the ultimate financial responsibility for the losses. Based upon the agreement and the applicable law, we hold that upon dissolution Mrs. Byrd's capital deficit, resulting from the special allocation of depreciation to her account as the general partner, was an asset of the partnership and her estate is to account to the partnership for that amount. Mrs. Byrd's estate is therefore presently liable to suffer the financial loss for this $1,987,344 as per the articles of agreement by contributing such amount to bring the balance of her capital account.

The *Park Cities* result is now the default in absence of an agreement to the contrary under Section 807 of the Revised Uniform Partnership Act.

Using capital accounting as the benchmark against which a special allocation is tested for tax purposes is far from ideal. As noted by the court in *Park Cities*, this accounting only means that there will be distant future cash consequences, probably of small present value, of the current tax deal. There is no ready alternative to using capital accounting, however. Capital accounting wins by default.

The deficit makeup requirement provides real problems in practice. With a deficit makeup, third-party creditors, as subrogees for an insolvent tax partnership, can proceed against the tax partners individually. Of course, negative capital accounts may not mean economic or legal insolvency. For example, negative balances may result from non-economic accelerated depreciation, as in *Park Cities*. But, when the negative balances reflect real losses, say from a tort judgment, the deficit makeup means personal liability even if the tax partnership is organized as a limited partnership or as an LLC. Business planners are quite reluctant to ask their investors to assume a risk of real liability—after all, not every risk can be insured against—just to make the tax advisor's life easier. Fortunately, the Section 704(b) regulations accommodate limited liability somewhat.

Read Section 1.704–1(b)(2)(ii)(*d*)'s alternate test for economic effect. Under this alternate test, an allocation will be respected, even if there is no deficit makeup, provided that 3 additional requirements are satisfied: First, the allocation cannot take the partner's account negative. The idea here is that, since creating or increasing a negative capital account balance of a limited partner or an LLC member probably has no economic impact on that partner or member (because the partner or member is not required to fund any negative balance created by such an allocation), such an allocation should not be respected under Section 704(b).[13] In contrast, (i) increasing a positive or negative balance or (ii) decreasing a positive balance is likely to reduce the cash to be received when the partnership liquidates (if not before), and, thus, should be respected for tax purposes.

The 2d additional requirement under the alternate test for economic effect is that a current allocation to a partner cannot be expected to result in a future negative capital account balance. This requirement backs up the requirement that an allocation cannot take a capital

---

13. It is possible that the negative balance will be offset against future profit allocations, so that the current loss reduces a future positive capital account balance, but this possibility is sufficiently unlikely that the regulations ignore it.

account negative by assuring that the current loss allocation is not a set-up for a future negative capital account balance.

Last, the 3d requirement under the alternate test for economic effect is that the partnership agreement must contain a "qualified income offset." This requirement backs up the no **expected** future negative capital account balance requirement just discussed. An expectations test, like the just-discussed second requirement, is notoriously hard to enforce. Thus, the third requirement specifies that the partnership agreement must provide that, if unexpected events occurring after the allocation of a loss to a partner cause the partner to have a negative capital account, later income is to be specially allocated to that partner as quickly as possible in order to get the balance back up to zero. Under these circumstances, any tax benefits from such a questionable loss allocation are likely to be short-lived. This later special allocation is called a "qualified income offset" in the regulations.

The student may wonder why anyone cares about a limit on allocations of losses that would otherwise create or increase a negative capital account balance since the losses will not be deductible immediately regardless because of Section 704(d). After all, (i) the capital account mirrors the outside basis and (ii) Section 704(d) disallows current loss deductions once the positive outside basis is exhausted. There are 2 reasons for caring about the loss limitations in the Section 704(b) regulations, however: First, Section 704(d) does not disallow losses for all time. Losses not allowed currently because of an inadequate outside basis are allowed in later years if the partner gets outside basis later as a consequence of being allocated income or making a later capital contribution to the partnership. In contrast, losses allocated away from a partner (to another partner) by Section 704(b) are lost forever. Second, a partner can get outside basis in excess of his capital account by operation of the debt pass-through rules of Section 752 (to be discussed in detail in the next chapter). If so, the outside basis exceeds the capital account, and the Section 704(b) prohibition against negative capital account balances restricts losses well before Section 704(d) has an effect.

REVIEW: Reg. §§ 1.704–1(b)(2)(ii)(*b*) and (*d*) and –1(b)(2)(iv)(*a*), (*b*), and (*q*)

Problem Set IV.C

1. George and Martha form a general partnership to practice law. Each contributes $10,000 initially. No further contributions are required. The partnership is cash basis and has a calendar-year tax year. George does divorce work mostly. Martha does trust and estate work primarily. George is entitled to 75% of the gross divorce billings and 25% of the trust and estate work. Martha gets 75% of the trust and estate work and 25% of the divorce work. All unbillable costs are shared evenly. Distributions are to be negotiated yearly. The partnership rents everything, so that its only asset at year-end is cash in the bank which earns

no interest. The partnership lasts 5 years, in which the results are as follows:

Year 1

Costs	$50,000
Divorce Revenues	200,000
Trust & Estate Revenues	150,000
Distributions	100,000 each

Year 2

Costs	$50,000
Divorce Revenues	100,000
Trust & Estate Revenues	300,000
Distributions	125,000 each

Year 3

Costs	$50,000
Divorce Revenues	200,000
Trust & Estate Revenues	150,000
Distributions	225,000 each

Year 4

Costs	$50,000
Divorce Revenues	200,000
Trust & Estate Revenues	150,000
Distributions	100,000 each

Year 5

Costs	$50,000
Divorce Revenues	200,000
Trust & Estate Revenues	250,000
Distributions	?

At the end of the 5th year, all bills are collected and all remaining cash is distributed to the partners in accordance with their agreement.

(a) As to each year, how are the partners taxed? (Assume that the partners' deal will be respected for tax purposes, which it would, as discussed immediately below.)

(b) What are the liquidating distributions and how are they taxed?

D. WHEN IS CAPITAL ACCOUNTING RESPECTED?

SKIM: Reg. § 1.704–1(b)(0)

READ: Reg. §§ 1.704–1(b)(1), (b)(2)(i)

Unfortunately, the capital account notion, as implemented through the "economic effect" requirement of Section 704(b), is not adequate to deal with all of the tax concerns that are presented by partnership special allocations. In some cases, even a partnership agreement cast in (or reinterpreted into) capital accounting terms should not be respected for tax purposes.

Consider the 50–50 partnership between Judy and Sue. Judy has a net operating loss carryover that will expire unused at the end of 2000. To use up this loss, Judy and Sue agree to modify their agreement (i) to give Judy all of the partnership's 2000 income, which will be tax-free to her because of the NOL carryover, then (ii) to give Sue all of the 2001 income, and finally (iii) to resume 50–50 sharing in 2002. Should this deal be respected for tax purposes? Well, first there is the question as to whether this really is the deal. What happens if the partnership does much better in 2001 than in 2000? One guesses that Judy would decide that this was a deal for tax purposes only. If the stated deal is not the real deal, obviously the tax law should look to the real deal. But, what if the stated deal really is the deal? The pre-tax economic effect likely will not vary much from 50–50 when the dust settles, yet the special allocation effects considerable tax savings. This is troubling. In some cases, the tax law should not respect the timing of partners' special allocations.

There is another type of special allocation that presents particular concern: different allocations for items of different tax character. Consider the Judy and Sue partnership again. Now, Judy is in a low tax bracket, while Sue is more heavily taxed. Their 50–50 deal says that Judy's 50% share is first to include ordinary income, while Sue's is first to include long-term capital gains, but that, in total, they will end up 50–50 notwithstanding the special allocations of items with different tax characters. This deal has no pre-tax impact. Thus, it makes sense to ignore the deal for tax purposes and allocate all items 50–50.

These concerns are addressed by the ·second requirement of the Section 704(b) regulations: that a valid "economic effect" (the first requirement) must be sufficiently "substantial" to support the underlying allocation. Read Section 1.704–1(b)(2)(iii) of the regulations. The pre-tax economic effect must be substantial **compared to the tax savings achieved**.

Specifically, an allocation is defective if (i) one partner's after-tax consequences improve and (ii) there is a strong likelihood that no other partner's after-tax results will be substantially hurt. (This analysis is done in present value terms.) In other words, an allocation cannot be an unequivocal win for all partners because of the associated tax outcomes. Read Example 5 in Section 1.704–1(b)(5) of the regulations. In the example, the allocation impacts the pre-tax economics: One partner is allocated more economic income, and the other less, than if there were no special allocation. These pre-tax economics get lost in the tax savings that the allocation would achieve, however: The partner who is giving up eventual cash distributions is saving tax in excess of the cash relinquished. The other partner gets cash in excess of the associated increase in taxes. In other words, the allocation is an after-tax win for both partners because of the associated tax savings. It lacks **substantial** economic effect.

Prior to the 1985 Section 704(b) regulations, some practitioners thought that the substantial economic effect requirement only mandated that an allocation of tax consequences serve some business purpose in the deal, so that a party could sell tax benefits for cash.[14] This view was rejected in the regulations. Tax allocations must follow a pre-tax deal. In other words, there must be an after-tax economic effect before an allocation is respected. A transfer of tax benefits for cash is unacceptable. In Example 5, since the special allocation has little non-tax effect, it is not respected for tax purposes.

This general test of substantiality is pretty mushy, however. Thus, the regulations also provide that 2 particular types of allocation automatically lack substantiality: First is the "shifting" allocation subject to Section 1.704–1(b)(2)(iii)(*b*). Read this provision. It goes after deals like the second Judy and Sue deal described above—where, in one tax year, items of different character are allocated differently between the partners, but in roughly offsetting amounts, so that the principle impact of the allocation is tax saving rather than effecting non-tax economics. Read Examples 6 and 10 in the regulations.

The second type of allocation singled out for lack of substantiality is the "transitory" allocation addressed by Section 1.704–1(b)(2)(iii)(*c*). Read it. It addresses multi-year allocations like the first Judy and Sue deal, above. Here, the problem is not offsetting items of different character in one tax year (the shifting allocation), but offsetting items in different tax years. Under the regulations, a current allocation is unacceptable if, at the time that it enters the agreement, there is a strong likelihood that the allocation will be offset by allocations in later tax years. Read Examples 7 and 8. An allocation that actually effects year-end capital account balances still is not respected if it is likely that the current capital account effect will be eliminated by special allocations in later tax years.

One may be puzzled as to why the regulations bother to identify shifting and transitory allocations as unacceptable. After all, nobody would think that such outrageous deals could work, right? But people

---

14. Note that the reverse argument was rejected in *Park Cities*. There, the pre-tax consequences of a tax allocation were stuffed down the estate's throat.

were doing such transactions prior to the Section 704(b) regulations. Also, note that shifting and transitory allocations are not the only allocations with economic effect that lack substantiality. The allocation in Example 5 of the regulations lacks substantiality even though it is neither shifting nor transitory.

There are 2 generous exceptions to the general substantiality rule, however. Read the last 5 sentences of Section 1.704–1(b)(2)(iii)(*c*). These exceptions apply, not only for purposes of the transitory allocation shoal, but also for purposes of the general test of substantiality. The first exception provides that, in testing an allocation for substantiality, one only looks 5 years out into the future for an offsetting allocation. Read Example 2 of the regulations. The apparent idea is that it is unreasonable to require taxpayers to look into the future indefinitely.

The 2d exception provides that, in testing an allocation for substantiality, one does not take into account that non-economic—"paper"—accelerated depreciation may be offset by an allocation of future non-economic—"paper"—gain because of the associated reduction in the tax basis of the depreciating property. Read Example 1(xi) of the regulations. (Reading this requires parsing through most of Example 1, which is annoying, but good exercise.) The idea underlying this exception is that, since non-economic accelerated depreciation is not associated with an economic effect, the most that any allocation of this tax item can do is to create future gain (as a consequence of the associated reduction of inside and/or outside basis) rather than impact cash distributions, so that providing expressly for such a gain offset is not troubling.

These 2 exceptions to the application of the general test of substantiality bless the real estate tax shelter and simple equipment leasing shelters for purposes of Section 704(b). In both, investors get paper losses attributable to accelerated depreciation and other tax accounting rules and then get later gain, perhaps capital gain, so that the shelter gives the investors, at least, a very valuable interest-free loan from Uncle Sam in addition to any underlying pre-tax economic gain.

REVIEW: Reg. §§ 1.704–1(b)(2)(i)–(iii)

Problem Set IV.D

1. Julie and Jane form a general partnership. Julie puts up 90% of the cash, while Jane only 10%. They agree to share everything 90–10. Does their agreement have substantial economic effect?

2. Assume the same facts as in Problem 1, except that they form an LLC. Now, does their deal have substantial economic effect?

3. Assume the same facts as in Problem 2 (an LLC), except that the deal is that expected early losses are to be allocated 99% to Julie and 1% to Jane, with any later profits also to be allocated 99–1 until Julie's capital account is back to her original cash contribution, at which point all profits are 90–10. Does this deal have substantial economic effect?

4.   Does the deal in Problem 3 of Problem Set IV.B have substantial economic effect?

E.   RESULT WHEN CAPITAL ACCOUNTING NOT RESPECTED

The basic rules regarding substantial economic effect are intricate, but, except for the uncertainty inherent in the general test of substantiality, are pretty mechanical. If the client is willing, the tax advisor can draft a partnership agreement that complies with the Section 704(b) regulations. Life rarely is this easy, however. For example, a client may not be willing to live with a qualified income offset. In fact, a client may not be willing to live with tax allocations in the partnership agreement at all. Under these circumstances, Section 704(b) provides that tax items are allocated in accordance with the partners' "interest in the partnership."

The Section 704(b) regulations provide some, but just some, guidance as to how to determine the partners' interests in the partnership. Read Sections 1.704–1(b)(3)(i) and (ii). Little help. But there is some assistance in Section 1.704–1(b)(3)(iii). Read it; assuming, for now, that "book value" means adjusted tax basis. Capital accounting comes in again. For example, under this partners' interests in the partnership rule, items of special tax character are allocated proportionately to the overall change in the capital accounts. Reread Example 5. In fact, as to loss allocations, Section 1.704–1(b)(3)(iii) resembles the alternate test for substantial economic effect without a requirement for a qualified income offset. Here, however, there is a rule for when a loss allocation takes a capital account of a limited partner or LLC member negative: One looks at how the allocation would affect the partners by comparing (i) how cash would have been distributed among the partners if, prior to the loss, every item of partnership property was sold for exactly its adjusted tax basis and all proceeds from this sale then distributed in liquidation to (ii) how cash would be distributed after a similar sale immediately after the loss was booked. This rule allocates a loss that otherwise would take the capital account of a tax partner negative back to tax partners with positive balances. The idea is that an economic loss reduces the total value of partnership assets, which value, when the partnership liquidates, affects only partners with positive capital account balances (or partners subject to deficit makeups). Read Examples 1(iv)–(vi) and (15).[15]

The student may wonder why the discussion of Section 704(b) has not included cases or rulings. After all, the regulations are over 16 years old. Nevertheless, there are no really interesting cases or rulings interpreting the regulations. One can speculate why. Recently, at least, it seems that the IRS prefers to attack a deal under general business

---

15. The Section 704(b) regulations are the only example of "designer" or "monogrammed" tax regulations. The initials of persons who had input, both inside and outside the government, appear in examples.

purpose and sham transaction law rather than deal with the intricacies of their own regulations.[16]

REVIEW: Reg. § 1.704–1(b)(3)

Problem Set IV.E

1. If *Park Cities* had been decided for the estate, how would the depreciation have been allocated for tax purposes?

2. If any of the allocations in Problem Set IV.D do not have substantial economic effect, how are they taxed?

F. ALLOCATION OF RECAPTURE

READ: Reg. §§ 1.1245–1(e), 1.1250–1(f)

The discussion above of leasing and real estate shelters noted that the usual structure specially allocates depreciation deductions (either directly or by a special allocation of a bottom line loss that reflects the depreciation) in the early years of the shelter to the outside investors, with these losses to be offset by special allocations of income or gain in later years (so that, overall, there is no net effect on the partner's capital account). Such special allocations are blessed in the Section 704(b) regulations. One justification for allowing these special allocations is that, since Congress intends for non-economic accelerated depreciation to be a tax incentive, it should be allocable relatively freely so as to have the broadest incentive effect. Even under this analysis, however, there should be a tax cost for benefitting from the tax incentive. A direct owner of depreciable property pays a price for accelerated depreciation: recapture. The regulations applicable to recapture on personal property owned by partnership pursue this notion and provide that recapture must be allocated back to the partners who received the associated depreciation. The amount of recapture allocated to a partner cannot exceed her share of gain on the relevant property. There are no regulations yet with regard to the partial recapture on realty enacted in 1997,[17] but the same rule should apply under the language of the old regulations, Section 1.1250–1(f).

REVIEW: Reg. §§ 1.1245–1(e), 1.1250–1(f)

Problem Set IV.F

A real estate partnership has 2 partners. They share all tax items except depreciation equally. Depreciation is allocated 75% to one partner and 25% to the other. These allocations have substantial economic effect. A building is sold, resulting in $100,000 of gain, all of which is Section 1250 recapture. How is this gain allocated between the partners?

---

16. *See, e.g., ACM Partnership v. Commissioner*, 157 F.3d 231 (3d Cir.1998). The blunderbuss of the Anti–Abuse Regulations is discussed below in Chapter XI.

17. I.R.C. § 1(h)(1)(D).

G. TAKING STOCK

The last few sections of this chapter have been hard going indeed. Complex rules were discussed alongside the presentation of difficult concepts. It is helpful at this juncture, therefore, to step back from the complexity in order to reflect on the difficult concepts.

Partners are taxed on the partnership's tax items as if earned directly. But, these items do not belong to the partners outright and may never be received or borne by them. Thus, some means of attributing partnership tax items to partners is needed. The partners' agreement, and in particular the capital accounting in it, is the only state-law instrument that tracks the partners' benefits and burdens associated with particular tax items. Thus, Section 704(b) and its regulations generally defer to a partnership agreement's allocations if they are properly accounted for in accounts that have economic consequences. In fact, in most cases, even if the partnership agreement does not provide for capital accounts, the partners' interests in the partnership rules of Section 1.704–1(b)(3) of the regulations reinterpret the partners' agreement into capital accounting terms.

Unfortunately, there are 3 basic problems with respecting even proper capital accounts for tax purposes (in a debt-free partnership, the case in this chapter). The first problem is timing. A current allocation of profit (loss) to a partner may be offset by an allocation of loss (profit) in a later year. If the later, offsetting allocation is not related to the current allocation, this is not troubling, as the current allocation still has an economic impact, albeit far into the future. The later allocation may be associated with the current allocation, however. For example, a partnership agreement can provide that a partner allocated losses currently is to be allocated any subsequent profits up to the amount of the current losses. In this case, the current losses may have no ultimate economic impact. The likelihood of economic consequences decreases as the likelihood of the offsetting allocation increases. This is troubling, as many old-school tax shelters were based on such timing strategies. Hence, the current regulations in general do not respect such transitory allocations, regardless of the quality of the partnership's capital accounting.

The second problem with respecting capital accounts is tax character. Capital accounting—which is a state-law mechanism, after all—pays no attention to the tax character of items. Under state (non-tax) law, income is income, regardless of whether it is treated for tax purposes as ordinary taxable income, long-term capital gain, tax-free muni bond income, or in some other tax-favored way. Yet, the tax law cares about tax character. It should not be possible to freely transfer tax benefits without a corresponding economic impact. Thus, Section § 1.704–1(b)(2)(iii)(c) prevents naked tax benefit transfers by requiring any allocation to have an after-tax consequence. Then, Section 1.704–1(b)(2)(iii)(b) prevents the most obvious form of tax benefit transfer, the shifting allocation.

The 3d problem is tax items that have no corresponding economic consequences at all, such as non-economic accelerated depreciation. As to such items, a requirement that an allocation have an economic effect would be artificial. (This problem is presented most clearly with non-recourse deductions, as to be considered in Chapter V, but has been seen here already.) The last 3 sentences of Section 1.704–1(b)(2)(iii)(c) and associated provisions allow quite free allocation of non-economic deductions. Then, Section § 1.1245–1(e) requires that the associated non-economic recapture income be allocated to the partners who received the associated non-economic deductions.

H. GROSS INCOME ALLOCATIONS, GUARANTEED PAYMENTS, AND SECTION 707(a)

READ: Code §§ 707(a)(1), (a)(2)(A), and (c) and Reg. § 1.707–1(c)

There is one final allocation problem presented by the simple partnership discussed in this chapter. This problem is best illustrated with an example: Beth and Ann form a partnership. Beth puts up 75% of the cash. Ann puts up the remaining 25%. Ann also is to work full time in the partnership's business. Beth and Ann's economic arrangement is that Ann receives reasonable compensation for her services, with any residual profit or loss allocated 75% to Beth and 25% to Ann. What should be the tax result in a year in which the partnership is profitable without regard to Ann's compensation, but, after taking Ann's compensation into account, the partnership shows a loss? One might want to allow the residual loss 75% to Beth and 25% to Ann (on top of her compensation income). Under this treatment, even though, taken together, the partners show a profit, Beth is allowed a loss (and Ann more income than the partners earned collectively). Many find this troubling.[18]

The first question presented here is whether the "manufactured" loss result can be achieved under the Section 704(b) regulations by allocating gross income first to Ann in an amount equal to her services compensation. The regulations are silent on allocations of gross income in excess of taxable income. Item allocations, like a special allocation of depreciation, can result in one partner having a loss and another showing profit and are blessed in the regulations, but a gross income allocation is not an item allocation.[19] Fortunately, Congress thought about this issue back in 1954, and adopted special rules, so that one need not face the Section 704(b) issue in many contexts.

The heart of the 1954 regime is the hybrid approach of Section 707(c). Under this provision, gross income allocations are allowed with

---

18. Chapter VI discusses the "ceiling rule" in Section 1.704–3 of the regulations, which applies to allocations of tax items associated with contributed property. These ceiling rule regulations go to breathtaking lengths to prevent just such a manufactured loss.

19. A qualified income offset can be of gross income, but this is a very special case. Treas. Reg. § 1.704–1(b)(2)(ii)(d).

respect to payments to a partner determined without regard to the income of the partnership. The partnership is allowed a deduction as long as the item would be deductible (and not capitalized under Section 263) if paid to a third party.[20] Under the regulations, the partner to whom the payment is made is taxed as if allocated a share of gross income—being taxed in her year that includes the end of the partnership's tax year in which paid.[21] Note that this rule only applies to payments. Accruals, mere bookkeeping entries, cannot be used to manufacture losses under Section 707(c).

Further rules also where provided in 1954. Section 707(a)(1) adopts the entity approach for situations where partners are acting in independent capacities. For example, a real estate broker may be a partner and provide occasional brokerage services to the partnership on the same terms as similar services are provided to third parties. Section 707(a)(1) amounts are treated just like any other amount paid or accrued. This rule, standing by itself, blesses a timing game: an accrual basis partnership accruing a deduction for unpaid Section 707(a)(1) amounts with respect to a cash basis partner. Congress responded in 1984 by expanding a general rule directed at abusive related-party transactions: Section 267(e), as amended in 1984, applies Section 267(a)(2) to defer any partnership deduction until the partner takes the item into income. Read Sections 267(a)(2) and (e).

Thus, now, the basic pattern is: Section 707(a)(1) amounts are accounted for under the partner's accounting method. Section 707(c) amounts are accounted for under the partnership's method. Beyond this, as to basic income tax consequences, there is little difference between the two types of amount.[22] Therefore, it is not surprising that there is little law distinguishing between them. The IRS' only attempt to distinguish them is in 2 1981 rulings, which conclude that, (i) as to a real estate partnership, a partnership management fee of 5% of gross rentals represents a guaranteed payment, while, (ii) as to a securities investment partnership, a management fee of 10% of gross income paid to a partner who provides similar services at the same rate to unrelated entities is a Section 707(a)(1) amount.[23]

---

20. It is unclear whether disallowance provisions such as Section 265 apply with regard to guaranteed payments.

21. A guaranteed payment is ordinary income to the payee partner, while a gross income allocation could be of, say, capital gain or other specially-treated income.

For capital accounting purposes, Treas. Reg. § 1.704–1(b)(2)(iv)(*o*), offsets the payee partner's income and distribution, so that only the partners' share of the associated deduction impacts the capital accounts.

22. There are numerous collateral differences, however. For example, the recipient of a Section 707(a)(1) amount for services may be treated as an employee for

fringe benefits and employment tax purposes. Similarly, a Section 707(a)(1) payment for capital is interest, subject to all of the special tax rules that apply to interest, while a guaranteed payment may not be for some purposes. There are similar issues presented when distinguishing these items from a regular distributive share.

23. Rev. Rul. 81–300, 1981–2 C.B. 143; Rev. Rul. 81–301, 1981–2 C.B. 144. Note that being measured by gross income, or at least gross rentals, as compared to being measured by net income, apparently does not disqualify an item from being a guaranteed payment.

Congress has dealt with the interaction between deductions of items paid to partners and gross income allocations in one additional context: Apparently, practitioners were trying to avoid deduction disallowance provisions by, rather than paying an item that would not be deductible, (i) admitting the payee as a nominal partner, (ii) allocating the payee income (in such a way that there is no guaranteed payment), and (iii) distributing cash to the nominal partner in an amount equal to the income allocation. It was hoped that the income allocation would have the effect of a deduction by allocating income away from the real partners. For example, a real estate partnership would bring an architect in as a partner to avoid having to capitalize her fee. While it is not clear that this strategy ever worked, Congress made a pre-emptive strike by enacting Section 707(a)(2)(A) in 1984.[24] It says that such a deal is treated as not involving a partner, so as to result in capitalization rather than an effective deduction.

REVIEW: Code §§ 267(a)(2) and (e) and 707(a)(1), (a)(2)(A), and (c) and Reg. §§ 1.704–1(b)(2)(iv)(o) and 1.707–1(c)

Problem Set IV.H

1.　Shelly is an architect. She wants to design and build a building for her practice. Sam is a friend with money. He will finance a partnership with Shelly to build the building which will be leased to Shelly to be used in her practice under a commercially reasonable lease. Their deal is that Shelly gets 3% of rents, with any excess cash flow being allocated proportionately to capital accounts until Sam has received distributions equal to his original capital. Any profit or loss (determined using tax accounting) after removing Shelly's 3% is first allocated proportionately to positive capital account balances at the beginning of the year until the year after the year in which Sam has received total distributions equal to his original contribution, after which time profit is allocated 50–50. Capital accounts are to be respected in liquidation, including a deficit makeup. How is this arrangement taxed? (Remember the discussion of Section 83 in Chapter II.)

2.　An alternative is for Shelly and Sam to (i) pay Shelly her 3%, (ii) pay Sam 10% annually on his capital account, and (iii) just allocate all profit after these amounts 50–50. Capital accounts are to be respected in liquidation. How is this taxed? (Consider whether Section 263A(f) applies.)

3.　Another alternative is the same as Problem 2 except that Sam's 10% return is paid out of profits only. How is this taxed? What if the amount due accrues, to be paid as cash is available? *See* Rev. Rul. 67–158, 1967–1 C.B. 188.

---

24. Section 707(a)(2)(A) can apply to disguised sales of property, but, because the allocation required by this section would mess up capital accounts with property transactions, in practice (A) has no effect with regard to property. Section 707(a)(2)(B) deals with the related property transaction, but since it does not involve an allocation, was discussed in Chapter II.

4.   A final alternative is the same as Problem 1 except that the flip in interests occurs when Sam has received distributions equal to his original investment plus a 10% annual yield on the unpaid balance (rather than just his original contribution) and then the interests go to 50–50 (rather than to 90–10). How is this taxed?

5.   Steve and Neil form a general partnership. Steve is to be allocated 25% of partnership income, but not less than $100,000, which is to be paid to him within 30 days after the end of the year. The remaining profit and any cash not needed by the partnership are Neil's. In a year, the partnership has $200,000 of income and Steve gets his $100,000. What is the tax treatment?

6.   Ellen is a partner in the Paris office of a law firm. She is paid $250,000 per year plus 14% of the profits of the Paris office. How much, if any, of her share is foreign earned income for purposes of Section 911? *See Miller v. Commissioner*, 52 T.C. 752 (1969), *acq.*, 1972–2 C.B. 2.

Chapter V

BORROWING AND RELATED ALLOCATIONS

A. INTRODUCTION

READ: Code §§ 704(d), 722, 731(a), 733, and 752(a)–(c)

Chapter III introduced Subchapter K's basic aggregate approach to debt. Last chapter's discussion of allocations did not reflect partnership debt, in the interests of simplicity. This chapter looks at how partnership losses attributable to borrowed money are allocated among the partners. Later chapters explore other situations where debt has tax consequences, such as distributions of property subject to debt.

The student may wonder why losses, particularly losses attributable to borrowed money, are so prominent in the lore of Subchapter K. The answer is that tax losses are common and Subchapter K provides the best vehicle for multiple taxpayers to benefit from debt-financed losses incurred in a common activity.

Tax losses are common. As the 1990s boom in high-tech demonstrated, businesses that still are growing, even very successful and valuable businesses, can show operating losses. Also, the tax law provides generous depreciation, which can provide such large deductions that businesses can show a tax loss even when they are showing a financial profit.

Subchapter K provides the best vehicle for using the losses of a joint enterprise. Corporate losses can be used only by that corporation (or other members of a consolidated group if a consolidated return is filed), either in past or future profitable years.[1] For a start-up corporation, there are no past profits to use losses against, so that losses can be used only in the future, when they have a lower present value. Investors in a tax partnership can use its losses immediately (subject, of course, to Section 704(d), the PAL rules, and the At–Risk rules discussed later in this chapter). Moreover, as discussed in this chapter, many losses attributable to money borrowed by a partnership can be used by its partners. Subchapter S, discussed below in Chapter XII, allows investors in certain

---

1. I.R.C. § 172.

closely-held corporations to use some of the entity's losses, but the Subchapter S corporation is not a very flexible vehicle, and debt-related losses do not flow through an S Corporation like they flow through a partnership.

Under these circumstances, the growth of partnerships has been linked closely to the increased use of tax losses, including debt-financed losses, so that such losses have played a key role in the development of Subchapter K.

B. THE BASICS OF SECTION 752

READ: Code § 752

Before discussing debt-related losses, it is necessary to expand upon Chapter III's analysis of Section 752, which contains the core rules applicable to partnership obligations.

Sections 752(a) and (b) use fictional cash contributions and distributions to achieve results similar to those under an aggregate approach. Under Section 752(a), a partnership borrowing is treated as a cash borrowing by the burdened partners followed by these partners making cash contributions to the partnership. Similarly, Section 752(b) treats partnership payments of debt principal as if cash were distributed to the partners to pay off the debt. Use of partnership (entity) resources to pay the debt is treated as a benefit to the partners, since Section 752, in effect, treats partnership borrowing as partner borrowing.

These rules achieve sound results in many contexts. For example, a key feature of accrual accounting is the creation of liabilities by accruing payable obligations for expenses prior to payment. Section 752 works soundly here. When an expense is accrued, there is no net effect on outside basis: The reduction in outside basis attributable to the deduction is exactly offset by the basis increase from the associated liability (which basis, in fact, supported the deduction for purposes of Section 704(d)). When the payable is satisfied, the outside basis goes down. Thus, outside basis is reduced only once, and only when an expense is paid.

Section 752(c) generally adopts the *Crane* rule, and expands it to recourse debt: The owner of property subject to debt, nonrecourse and recourse, is treated as the obligor of any debt the property is subject to. This rule normally comes into play with regard to the taxation of contributions and distributions of encumbered property, as discussed later in this chapter and in Chapters II, VII, and VIII.

Section 752(c) has another feature not present in *Crane* itself: a limitation on its application to an amount of debt not greater than the fair market value of the encumbered property. This limitation presented considerable interpretative problems. Finally, the Supreme Court, in *Tufts*, below, was forced to clear things up. This is the same *Tufts* taught in basic tax courses with the Subchapter K issue edited out. Below is the case edited with the *Crane* issue edited out so that the student can focus on the Subchapter K issue:

COMMISSIONER v. TUFTS

Supreme Court of the United States, 1983.
461 U.S. 300, 103 S.Ct. 1826, 75 L.Ed.2d 863.

JUSTICE BLACKMUN delivered the opinion of the Court.

On August 1, 1970, respondent Clark Pelt, a builder, and his wholly owned corporation, respondent Clark, Inc., formed a general partnership. The purpose of the partnership was to construct a 120–unit apartment complex in Duncanville, Tex., a Dallas suburb. Neither Pelt nor Clark, Inc. made any capital contribution to the partnership. Six days later, the partnership entered into a mortgage loan agreement with the Farm & Home Savings Association (F & H). Under the agreement, F & H was committed for a $1,851,500 loan for the complex. In return, the partnership executed a note and a deed of trust in favor of F & H. The partnership obtained the loan on a nonrecourse basis: neither the partnership nor its partners assumed any personal liability for repayment of the loan. Pelt later admitted four friends and relatives, respondents Tufts, Steger, Stephens, and Austin, as general partners. None of them contributed capital upon entering the partnership.

The construction of the complex was completed in August 1971. During 1971, each partner made small capital contributions to the partnership; in 1972, however, only Pelt made a contribution. The total of the partners' capital contributions was $44,212. In each tax year, all partners claimed as income tax deductions their allocable shares of ordinary losses and depreciation. The deductions taken by the partners in 1971 and 1972 totaled $439,972. Due to these contributions and deductions, the partnership's adjusted basis in the property in August 1972 was $1,455,740.

In 1971 and 1972, major employers in the Duncanville area laid off significant numbers of workers. As a result, the partnership's rental income was less than expected, and it was unable to make the payments due on the mortgage. Each partner, on August 28, 1972, sold his partnership interest to an unrelated third party, Fred Bayles. As consideration, Bayles agreed to reimburse each partner's sale expenses up to $250; he also assumed the nonrecourse mortgage.

On the date of transfer, the fair market value of the property did not exceed $1,400,000. Each partner reported the sale on his federal income tax return and indicated that a partnership loss of $55,740 had been sustained.[2] The Commissioner of Internal Revenue, on audit, determined that the sale resulted in a partnership capital gain of approximately

---

2. [Court's Note 1:] The loss was the difference between the adjusted basis, $1,455,740, and the fair market value of the property, $1,400,000.

$400,000. His theory was that the partnership had realized the full amount of the nonrecourse obligation.[3]

[The IRS' position was that, since Tufts had been allocated a share of the partnership's debt under the Section 752 regulation, which share had increased his outside basis so as to support deductions in excess of his capital investment, he must include his share of the debt in his amount realized upon sale of his interest.]

Section 752(d) specifically provides that liabilities involved in the sale or exchange of a partnership interest are to "be treated in the same manner as liabilities in connection with the sale or exchange of property not associated with partnerships." Section 1001 governs the determination of gains and losses on the disposition of property. Under § 1001(a), the gain or loss from a sale or other disposition of property is defined as the difference between "the amount realized" on the disposition and the property's adjusted basis. Subsection (b) of § 1001 defines "amount realized": "The amount realized from the sale or other disposition of property shall be the sum of any money received plus the fair market value of the property (other than money) received." At issue is the application of the latter provision to the disposition of property encumbered by a nonrecourse mortgage of an amount in excess of the property's fair market value.

Section 752 prescribes the tax treatment of certain partnership transactions, and § 752(c) provides that "[for] purposes of this section, a liability to which property is subject shall, to the extent of the fair market value of such property, be considered as a liability of the owner of the property." Section 752(c) could be read to apply to a sale or disposition of partnership property, and thus to limit the amount realized to the fair market value of the property transferred. Inconsistent with this interpretation, however, is the language of § 752(d), which specifically mandates that partnership liabilities be treated "in the same manner as liabilities in connection with the sale or exchange of property not associated with partnerships." The apparent conflict of these subsections renders the facial meaning of the statute ambiguous, and therefore we must look to the statute's structure and legislative history.

Subsections (a) and (b) of § 752 prescribe rules for the treatment of liabilities in transactions between a partner and his partnership, and thus for determining the partner's adjusted basis in his partnership interest. Under § 704(d), a partner's distributive share of partnership losses is limited to the adjusted basis of his partnership interest. When partnership liabilities are increased or when a partner takes on the liabilities of the partnership, § 752(a) treats the amount of the increase or the amount assumed as a contribution by the partner to the partner-

---

3. [Court's Note 2:] The Commissioner determined the partnership's gain on the sale by subtracting the adjusted basis, $1,455,740, from the liability assumed by Bayles, $1,851,500. Of the resulting figure, $395,760, the Commissioner treated $348,661 as capital gain, pursuant to § 741 of the Internal Revenue Code of 1954, and $47,099 as ordinary gain under the recapture provisions of § 1250 of the Code. The application of § 1250 in determining the character of the gain is not at issue here.

ship. This treatment results in an increase in the adjusted basis of the partner's interest and a concomitant increase in the § 704(d) limit on his distributive share of any partnership loss. Conversely, under § 752(b), a decrease in partnership liabilities or the assumption of a partner's liabilities by the partnership has the effect of a distribution, thereby reducing the limit on the partner's distributive share of the partnership's losses. When property encumbered by liabilities is contributed to or distributed from the partnership, § 752(c) prescribes that the liability shall be considered to be assumed by the transferee only to the extent of the property's fair market value.

The legislative history indicates that Congress contemplated this application of § 752(c). Mention of the fair market value limitation occurs only in the context of transactions under subsections (a) and (b). The sole reference to subsection (d) does not discuss the limitation. While the legislative history is certainly not conclusive, it indicates that the fair market value limitation of § 752(c) was directed to transactions between a partner and his partnership.

By placing a fair market value limitation on liabilities connected with property contributions to and distributions from partnerships under subsections (a) and (b), Congress apparently intended § 752(c) to prevent a partner from inflating the basis of his partnership interest. Otherwise, a partner with no additional capital at risk in the partnership could raise the § 704(d) limit on his distributive share of partnership losses or could reduce his taxable gain upon disposition of his partnership interest. There is no potential for similar abuse in the context of § 752(d) sales of partnership interests to unrelated third parties. In light of the above, we interpret subsection (c) to apply only to § 752(a) and (b) transactions, and not to limit the amount realized in a sale or exchange of a partnership interest under § 752(d).

REVIEW: Code § 752

Problem Set V.B

If *Tufts* had gone the other way on the Section 752(c) issue, how would the partners have been taxed differently over the life of the partnership?

C. PARTNERSHIP RECOURSE DEBT: THE EASY CASE

READ: Code §§ 704(d) and 752 and Reg. §§ 1.752–1(a)(1) and 1.752–2(a) and (b)

With the basics of Section 752 as background, the analysis can focus on the allocation of partnership losses associated with borrowings among the partners. Fortunately, most of the concepts needed already were introduced in the last chapter. There, the capital accounting rules that implement the requirement that a loss allocation have economic effect worked mightily to assure that a partner not be allowed losses that will be borne by another partner's capital. Here, the idea is that a partner not be allocated deductions related to a debt that is borne by another partner. Thus, the only additional analyses required are of (i) how the partners bear partnership borrowing and (ii) which losses relate to borrowing. This section of this text reviews these analyses as to partnership obligations for which at least one partner is personally liable (directly or indirectly as a consequence of side agreements, like guarantees), which are called "recourse" obligations in the Sections 704 and 752 regulations.[4]

This issue of how to allocate debt among partners was avoided thus far in this text by assuming that debt is shared by the partners pro-rata. The student may have been troubled by this assumption. After all, as to the usual recourse liabilities of a state-law general partnership, liability is joint and several.[5] Perhaps all partners should be treated as liable on recourse debt for Subchapter K purposes.

If Section 752(a) were interpreted to treat all partners as fully liable for all partnership recourse debt, the mechanics of Subchapter K would not work properly. Partnership debt would increase the outside basis of each partner even though the partnership's inside basis includes its debt only once. This multiple counting of debt in the partners' total outside basis would immediately throw the symmetry between inside and outside basis out of whack.

Section 1.752–2 of the regulations solves this problem by giving each partner only a share of partnership recourse debt.[6] This share is determined on an "after the dust settles" basis. Specifically, one works through the maze of state-law relationships, including guarantees, indemnity, and contribution, by assuming (i) that the partnership liquidates at a time when all of its assets are worthless (adjusting the capital accounts for the associated losses), (ii) that everybody sues everybody on every possible claim under the partnership agreement and otherwise, and, (iii) that, finally, after the dust settles on all of the litigation, all losers fulfill their legal obligations. Then, the Section 752 regulations treat a partner as obligated on recourse debt to the extent that she would make payment under these circumstance. Normally, in a pro-rata general partnership, this rule means that the partners share recourse debt pro-rata. Generally, Section 807 of RUPA, as in *Park Cities*, allocates ultimate liability for partnership debt in excess of partnership assets proportionately to negative capital account balances.[7] In the usual

---

4. Treas. Reg. §§ 1.704–2(b)(2), 1.752–1(a).

5. Section 306(a) of the 1997 Revised Uniform Partnership Act provides:

   Except as otherwise provided ..., all partners are liable jointly and severally for all obligations of the partnership unless otherwise agreed by the claimant or provided by law.

6. All of the debt regulations have related-party anti-abuse rules which are not reviewed in the text in the interests of simplicity.

7. RUPA Section 807 provides in part:

§ 807. Settlement of Accounts and Contributions Among Partners

   (a) In winding up a partnership's business, the assets of the partnership, incase, a negative capital account is created by allocations of losses. Thus, under the after-the-dust-settles approach to recourse debt of the Section 752 regulations, since the partners' capital accounts go negative when all assets are treated as sold for nothing proportionately to the partners' loss sharing ratios, these ratios usually control the allocation of recourse debt between the partners.[8] Read Sections 1.752–2(f)(Example 1) and (Example 2) of the regulations.

Thus, as to recourse debt, the partners usually share the debt as they would share economic losses in excess of their capital. With this rule in place, matters still are involved, but with few surprises. For example, when a partnership borrows, the partners get outside basis for their respective shares of the debt. Thus, they may withdraw cash in an amount at least equal to their Section 752 share of the debt without being taxed under Section 731. As the debt is paid down, so that the partners' respective shares of the debt are reduced, deemed distributions under Section 752(b) appropriately reduce basis. The deemed distributions usually do not result in tax, because the cash used to pay the debt is generated by income that increased the partners' outside bases.[9] Thus, while Section 752 operates on an ongoing basis, it usually has no tax effect and can be ignored.

One aspect of the operation of Section 752(c) that was discussed briefly in Chapter II can be amplified at this point. Section 752 comes into play when property subject to debt is contributed to a partnership. Under Section 752(c), the partnership is treated as the obligor for tax purposes. The non-contributing partners increase their outside bases for their respective shares of the debt. The contributing partner has a deemed cash distribution for her net decrease in liability (from 100% to her share of the debt under Section 752(a)).[10] This deemed cash contribution can be treated as a partial sale under the Section 707(a)(2)(B) regulations, as discussed in Chapter II.

Having determined a partner's share of debt, it is possible to complete the analysis of loss allowance. A partner being allocated a share

---

cluding the contributions of the partners required by this section, must be applied to discharge its obligations to creditors . . . Any surplus must be applied to pay in cash the net amount distributable to partners in accordance with their right to distributions under subsection (b).

(b) Each partner is entitled to a settlement of all partnership accounts upon winding up the partnership business. In settling accounts among the partners, the profits and losses that result from the liquidation of the partnership assets must be credited and charged to the partners' accounts. [Note that this did not happen in *Park Cities*.] The partnership shall make a distribution to a partner in an amount equal to any excess of the credits over the charges to the partner's account.

A partner shall contribute to the partnership an amount equal to any excess of the charges over the credits in the partner's account . . .

8. In fact, prior to 1991, the Section 752 regulations allocated recourse debt among the partners proportionately to the respective loss-sharing ratios.

9. Rev. Rul. 94–4, 1994–1 C.B. 196.

10. Under Section 1.752–1(f) of the regulations, the decrease in personal debt is netted against the increase in the partner's amount of partnership liabilities, rather than being treated as a gross distribution followed by a gross contribution, as this alternative could trigger a tax, which seems inappropriate.

of partnership debt under the Section 752 regulations enables the partner to deduct losses attributable to partnership borrowing notwithstanding Section 704(d). A partner's deductible losses from her partnership are limited by Section 704(d) to her outside basis in the partnership, as discussed in Chapters III and IV. Thus, a partner in a debt-free partnership can deduct cumulative net losses only up to her actual investment. With partnership borrowing in the picture, however, Section 704(d)—working with Sections 722 and 752(a)—allows cumulative net losses up to the partner's investment **plus** her share of debt. In the usual case, this rule makes perfect sense. If a partner bears a partnership debt used to fund a loss, she should not have to wait until the debt is paid out of her share of partnership profits or out of her outside resources to be being allowed the appropriate deduction.[11]

Which, as with most Subchapter K issues, gets us back to Section 704(b). What flexibility is there in allocating tax losses[12] attributable to borrowing among the partners? Answering this question requires another visit to the substantial economic effect regulations.

Partnership borrowing has no effect on the partners' capital accounts.[13] Thus, in general, a partner's outside basis equals her capital account plus her share of partnership debt.[14] Intuitively, the capital account is the partner's share of the partnership's (net) equity, while the outside basis is her share of the partnership's (gross) assets.

That capital accounts do not include debt presents the central problem here. In Chapter IV, where no partnership debt was involved, we were not particularly troubled by the Section 704(b) regulations' skepticism about losses taking a capital account negative, as any such loss would have bumped into the limitation of Section 704(d) regardless. Here, we have a higher limit under Section 704(d) and therefore want to be able to take partners' accounts negative.[15]

Section 1.704–1(b)(2)(ii)(*b*)(3) of the regulations is the general rule controlling the impact of recourse debt of a general partnership on allocations. Assuming substantiality, one can allocate as many losses to a partner in excess of her capital account as desired as long as, under the partnership agreement and all of any other state-law agreements, the

---

11. At such time, the loss, which was carried forward under the second sentence of Section 704(d), is allowed by Section 704(d).

12. State-law losses are allocated under the partnership agreement and control the allocation of the debt under the Section 752 regulations.

13. Of course, interest expense allocated to a partner reduces her capital account.

14. This rule breaks down (i) when property is contributed or distributed by a partnership and (ii) when the composition of a partnership changes by the transfer of a partnership interest or the admission of a new partner.

15. All partners having negative tax capital accounts does not mean that the partnership is financially insolvent (liabilities exceeding assets). Since tax capital accounts are kept under tax accounting, a total negative capital account means only that the total partnership debt exceeds the total adjusted tax basis of the partnership's assets. Assets' adjusted tax basis frequently is well below fair market value, particularly if the assets are being depreciated under Section 168, which generally provides cumulative depreciation in amounts that exceed the true economic decline in the value of assets.

partner is liable for any deficit in her capital account. In other words, since debt-related losses take a capital account negative, for such losses to have economic effect, the partner to whom such a loss is allocated must be responsible for the associated negative capital account balance. Then, the Section 752 regulations allocate to the partner an amount of debt at least equal to the negative balance so that the losses allocated under Section 704(b) are not limited by Section 704(d). All of which makes perfect sense. A partner who bears a partnership loss **should** get the deduction therefor when booked by the partnership.

The basic test for economic effect requires more than that a partner allocated a loss must be liable for that particular loss, however. It requires that the partner be personally unlimitedly liable for **all** losses that **could** be allocated to her. In a general partnership, this happens by operation of law in the absence of some side agreement to the contrary. But frequently the partners will agree among or with lenders to limit the liability of one or more partners themselves (as in a limited partnership or LLC). Section 1.704–1(b)(2)(ii)*(c)* of the regulations accommodates this by modifying the basic test of economic effect to allow losses up to any amount a partner is obligated to restore, even if the partner is not unlimitedly liable.[16]

To summarize the discussion thus far, which focused on recourse debt of general partnerships, Subchapter K works as one would expect. When a partnership loses borrowed money, the partners' that bear the loss under state law are allocated the associated tax loss under Section 704(b) and are given the basis that is required to support this tax loss under Section 752. The hard issues involve nonrecourse debt and LLCs, which are discussed below.

REVIEW: Code §§ 704(d) and 752 and Reg. §§ 1.704–1(b)(2)(ii)*(c)* and *(d)* and 1.752–1(a)(1), –1(f), –2(a), –2(b), and –2(f) (Example 1) and (Example 2)

Problem Set V.C

1. P1, Inc. and The P2 Company form a 50–50 general partnership to engage in a service business that requires no material assets. Each contributes $10 million in cash.

    A. In the partnership's first year, the partnership loses its entire $20 million of capital. How are the partners taxed?

    B. In the 2d year, the partnership borrows another $20 million on a fully recourse basis. Again, the entire $20 million is lost. How are the partners taxed?

    C. In the 3d year, the partnership borrows yet another $20 million. The terms of the borrowing and the partnership agreement

---

16. Note that the alternate test for economic effect in Section 1.704–1(b)(2)*(d)* of the regulations, while helping with the allocation of equity-funded losses to limited partners and LLC members, as discussed in Chapter IV, usually is of little help with regard to allocations of deductions attributable to debt, as such losses usually involve taking a partner's capital account negative, which the alternate test does not address.

provide that the creditor cannot pursue the non-partnership assets of P1 to satisfy the debt. Yet again, the entire $20 million is lost. How are the partners taxed?

    D.   Finally, in the 4th year, the partnership borrows $20 million. The terms of the borrowing and the partnership agreement provide that the lender can proceed only against the partnership's receivables if there is a default in making payments on the lending. In a side agreement between all parties signed at the same time as the loan papers, P1 guarantees the debt. All $20 million is lost. How are the partners taxed?

    2.   What would be the outcomes under the facts of Problem 1 if, to reflect the partners' non-capital contributions to the partnership, P1 put up 50% of the capital and shared 75% in the partnership's profits and losses and P2 put up 50% and received the remaining 25% of profits and losses?

D.   PARTNERSHIP NONRECOURSE DEBT

READ: Code §§ 465(a), (b), (c)(3), and (e) and Reg. §§ 1.704–2(b)(1), (b)(2), (c), (d), (e), (f)(1), (f)(6), (g), (j)(1)(ii), and (j)(2) and 1.752–3(a)

With classic nonrecourse debt, a lender agrees that, in the event of default on the debt, she will look solely to specified property, usually property subject to a mortgage associated with the nonrecourse debt, to recover her debt. Classic nonrecourse lending is common in real estate transactions and became fashionable in tax shelters. Still, classic nonrecourse debt is not something the average tax advisor sees every day. However, the rules that control the impact of nonrecourse debt on partnership allocations also apply with regard to borrowings by LLCs, which are quite common today. It is helpful to examine the nonrecourse debt rules in their native environment before looking at more exotic settings, however. Thus, this section looks at classic nonrecourse debt, with LLC borrowings to be examined later in this chapter.

The economics of classic nonrecourse lending are a bit involved. Most importantly for present purposes, the lender, rather than the property owner, bears the risk that the property that secures the loan will become worth less than the outstanding unpaid balance of the loan at some point in the future. At this future point, if the borrower defaults, she will have lost her equity in the securing property, but the lender will lose the difference between the outstanding balance of the loan and the value of the property. Lenders are compensated for this risk through higher interest payments, and guard against it by requiring amortization of the loan principal.

These economics interact with the tax law. Consider depreciation. In theory, the depreciation expense is allowed to reflect the loss in value of the depreciating asset. Thus, when property is subject to classic nonrecourse debt, once depreciation has reduced the adjusted basis of the property to below the balance of the debt at that time, any future loss in value (economic depreciation) should impact the lender rather than the property owner. Under *Crane* and *Tufts*, however, any subsequent tax depreciation still is allowed to the owner.[17]

Subchapter K's rules for losses attributable to classic nonrecourse debt reflect these underlying economics: Nonrecourse debt in general is treated as other debt. There are special rules for deductions that are treated as being attributable to nonrecourse debt, however. Read Sections 1.704–2(c), (d)(1), (d)(2), and (j)(1)(ii) of the regulations. Ignoring distributions of borrowed money, which are discussed later in this chapter, a year's amount of nonrecourse deductions is the increase (over the year) in the total amount determined by adding together the respective amounts for each nonrecourse debt by which the balance of the debt exceeds the securing property's (or properties') adjusted (net of depreciation) tax basis (or bases).[18] In other words, in the usual case, the nonrecourse deductions in a year are the year's depreciation (i) that took the basis of property subject to nonrecourse debt below the amount of the associated nonrecourse debt or (ii) that increased the amount by which the debt exceeded the adjusted basis.

Special, liberal allocation rules apply to these deductions. Section 1.704–2(e)(2) allows partnership nonrecourse deductions to be allocated in any way that is "reasonably consistent with allocations that have substantial economic effect of some other significant partnership item attributable to the property securing the nonrecourse liabilities." The partner allocated the loss must be allocated the associated future built-in (*Tufts*) gain (a share of the amount by which the nonrecourse liability exceeds the tax basis, which total amount is called "minimum gain" in the regulations), since that gain is present regardless of what happens to the value of the property under *Tufts*.[19] Then, Section 1.752–3(a)(1) allocates the partner an amount of the nonrecourse debt equal to the loss (minimum gain), which increases the partner's outside basis sufficiently that the partner can use the loss allocated to her in the face of Section 704(d). Note how the regulations under Sections 704(b) and 752 work together to achieve this result.

As this discussion suggests, the basic notion underlying Section 1.704–2 of the regulations is that nonrecourse deductions have no economic effect to the partners, so that their allocation among the partners cannot have substantial economic effect. A logical consequence of this view would be that nonrecourse deductions should be allocable in any way so long as the partner to whom an allocation is made bears the associated minimum gain. The actual regulations, however, stop short of

---

17. The borrower is responsible for tax gain that recaptures the excess noneconomic depreciation should the lender end up really bearing any loss. This regime makes particular sense today, since current Section 168 of the Code provides accelerated depreciation that is much faster than the economic decline in value of most depreciat-ing assets as an incentive to business to invest in machinery and equipment.

18. Section 1.704–2(d)(2) of the regulations provides rules for when a property is subject to more than one nonrecourse obligation.

19. Treas. Reg. § 1.704–2(e)(3).

so allowing free transferability of nonrecourse deductions. An allocation of nonrecourse deductions must be "reasonably consistent with allocations that have substantial economic effect of some other significant partnership item attributable to the property securing the nonrecourse liabilities."[21] There is little guidance on the 2 key ideas here: "reasonably consistent" and "significant item."[22]

Paragraph (ii) of Example 1 in Section 1.704–2(m) gives some examples. There, the basic deal is that items other than nonrecourse items are allocated (i) 90% to the limited partner and 10% to the general partner, reflecting the proportions of their respective capital contributions, until such time as the limited partner has received cumulative income allocations equal to the cumulative prior losses allocated to her, and, (ii) thereafter, 50–50. With no analysis, the example concludes that any allocation of nonrecourse deductions between 90–10 and 50–50 is "reasonably consistent." The spread between 90–10 and 50–50 seems to be motivated by concerns (i) that the limited partner investor should not be allocated a greater share of nonrecourse deductions than she provided cash and (ii) that a general partner who provides capital in an amount that is less than her pro-rata share of residual profits should not be allowed deductions in excess of that pro-rata share. Thus, the example is little help outside the limited partnership context—little help with general partnerships or with LLCs.

As noted above, in order to meet the regulations' requirements, the partnership agreement must provide that an allocation of nonrecourse deductions is associated with a "minimum gain chargeback," an allocation of the associated future built-in gain. The contours of a minimum gain chargeback are elaborated in Section 1.704–2(f)(1). The chargeback is triggered by a reduction in the partnership's total minimum gain. This usually happens only when property is sold or debt is paid down. For example, when property subject to nonrecourse debt is sold, the amount, if any, by which, the debt exceeded the property's basis is removed from the determination of partnership minimum gain, so that minimum gain is reduced. Under *Tufts* there should be sufficient gain to cover the reduction. This gain, up to the net reduction in the partnership's total minimum gain (minimum gain on other partnership assets may be increasing) is then allocated among the partners proportionately to how they shared the associated nonrecourse deductions under Section 1.704–2(g)(2).[23] Read Section 1.704–2(f)(1).

As just noted, a reduction in the principal of nonrecourse debt encumbering property in a year (due to partial repayment) in an amount

---

21. Treas. Reg. § 1.704–2(e)(2). As to limited partnerships, this rule creates further pressure to comply with the only substantial economic effect rule applicable to limited partnerships, the alternate test for economic effect (including the requirement for a qualified income offset) as to other items.

22. For example, it is unclear whether significance is measured (i) in absolute dollars, (ii) relative to the partnership's gross or net value, or (iii) relative to all items associated with the property subject to the nonrecourse debt.

23. The minimum gain chargeback usually consists of gain (recapture), hence the name, but can be of other items, say, when debt is paid down. Treas. Reg. § 1.704–2(j)(2).

in excess of that property's depreciation for that year reduces that property's contribution to partnership minimum gain. If the reduction is sufficiently large that there is a net decrease in total minimum gain, a minimum gain chargeback is triggered. Here, however, there is no gain triggered by the event that is responsible for the reduction in minimum gain. Section 1.704–2(f)(6) of the regulations requires an allocation of other income items, if enough.[24] If there is not enough, the partnership agreement must provide for allocations of income in later years.

The question arises as to the relationship between the special rules for deductions associated with nonrecourse debt and the remainder of the Section 704(b) regulations. Read the last sentence of Section 1.704–2(g)(1). This apparently insignificant sentence says that, for purposes of applying the alternate test for economic effect, one treats a partner's share of the partnership's minimum gain as if the partner was obligated to restore any negative balance in her capital account up to the amount of such share. This makes sense, since the partner, in effect, is required to repay the amount through the minimum gain chargeback. But, this is pretty significant, as it means that the rules for nonrecourse deductions work independently from the other rules in the only cases where it matters, those situations where the partners do not bear all debts pro-rata. In these cases, an allocation of nonrecourse deductions does not (i) impact the partners' ability to take other losses or (ii) affect the timing of any qualified income offset.

Failure to comply with the special nonrecourse deduction regulations still results in the allocation being tested under the general rules regarding the partners' interests in the partnership: Section 1.704–1(b)(3).[25] Since nonrecourse deductions generally take the partners' capital accounts negative (or further negative), and, thus, do not affect liquidation proceeds for purposes of Section 1.704–1(b)(3)(iii), nonrecourse deductions must be tested under the mushy standard of Section 1.704–1(b)(3)(ii). Thus, these amounts probably are allocated either proportionately to general profit or loss shares or proportionately to capital contributions.

Section 1.752–3(a) has a few additional rules worth noting. Paragraph 1 is the most important and has been discussed already. Paragraph 2 is discussed in Chapter VI along with the discussion of Section 704(c). Paragraph 3 allocates any nonrecourse debt not allocated under Paragraphs 1 or 2 among the partners proportionately to their respective shares of profits. This provides a default rule just to have a rule for those cases where the allocation of liabilities has no tax consequences. For example, if the relevant partnership interest is sold, any outside basis created under Section 752(a) will be offset by an amount realized under

---

24. Note that, in accordance with the regulations' general skepticism of gross income allocations based on bookkeeping alone, they are not authorized.

25. Section 1.704–2 of the regulations interprets "partners' interest in the part-

nership," not "substantial economic effect." Nonrecourse deductions, lacking economic effect, cannot be allocated under the general substantial economic effect rules.

Section 752(d), so that the allocation of the debt has no net effect. But, Paragraph 3 also provides other elective methods for the rare case where the allocation matters and is not covered by Paragraph 1 or 2.

There is one further concern with regard to classic nonrecourse debt. Chapter I discussed the connection between the evolution of the taxation of partnerships and the growth of tax shelters. In the interests of simplicity, this discussion did not examine the At–Risk rules contained in Section 465, which were enacted in 1976 and expanded in 1978. These rules were enacted to limit the use of nonrecourse debt in tax shelters, but apply much more broadly.

Section 465 reflects reasonable reservations about the *Crane* rule. The *Crane* rule treats nonrecourse debt like recourse debt. When the debt is less than the value of the property, *Crane* rule treatment makes perfect sense: The owner of the property, even though not legally liable, almost certainly will pay the nonrecourse debt, just as if the debt were recourse, to protect her valuable equity, and, thus, has the benefits and burdens of any owner of mortgaged property. Thus, in this usual case, it makes sense to allow depreciation to the owner of property subject to nonrecourse debt. On the other hand, when the property is worth less than the debt, the owner has a much reduced incentive to pay the debt and keep the property. The lender really bears the risk of any further loss in value of the property. In other words, once the owner has lost her equity interest as a consequence of economic depreciation (so as to no longer have an amount at risk) no further depreciation is appropriate. Section 465 pursues this insight by assuming that a property's value equals its adjusted tax basis.[26] If tax depreciation reduces a property's basis to less than the amount of encumbering unpaid nonrecourse debt (the original amount of which was included in the initial cost basis under the *Crane* rule), the owner is not allowed that depreciation (until such time as the owner makes a further investment, including by applying his profits from the property to paying down the debt). In the case of a partnership, this means that Section 465 adds, as a shadow to Section 704(d), a further limitation on losses allowed to a partner in a year equal to the outside basis **reduced by the share of nonrecourse debts included therein** (with an appropriate infinite carryforward of any currently-disallowed loss).[27] Certain traditional nonrecourse real estate financing is exempted from the At–Risk rules by Section 465(b)(6).

REVIEW: Code §§ 465(a), (b), (c)(3), and (e) and Reg. §§ 1.704–2(b)(1), (b)(2), (b)(3), (c), (d), (e), (f)(1), (f)(6), (g), (j)(1)(ii), (j)(2), and (m)(Example 1) and 1.752–3(a)

Problem Set V.D

1. Gargantuan Promoters, Inc. (GP) and The Little, Tiny, and Defenseless Corporation (LTD) form a limited partnership, with GP as

---

26. Of course, current tax depreciation usually is faster than economic depreciation, so this assumption is questionable. This is why Section 465 customarily is viewed, not as a sharp policy instrument, but rather as a dull bludgeon against tax shelters.

27. *See* Prop. Treas. Reg. § 1.465–24(a)(2) (1979).

the general partner and LTD as the limited partner. The partnership is going to purchase and lease an office building. The building will cost $40 million. $30 million of the purchase price will be financed on a nonrecourse basis (secured by a first mortgage on the property) from a third-party bank that qualifies under 465(b)(6). The partnership's $10 million downpayment will be provided 5% ($500,000) by GP and 95% ($9.5 million) by LTD. Because of accelerated depreciation, the partnership will show "paper" losses for its first few years. The cumulative initial losses will exceed $10 million, which is the total amount of the partners' original capital contributions.

A.   If the limited partnership agreement provides that everything (profits, losses, and cash distributions) is to be allocated 5% to GP and 95% to LTD, how are the partners taxed with regard to the initial losses? (See Treas. Reg. § 1.704–1(b)(2)(ii)(*i*).) Is a qualified income offset required?

B.   If the limited partnership agreement provides that all profits and losses are to be allocated 5% to GP and 95% to LTD, but nonrecourse deductions (as defined in Section 1.704–2(c) the regulations) are to be allocated 1% to GP and 99% to LTD (with an appropriate gain chargeback), how are the partners taxed with regard to the initial losses?

C.   If the limited partnership agreement provides that everything is to be allocated 5% to GP and 95% to LTD, except that nonrecourse deductions (as defined in the regulations) are to be allocated 10% to GP and 90% to LTD (with an appropriate gain chargeback), how are the partners taxed with regard to the initial losses?

D.   If the limited partnership agreement provides that profits, losses, and non-liquidating cash distributions are to be allocated 20% to GP and 90% to LTD, except that, (i) upon liquidation, distributions are to be made in accordance with positive capital account balances (and GP has to fund any negative balance) and (ii) nonrecourse deductions (as defined in the regulations) are to be allocated 10% to GP and 90% to LTD (with an appropriate gain chargeback), how are the partners taxed with regard to the initial losses? Is a qualified income offset required?

E.   If the limited partnership agreement provides that profits, losses, and non-liquidating cash distributions are to be allocated 1% to GP and 99% to LTD, except that, (i) upon liquidation, distributions are to be made in accordance with positive capital account balances (and GP has to fund any negative balance) and (ii) nonrecourse deductions (as defined in the regulations) are to be allocated 20% to GP and 80% to LTD (with an appropriate gain chargeback), how are the partners taxed with regard to the initial losses?

2.   How would your analysis of Problem 1 differ if the debt does not qualify under Section 465(b)(6)?

E. "PARTNER NONRECOURSE DEBT"

The Section 704 regulations, but not the Section 752 regulations, provide rules for a 3d distinct type of debt in addition to recourse and nonrecourse debt: "partner nonrecourse debt," as defined in Section 1.704–2(b)(4). This is debt that is nonrecourse at the entity level but is owed to or guaranteed by a partner (or a related person), so that a partner effectively bears the residual risk with respect to the obligation. Regardless of the terms of the partnership agreement, all deductions related to such debt (determined using the same methodology that is used to determine the amount and character of deductions attributable to nonrecourse debt, as discussed above) are allocated to the lending partner, with a corresponding minimum gain chargeback (determined solely with regard to such debt), under Section 1.704–2(i). The debt (which is recourse for purposes of the Section 752 regulations because a partner is liable) is allocated to the guaranteeing partner.

Under the general rules for recourse deductions, these losses otherwise might be allocable to other partners because they bear other partnership debt. Apparently, Treasury thought the right deduction allocation rule here is so clear as to merit a special rule.

REVIEW: Reg. §§ 1.704–2(b)(4) and (i)

F. LLC DEBT

The Sections 704 and 752 regulations predate the precipitous rise of LLCs after the check-the-box regulations. It is not surprising, therefore, that the regulations work awkwardly with regard to LLCs.

An LLC is used to protect all of its members from liability for the business' obligations. Read Section 1.752–1(a)(2) of the regulations. A liability that is nonrecourse as to the owners of an entity taxed under Subchapter K is nonrecourse for purposes of these regulations even if the liability is recourse as to the entity.

Under these circumstances, in order to work out the taxation of LLCs, it is necessary to determine how the regulations deal with debt that is recourse as to the entity but nonrecourse as to the equity owners:[28] The LLC has nonrecourse deductions when it has minimum gain under Section 1.704–2(c). The general, unsecured obligations of an LLC, in effect, are secured by all of the LLCs assets. Thus, in the usual case, an LLC has minimum gain only when the total amount of all liabilities exceeds the total inside basis of the LLC's assets.[29] If so, associated deductions can be allocated as the members see fit, subject to

---

28. This problem should not be overstated, however. LLCs do not lose borrowed money every day, so that the issue of debt-related deductions does not arise that often. Moreover, if an LLC is in financial trouble, lenders will want member guarantees, in which case the debt is recourse for Subchapter K purposes.

29. Treas. Reg. §§ 1.704–2(b)(3), (4).

the reasonable consistency standard of Section 1.704–2(e). As noted above, that standard is particularly unclear as applied to LLCs. As always, an allocation of nonrecourse deductions also must be associated with a minimum gain chargeback under Section 1.704–2(f).

Once the nonrecourse deductions are allocated, Section 1.704–2(g)(1)(i) allocates the increase in minimum gain to the partners who were allocated the deductions so that Section 1.752–3 gives them basis to support the allocations. Fortunately, in the usual pro-rata LLC, once one wades through these remarkably involved rules for fairly common and straightforward transactions, one concludes that the pro-rata allocations are valid. (The losses are allocated pro-rata, consistently with all other tax items, so that the allocation is respected and carries debt basis with it.) Of course, technically, a qualified income offset is required, but many lawyers are willing to take the risk of omitting one.

Unfortunately for the tax lawyer, many LLCs cannot borrow on their own credit alone. Member guarantees may be required to get one or more loans. If a member guarantees a loan that is recourse at the entity level, the loan is subject to all of the rules for partnership recourse obligations:[30] Only the guaranteeing member gets the associated outside basis. Allocations (other than of nonrecourse deductions) are subject to the regular substantial economic effect and partner's interest in the partnership rules. On the other hand, if a member guarantees an obligation that is nonrecourse at the entity level, the loan is treated as a partner nonrecourse obligation that is subject to the rules discussed in the preceding section of this text, most importantly, to the reasonable consistency requirement. While this distinction makes sense by analogy with the comparable partnership arrangements, looked at in isolation it is hard to see why somewhat different allocation rules apply to LLC debt depending upon the entity-level character.

It is unclear how Section 465 applies to LLCs. Under proposed regulations Section 1.465–6(d), which was promulgated in 1979, well before the modern LLC era, and has been merely proposed for over 20 years, a mere guarantor has no amount at risk for Section 465 purposes. The only way an LLC member can be economically at risk for LLC debt is through guarantees, however. Thus, applying the proposed regulation to LLCs would mean that no member is allowed an amount at risk with respect to LLC borrowing, including borrowing guaranteed by the members. This would be a surprising result today given that the current Section 752 regulations, which were promulgated in 1991, provide that a guarantor gets basis with regard to debt that is otherwise nonrecourse.[31]

---

30. Treas. Reg. § 1.752–1(a).

31. The old proposed Section 465 regulations are consistent with the general tax principal that a guarantor is treated as being only contingently liable. In 1984, however, Congress instructed the Treasury not to follow this principal under Section 752; hence, the new regulations. H.R. Conf. Rep. No. 861, 869 (1984).

REVIEW: Prop. Reg. § 1.465–6(d) and Reg. §§ 1.704–2(c), (d), (e), (f), and (g) and 1.752–1(a)(2) and –2

Problem Set V.F

1. Natalie and Nate form an LLC, each putting up $1 million for the LLC's equity. The LLC borrows $1 million solely on the basis of its general credit. Under the relevant organizing documents, losses are to be allocated 35% to Natalie and 65% to Nate, while profits are to be allocated 65% to Natalie and 35% to Nate, except that, if there have been any losses, profits are to be allocated 35% to Natalie and 65% to Nate until the total amount of profits so allocated equals the total amount of losses. Proper capital accounts are to be kept. Operating cash distributions are to be made 65% to Natalie and 35% to Nate. Upon liquidation, proceeds are to be distributed proportionately to the members' respective capital account balances. There is no obligation to restore negative capital account balances.

Unfortunately, the LLC starts up by losing $2.25 million. (Ignore Section 195.) How are the losses allocated between Natalie and Nate?

2. How would your analysis of Problem 1 differ if the debt was guaranteed by Natalie? By Nate? By both, jointly and severally, with each being entitled to reimbursement from the other to the extent more than 50% is paid?

G. DISTRIBUTIONS OF THE PROCEEDS OF NONRECOURSE BORROWING

READ: Section 731(a)

The 704(b) regulations work with the Section 752 regulations to facilitate fairly free allocation and utilization of nonrecourse deductions, deductions that create or increase minimum gain, with a minimum gain chargeback as the only price for being allocated the deductions. There is another situation where a current transaction related to partnership nonrecourse debt can create or increase minimum gain: when the proceeds of a nonrecourse borrowing are distributed to the partners. Here also, the regulations work to allow the partnership to distribute the borrowed money among the partners as desired tax free, but the partners receiving the borrowed cash must bear a minimum gain chargeback.[32]

Read Sections 1.704–2(e)(3), (g)(1), and (h)(1) of the regulations. They treat distributions of the proceeds of partnership nonrecourse borrowing (borrowing associated with an increase in partnership minimum gain) similarly to allocations of nonrecourse deductions (deductions

---

32. Also, the distribution reduces outside basis. Thus, for example, if the distributee partner had a zero basis prior to the borrowing and the entire proceeds of the borrowing were distributed, the partner would be allocated debt equal to the amount received, so that there is no net effect on outside basis, which assures that the partner has deemed distributions or gain as the debt is satisfied.

associated with an increase in partnership minimum gain).[33] Both give the partner a share of partnership minimum gain. Given the fungibility of money, there is no perfect way to determine whether distributions so relate to nonrecourse debt. Thus, Section 1.704–2(h)(2) authorizes the use of any reasonable allocation method. If cash distributions are less than the increase in minimum gain caused by the borrowing, however, there may be no reasonable method to allocate this increase in minimum gain among the partners. If so, under Section 1.704–2(h)(4), the unallocated excess carries over to be allocated to the partners as a consequence of future distributions. The allocation of minimum gain to a partner also allocates a portion of the underlying debt to the partner under Section 1.752–3(a)(1) of the regulations, which shelters the distribution for purposes of Section 731(a).

An example illustrates the operation of these rules: A limited partnership has one general partner and numerous limited partners. The general partner is allocated 10% of all profits and the limiteds are allocated 90%. The partnership's sole material asset is a piece of real property with a basis of $1 million and a value of $4 million. The partnership has no pre-existing debt. It then borrows $2 million on a nonrecourse basis, granting the lender a first mortgage in the real estate as security. The $2 million is distributed to the limited partners.

The borrowing creates $1 million of partnership minimum gain (the amount by which the nonrecourse debt exceeds the encumbered property's basis). It is reasonable to allocate this among the partners in the same proportions in which they received the $2 million distribution. This means that, in order to satisfy the Section 704(b) regulations, each limited partner must be allocated 50¢ of minimum gain chargeback for each $1 received. Thus, under the Section 752 regulations, $1 million of the debt is allocated solely to the limited partners (with only 90% of the remaining $1 million allocated to the limited partners under Section 1.752–3(a)(3)). This gives the limited partners sufficient basis that the distribution is not taxable under Section 731(a). The first $1 million of future gain on the property is allocated to the limited partners, with all remaining gain going 90–10. Overall, this treatment tailors the tax treatment to how the loan proceeds were distributed.

REVIEW: Code § 731(a) and Reg. §§ 1.704–2(e)(3), (g)(1), and (h) and 1.752–3

Problem Set V.G

1. What would be the analysis in the example in the text above if only $500,000 of the $2 million nonrecourse borrowing were distributed, all to the limiteds?

---

33. If the loan proceeds are not distributed, under the rules described above, the increase in partnership minimum gain turns deductions, including deductions not related to the leveraged property, into nonrecourse deductions that carry with them a minimum gain chargeback. Treas. Reg. § 1.704–2(c). Under Section 704(b), these deductions are allocated under the deduction rules above rather than other the rules for allocating distributions of the proceeds of nonrecourse borrowing.

2.   What would be the analysis in the example if $1 million in cash is distributed to the limiteds, but minimum gain went up $1.25 million during the year, the extra $250,000 of minimum gain arising from depreciation?

Chapter VI

ALLOCATIONS: PROPERTY CONTRIBUTIONS AND PARTNERSHIP INTEREST TRANSFERS

A. INTRODUCTION

Chapters IV and V introduced Section 704(b)'s basic regime regarding the allocation of tax items among the partners. These rules look to the allocation rules in the partnership agreement for the underlying economics. Some tax items have no connection with allocations in the partnership agreement, however. In particular, contributions of non-cash property and transfers of partnership interests raise important non-Section 704(b) allocation concerns. This chapter examines the rules that apply to these 2 situations.

B. NON–CASH PROPERTY CONTRIBUTIONS: SECTION 704(c)

1. The Basic Concern

READ: Code §§ 704(c)(1)(A) and 723 and Reg. § 1.704–1(b)(2)(iv)(d)(1)

When property is contributed to a partnership, the requirement that the capital accounts reflect the property's value means that the partnership's allocations of future profit and loss do not take into account any built-in gain or loss.[1] That gain or loss already was priced into the determination of the new partner's share of the ongoing partnership. Section 723, however, gives the partnership a transferred basis in the contributed property, so that the partnership is taxed on any built-in gain or loss. Special tax rules, in Section 704(c)(1)(A) and its regulations, control the allocation of this tax-book difference.

An example illustrates the economics of non-cash property contributions: Assume that Greg and Jim form a 50–50 partnership, Greg putting

---

1. Treas. Reg. § 1.704–1(b)(2)(iv)(d)(1).

in $1 million cash and Jim putting in Blackacre, which is worth $1 million, but has a tax basis to Jim of $10,000. The cash is put in the bank. (For simplicity, interest on this is ignored.) Under Section 723, the partnership gets a $10,000 transferred basis in Blackacre from Jim. Later, the partnership sells Blackacre for $1.5 million in one tax year, recognizing $1.49 million of gain, and distributes the $1.5 million 50–50 during the following tax year. Assume, for now, that this gain is allocated 50–50 for tax purposes. If so, after this gain allocation, Greg would have an outside basis of $1.745 million and Jim would have an outside basis of $755,000. When they each get their $750,000 cash distribution, Greg ends up with an outside basis of $995,000 and Jim has a $5,000 basis. The total outside basis equals the total inside basis, both $1 million, which is right, but the outside basis is allocated strangely, Greg having a $995,000 basis in an interest worth $500,000 and Jim having a $5,000 basis in the other interest, which also is worth $500,000. More importantly, Greg has paid tax on $745,000 of gain, even though his profit has only been $250,000 ($750,000 cash + $500,000 in value of partnership interest—$1 million investment), which explains the excess $495,000 of outside basis. The reverse, undertaxation and understated basis, is true for Jim.

The aggregate view shows what is wrong. Under a pure aggregate approach, formation of the partnership would be viewed as Jim selling 1/2 of Blackacre to Jim for $500,000. This would trigger $495,000 of gain. Greg would get a $500,000 basis in his 1/2 of Blackacre. Jim's basis in the 1/2 not sold would continue to be $5,000. Then, when Blackacre is sold for $1.5 million—$750,000 each—Greg would have $250,000 of gain and Jim would have $745,000 of gain, for a total gain of $1.24 million. Thus, taking into account that Jim was taxed on the $495,000 of gain when the partnership was formed, overall, Jim would pay tax on the total gain at the time of partnership formation ($990,000), with the $500,000 of gain accruing while the property was held by the partnership being shared 50–50. Economically, Jim got the full benefit from the property being worth $1 million at the time the partnership was formed, as that value was used in determining his share of the partnership, so that he should bear all taxes associated with that value. As noted in the Rabkin and Johnson quotation in Chapter I, the aggregate approach best captures partnership economics.

Current law's Section 704(c)(1)(A) avoids the mistaxation that would result from 50–50 sharing of the entire taxable gain, without adopting the aggregate approach: Jim pays no tax when the partnership is formed, but remains responsible for the $990,000 of gain built-in at the time that the property was contributed to the partnership, so that when the partnership sells the property he pays tax on the first $990,000 of gain, with the excess taxed 50–50. Jim pays tax on $1.24 million, the same as under the aggregate approach, but gets to delay paying any tax until the partnership disposes of Blackacre. Read Example 1 of Section 1.704–3(b)(2) of the regulations.

This regime contrasts interestingly with that under Subchapter C's entity approach. If Jim and Greg were to form a corporation under Section 351, each taking 1/2 of the corporation's stock, the transaction would be tax-free, and the corporation would get a $10,000 transferred basis in Blackacre under Section 362. Thus, if the corporation were to sell the property for $1.5 million, the corporation would bear tax on the full gain of $1.49 million. Greg would bear 1/2 of this tax, as payment of the tax impacts the value of all shares equally. Thus, in the real world, Greg would demand more than 1/2 of the company to reflect that Jim's property comes burdened with a built-in tax liability. In other words, real businesspeople price deals on an after-tax basis. Under Subchapter K, the taxation follows the economics more precisely than under Subchapter C, so that the tax law takes care of itself and the parties do not need to price taxes into their deal under these circumstances.

Note how the view of a property contribution by a partner to her partnership reflected in Section 704(c) dovetails with that in Section 707(a)(2)(B), which was discussed in Chapter II. Both view arrangements between the partners not involving future partnership activities as being different from prospective partnership matters.

Before dealing with hard cases, a further feature of Section 704(c)(1)(A) should be noted. It applies to built-in losses as well as to built-in gains. Modify the example so that Jim's basis in Blackacre is $2 million rather than $10,000. Also assume that, while the property was worth $1 million when contributed, it is worth only $500,000 when sold. Then, under Section 704(c)(1)(A), the first $1 million of the partnership's $1.5 million loss, the precontribution built-in loss, is allocated to Jim, with the remaining $500,000 loss allocated equally between the partners.

Section 704(c)(1)(A) is complicated by 3 concerns (i) depreciating[2] assets, (ii) interaction with Section 704(b), and (iii) the so-called "ceiling rule." These concerns are discussed in order in the succeeding sections of this text.

REVIEW: Code §§ 704(c)(1)(A) and 723 and Reg. §§ 1.704–1(b)(2)(iv)(*d*)(1) and 1.704–3(b)(2)(Example 1)

2. Depreciating Assets

The first problem under Section 704(c)(1)(A) is presented by assets that will contribute to the business, not by being sold, but by being consumed in generating profits. When a property's contribution to a business is from being sold, the example thus far, it is easy to allocate gain or loss among the partners so that the contributing partner is taxed on any built-in gain or loss at the time that the property was contributed. But what if the property will generate less taxable gain or loss than

---

2. This text treats amortization, including recovery of basis in debt instruments, as a form of depreciation.

built in at the time of contribution because the property is going to be depreciated? Then, one must allocate depreciation so as to deal with the built-in gain or loss problem.

Again, let us modify our hypothetical. Assume, in the interests of simplicity, that Jim's contributed an asset that is subject to 10–year straight-line amortization[3] after contribution, that was worth $1 million at the time of contribution, and that had a $600,000 adjusted basis to Jim at the time of contribution. Jim should be taxed on the $400,000 of built-in tax gain at some point. One way to do this is to allocate each year's $60,000 of amortization (one-tenth of $600,000) $10,000 to Jim and $50,000 to Greg. Greg gets the same deductions that he would have had if the partnership had purchased the amortizing asset. Jim gets $40,000 a year less depreciation than he would have had if he had sold the asset to the partnership so that, over the 10 years, he is taxed, in effect, on the $400,000 of built-in gain.[4] This approach is used under Section 704(c)(1)(A). Read Section 1.704–3(b)(1)(first 6 sentences) of the regulations.

REVIEW: Reg. § 1.704–3(b)(1)

3. Interaction with Section 704(b)

The question then arises as to how Section 704(c) interacts with Section 704(b), particularly the basic capital accounting rules. Prudently, the Section 704(b) regulations adopt the basic analysis of the Section 704(c) problem presented above: Pre-contribution gain or loss is not subject to allocation in the partner's capital accounts and thus cannot be subject to Section 704(b). The Section 704(b) regulations accomplish this by treating the contributed non-cash property as if it had been transferred to the partnership at fair market value, rather than at tax basis, for capital accounting ("book") purposes. Read Sections 1.704–1(b)(2)(iv)(*d*)(1) and (*d*)(3) of these regulations. Thus, there is a difference between the capital accounts and the tax accounts, which usually is referred to as a "book-tax difference." Gain or loss or depreciation of contributed property for capital accounting purposes is based on this book value rather than on the property's tax basis (but is determined using the same method as the tax depreciation, so that the book depreciation is proportional to the tax depreciation). Read Sections 1.704–1(b)(2)(iv)(*g*)(1) and (3). This creates a difference between book income determined for Section 704(b) capital accounting purposes and taxable income. The book income is allocated under the allocations provided in the partnership agreement—of course, subject to Section

---

3. Also assume that the partnership is entitled to a full year's amortization in the contribution year.

4. Note an arguable defect in this rule. If Jim had sold the asset for $1 million rather than contributing it to the partnership, the gain may have been capital or Section 1231 gain. Section 704(c), in effect, taxes him on ordinary income by taking away an ordinary deduction. Given that the ordinary tax is deferred, and that the immediate gain may have consisted of Section 1245 recapture, this defect does not concern people much, however.

704(b). Taxable income is allocated to eliminate the book-tax difference: Tax items are allocated to the non-contributing partners to match their book items, with any tax items left over allocated to the contributing partner. Accordingly, the tax-book difference, the amount subject to Section 704(c), is left to the contributing partner, so that the non-contributing partners are taxed the same as if the partnership had purchased the property. In other words, the contributing partner is stuck with the tax consequences of the partnership's basis in the contributed asset having transferred from her to the partnership under Section 723.

Consider this bookkeeping in the first Greg and Jim example, above. Immediately after the partnership is formed, the book and tax accounts would look as follows:

Book Accounts

Assets		Liabilities	
		–0–	
Cash	$1 million		
Blackacre	1 million	Equity	
	2 million		
		Greg	$1 million
		Jim	1 million
			2 million

Tax Accounts

Assets		Liabilities	
		–0–	
Cash	$1 million		
Blackacre	10,000	Equity	
	1,010,000		
		Greg[5]	$1 million
		Jim	10,000
			1,010,000

There is a $990,000 difference between the tax accounts and the book accounts, reflecting the $990,000 of pre-contribution gain. That built-in gain is taxed under Section 704(c)(1)(A), while everything on the book accounts is subject to Section 704(b). Read Sections 1.704–3(b)(2) (Example 1) (¶¶ (i)–(iii)).[6] When the land is sold for $1.5 million, there is a $1.49 million gain for tax purposes and a $500,000 gain for book purposes. The book gain is allocated 50–50, with Greg's share thereof being $250,000. Thus, the first $250,000 of taxable gain is allocated to

---

5. Note that, since there is no partnership debt, each partner's tax capital account exactly equals his outside basis at this juncture.

6. The "–3" regulations implement Section 704(c).

Greg, the non-contributing partner. All remaining gain, $1.24 million, is allocated to Jim. In total, Jim is taxed on his $250,000 of book gain and his $990,000 of precontribution gain.

This example illustrates how the Section 704(c)(1)(A) regulations achieve the intuitive result described above, but using capital account mechanics. Moreover, all of the tax-book difference is recognized and properly allocated so that the tax and book accounts become identical after Section 704(c)(1)(A) does its job. The complexity here, including the need for 2 sets of books, is troubling, but is acceptable to most, since the basic regime achieves tax results that are consistent with the basic economics of transactions.

REVIEW: Reg. §§ 1.704–1(b)(2)(iv)(d)(1), (d)(3), (g)(1), and (3) and 1.704–3(b)(2)(Example 1)(¶¶ (i)–(iii))

Problem Set VI.B.3

1. Hillary and Irene form a 50–50 partnership. Hillary contributes an office building on land. The land has a $500,000 basis and a value of $800,000. Assume, for simplicity, (i) that the recovery period for buildings is 20 years, and (ii) that property is depreciated a full year for the year in which placed in service, and not at all in the year disposed of, rather than current law's half-year and other conventions. The building cost $800,000, has been subject to $400,000 of depreciation (19 years worth, so that the building's adjusted basis to Hillary is $400,000), and is worth $700,000. Irene contributes $1.5 million of cash. (Ignore how the cash is used). How is depreciation on the building determined and allocated for book and tax purposes? (Remember Section 168(i)(7).)

2. Under the facts above, what are the book and tax consequences if the land and building are sold 4 years after being acquired for sales prices of $1 million and $600,000, respectively?

4. The Ceiling Rule

Section 1.704–3(b)(1) of the regulations contains the so-called "ceiling rule." It increases the complexity of applying Section 704(c)(1)(A) an order of magnitude, but, unfortunately, with no associated improvement in tax results.

Here is the basic problem: Assume that, in the Greg and Jim example above, the land is sold for $750,000 (rather than $1.5 million). For book purposes, there is a $250,000 loss ($750,000 sale price less $1 million book value), or $125,000 book loss per partner. For tax purposes there is a $740,000 gain. This tax gain should be allocated to eliminate the tax-book difference. This would require (i) that Jim be allocated the tax-book difference, a $990,000 gain, and (ii) that the $250,000 book loss be allocated 50–50, with the result that Jim has $865,000 of net gain and Greg have a loss of $125,000. (Note that this nets out to the $740,000 of actual taxable gain recognized by the partnership.) Then, each partner would have an outside basis and (tax and book) capital account of

$875,000; which is right, as each partner owns 1/2 of a partnership whose only asset is $1.75 million of cash.[7]

Unfortunately, there is a problem with this theoretically perfect accounting. Up until this example, Section 704(c)(1)(A) merely allocated a total tax gain or loss among partners. The perfect accounting in the current example goes one step further. It turns $740,000 of gain into a bigger gain for one partner ($865,000 to Jim) and a **loss** to the other (Greg's $125,000). A notional tax loss **that nobody recognized** is manufactured by fancy bookkeeping. This just seems funny. In particular, it seems that allowing taxpayers to manufacture notional losses would open the door to tax avoidance transactions. Hence, the regulations contain the ceiling rule in the next-to-the-last sentence of Section 1.704–3(b)(1) of the regulations. It provides a ceiling on the total gain or loss allocable under Section 704(c)(1)(A) that is equal to the total gain or loss actually recognized.[8] Thus, in the current example, the total amount allocable under Section 704(c)(1)(A) would be $740,000, all of which would be allocated to Jim. The additional $125,000 of manufactured, "notional," gain to Jim (offset by $125,000 of notional loss to Greg) required to fully eliminate the tax-book difference is not allowed.

The problem with the ceiling rule can be seen in the example. After the ceiling-rule-limited allocation, the books would look as follows:

Book Accounts

Assets		Liabilities
Cash	$1.75 million	–0–

		Equity
Greg		$875,000
Jim		875,000
		1.75 million

Tax Accounts

Assets		Liabilities
Cash	$1.75 million	–0–

		Equity
Greg		$1 million
Jim		750,000
		1.75 million

---

7. Jim got 1/2 of the partnership for $1 million in property and then the property lost $250,000 in value while owned by the partnership, of which Jim bore half. Greg got 1/2 of a partnership for $1 million cash, and then bore half of a $250,000 loss that accrued while property was owned by the partnership. The accounting suggested in this paragraph perfectly reflects these economics.

8. Remember that back in Chapter IV some concern was expressed with regard to gross income allocations manufacturing losses. That concern was based on the same policies as are behind the ceiling rule.

There still is a tax-book difference. The book accounts control liquidating distributions, so the pre-tax economics are not impacted, but Greg has yet to be allowed the $125,000 loss that he experienced economically, and Jim has managed to avoid taxation on $125,000 of gain from which he benefitted. As to be discussed in Chapter VIII, Section 731 will straighten things out when the partnership liquidates by, as to each partner, creating taxable gain or loss to reflect the difference between the cash received and the outside basis, but this may be cold comfort today if liquidation is not expected to occur for some time.

As this example suggests, there is a ceiling rule problem when an asset contributed with built-in gain is sold for a taxable gain if the taxable gain realized does not cover the remaining built-in gain (the original built-in gain reduced by any special allocations of depreciation under Section 704(c)). If sold for a tax loss, the ceiling rule applies if the tax loss is less than the noncontributing partners' share of the book loss. Similarly, there is a ceiling rule problem when depreciable built-in gain property is contributed to a partnership if the proportion that the built-in gain was of the total value at the time of contribution exceeded the contributing partner's share of the asset's future depreciation. Note that the gain and loss problems depend on a future event, the value of the contributed property when sold, while the depreciation problem does not.

Built-in losses can present a ceiling rule problem. As to sales, the ceiling rule applies if a tax loss realized does not equal the remaining built-in loss or if a tax gain does not cover the noncontributing partners' book gain. There is no problem with depreciation here, however, as there are always enough depreciation deductions to go around with built-in loss property.

The Section 704(c) regulations contemplate allowing partnerships to deal with tax-book difference problems associated with the ceiling rule by using "curative" or "remedial" allocations. Under a "curative" allocation, some tax item not subject to the ceiling rule is allocated specially solely for tax purposes (and not on the Section 704(b) "book" capital accounts) so as to reduce or eliminate the tax book difference. Read Section 1.704–3(c)(1) of the regulations. In the example just above, if the partnership were to have $250,000 of gain on another asset in a later year that otherwise would be allocated 50–50, the partnership could allocate all of that gain to Jim for tax purposes, but still 50–50 for book purposes, so as to then eliminate the tax-book difference. This special allocation would be valid despite (i) lacking substantial economic effect and (ii) not being in accordance with the partners' interests in the partnership. Similarly, when there is a ceiling rule problem with depreciation of a contributed asset, other tax items can be allocated while the asset is being depreciated, or later.

An alternative method of dealing with ceiling rule problems also is contemplated by the regulations. These "remedial" allocation rules allow the creation of notional items of income and loss, which otherwise is forbidden by the ceiling rule, but reduce the opportunities for tax avoidance. The heart of the remedial allocation rules is an arbitrary method of book depreciation. Under the regular rules (referred to in the regulations as the "traditional" method) depreciation for tax and book purposes is determined under the same method.[9] For example, if an asset that is 15–year recovery property only has 3 years left in its recovery period remaining is contributed to a partnership, the adjusted tax basis[10] and the book value are recovered over the remaining 3 years of the asset's original recovery period. In contrast, under the remedial allocation regime, when the book value exceeds the tax basis, the excess book value is treated as a new asset with the same character as the associated real asset, which must start its recovery period anew for book purposes.[11] In the example, the remaining tax basis of the 15–year asset would be recovered over 3 years, but the tax-book difference would be recovered over 15 years for book purposes. Read Sections 1.704–3(d)(1)–(5)(i).

If a partnership adopts the remedial allocation method to deal with ceiling rule problems, the ceiling rule does not apply, either to allocations of depreciation or to gain or loss (even for nondepreciable property, like land[12]). In the Greg and Jim example, since there is no depreciation, a remedial allocation would work identically to simply ignoring the ceiling rule, allocating $865,000 of gain to Jim and $125,000 of loss to Greg.

An example can be used to illustrate the differences between the 3 methods (traditional, curative, and remedial) of dealing with the ceiling rule as to depreciable property: Assume that, at the beginning of a tax year, a 5% pro-rata partner contributes our 15–year property with exactly 3 full years of straight-line depreciation of a remaining basis of $300,000 left. The asset is worth $450,000. Thus, there is a $150,000 tax-book difference. Under the traditional method, the book depreciation is $150,000 per year (1/3d of the $450,000 initial book value). Each year, for tax purposes, the partners other than the contributing partner should be allocated total depreciation deductions equal to 95% of the $150,000, or $142,500 of depreciation, to fully eliminate the tax-book difference over the 3 years remaining in the asset's recovery period. But there is only $100,000 of tax depreciation (1/3d of the $300,000 tax basis) to go around. Thus, the ceiling rule says that only $100,000 of depreciation is allocated to the non-contributing partners, resulting in a $42,500 shortfall each year. A curative allocation would allocate to the non-

9. Treas. Reg. §§ 1.704–1(b)(2)(iv)(*d*) and (*g*).

10. I.R.C. § 168(i)(7).

11. There is no ceiling rule problem, as to depreciation, with built-in loss property.

The regulations focus on depreciation and do not address the availability of remedial allocations with regard to partnership dispositions of built-in loss property.

12. *See* Treas. Reg. § 1.704–3(d)(7)(Example 2).

contributing partners, solely for tax purposes, $42,500 of deductions that are allocated to the contributing partner for book purposes.[13]

The remedial result is more complicated. First, the $300,000 tax basis would be depreciated over 3 years for tax and book purposes, resulting in $100,000 of annual depreciation for these purposes. Also, a $150,000 notional asset (the excess of the $450,000 book value of the asset over its $300,000 transferred tax basis) with a new 15–year life would appear on the book accounts only. (For simplicity, assume that this asset is depreciated (i) for a full year in its first year and (ii) using the straight-line method.) This asset would generate $10,000 of notional depreciation each year for 15 years. In the first 3 years after the contribution, there would be a total of $110,000 of book depreciation, which would be allocated 95–5, $104,500 to the non-contributing partners and $5,500 to the contributing partner. But, there is only $100,000 of tax depreciation to go along. Thus, $4,500 of notional, "remedial" income is created for the contributing partner, so that the non-contributing partners can be allocated the same $104,500 of tax depreciation as for book purposes.[14] In years 4 through 15, there is $10,000 of book depreciation and no tax depreciation. To give the non-contributing partners tax depreciation equal to their $9,500 of book depreciation, the contributing partner must be allocated a remedial $9,500 of income. Thus, over each of 15 years, the contributing partner has $10,000 more taxable income than book income, eliminating the total $150,000 book-tax difference, as desired.

To compare the tax results under the 3 ways of dealing with the ceiling rule:

	Traditional	Curative[15]	Remedial
Non–Contributing Partners			
Yrs 1–3	100,000 ded.	142,500 ded.	104,500 ded.
Yrs 4–15			9,500 ded.
Contributing Partner			
Yrs 1–3		42,500 inc.	4,500 inc.
Yrs 4–15			9,500 inc.

13. Note that the contributing partner is only allocated a total of $127,500 of taxable income, not the full $150,000 of built-in gain, as the contributing partner also gives up the $22,500 of depreciation (5% of $450,000) she would have received if the asset had been worth $450,000 when contributed, so that the total effect under Section 704(c) is to tax the contributing partner on $150,000 more than if the asset had been worth $450,000.

14. The contributing partner is being allocated $5,000 of depreciation on the $300,000 tax asset and $9,500 of income with regard to the book-only asset (so that the tax depreciation of the non-contributing partners can equal their book depreciation), which nets to $4,500 of income.

15. This assumes that the partnership has enough other deductions in the relevant tax years to achieve the same effect as ignoring the ceiling rule.

If the asset is sold, (i) for book purposes, the gain or loss is measured by the difference between the amount realized and the unrecovered amounts for the tax and notional assets, which gain or loss is allocated under Section 704(c)(1)(A) principles, and, then, (ii) the tax gain is so allocated, with a notional loss created as necessary. Read Section 1.704–3(f)(7) of the regulations.

In summary, the ceiling rule creates a problem. The curative method solves the problem if there are sufficient deductions or other needed tax items that otherwise would be allocated to the contributing partner. The remedial method solves the problem, but can take its time getting there.

Then, the question arises as to the freedom allowed partnerships to chose their method for dealing with ceiling rule problems. Under the last sentence of Section 1.704–3(b)(1) of the regulations, the traditional rule is acceptable as long as there are no ceiling rule problems. Otherwise, under Section 1.704–3(a)(1), the Section 704(c)(1)(A) method must be reasonable. Specifically, the 7th sentence seems to preclude methods other than curative and remedial allocations. Additionally, under Section 1.704–3(a)(2), different methods can be used for different properties, but the methods' aggregate effect must be reasonable. An allocation designed to reduce the partners' aggregate taxes by shifting the tax consequences of built-in gain or loss among partners is unreasonable under Section 1.704–3(a)(10). The regulations do not require that the ceiling rule allocation method be in the partnership agreement. The solution to any ceiling rule problem impacts the after-tax economics of all partners, however. Thus, good lawyers spell out the tax rules prior to a contribution of property that poses a ceiling rule problem, usually in the partnership agreement.

Most practitioners believe that it would be easier just to get rid of the ceiling rule, particularly given some of the flexibility afforded by the more recent Section 704(b) regulations. Recent Treasury amendments to the Section 704(c)(1)(A) regulations clarifying the rules mitigating the ceiling rule suggest that the ceiling rule still reflects Treasury policy, however. Congress does not seem interested. Nevertheless, the student is encouraged not to get bogged down in the details, but to remain focused on the basic problems here.

REVIEW: Reg. § 1.704–3

Problem Set VI.B.4

Redo Problem Set VI.B.3 on the new assumption that the building had been worth $880,000 when contributed and that the sales prices for the land and building 4 years later were $800,000 and $400,000, respectively.

C. CASH CONTRIBUTIONS: REVERSE SECTION 704(c)

When only cash is contributed in exchange for an interest in a new partnership, Section 704(c)(1)(A) taxes any other partner who contributes non-cash property on any built-in gain or loss, so that the partner that contributed cash is not taxed on any built-in gain or loss on property contributed by others. The same basic problem arises when cash is contributed for an interest in an existing partnership. The cash contributor should not be taxed on the built-in gain or loss in the partnership's assets. Section 704(c) does not apply, however, as no new non-cash property has been transferred to the partnership. A new economic partnership has been formed, but not a new tax partnership.

The Section 704(b) regulations contemplate special allocations, referred to as "reverse Section 704(c)"[16] allocations, to deal with this problem. The basic idea behind the reverse Section 704(c) rules is to bifurcate the life of the partnership so as to reflect that a new economic partnership has been formed. When the new interest is created for cash, the partnership's assets (including intangibles) are rebooked to fair market value for book capital accounting purposes.[17] In effect, a new partnership, with assets at book values equal to their fair market values, is created for book purposes. The resulting tax-book difference, when realized, is allocated among the old partnership interests much like Section 704(c)(1)(A) allocates a tax-book difference to a contributing partner.[18] And, yes, there can be a ceiling rule problem and curative and remedial allocations. Read Section 1.704–1(b)(2)(iv)(f) of the regulations.

In the discussion above, no real issue of how the special Section 704(c)(1)(A) items are allocated among partners was presented, as the items just went to the contributing partner. With a reverse Section 704(c) allocation, however, gain of loss built into the partnership's assets when the new interest is created must be allocated among the old partners. If there was a special allocation among the old partners, the issue arises as to how to allocate any reverse Section 704(c) items among

---

16. These allocations are the "reverse" of Section 704(c) allocations because cash, not non-cash property, is being contributed to the partnership. The 704(c) problem is taxing the contributing partner with regard to the contributed property, while the reverse Section 704(c) problem is taxing the old partners with regard to built-in gain or loss on partnership property at the time a new interest is sold. Thus, the reverse Section 704(c) problem is presented not only when cash is paid for a new interest, but also when non-cash property is contributed to a partnership in exchange for a partnership interest, in which case the contributing partner has a Section 704(c) problem and the old partners have a reverse Section

704(c) problem, but the text does not reflect this complexity. The reverse Section 704(c) problem presented by complete or partial redemption of a partnership interest is discussed at the end of this chapter.

17. This obviously is easier said than done, as assets' values, particularly intangibles, can be nearly indeterminable.

18. In practice, a reverse Section 704(c) allocation is more burdensome than a regular Section 704(c)(1)(A) allocation, as a reverse Section 704(c) allocation applies not just to a contributed asset, as does a Section 704(c)(1)(A) allocation, but to all partnership property at the time that the new partnership interest is created.

the old interests. There is no guidance in the regulations. Presumably, any special allocations are respected, subject to the limits imposed by Section 704(b).

An example is helpful: Ann and Beth form a 50–50 partnership, each contributing $100,000 of cash. They buy a parcel of land with the $200,000. At a time when the land is worth $1 million, Ann and Beth admit Carl as a 1/3d partner for $500,000 cash. They use all of this cash to buy another parcel of real estate. Years later, they sell (i) the first parcel for $1.9 million, recognizing $1.7 million of tax gain, and (ii) the second parcel for $2.3 million, recognizing $1.8 million of tax gain. Under a reverse Section 704(c) allocation, the first parcel was rebooked to $1 million upon Carl's admission. Thus, only $900,000 of the gain on the first parcel, the gain while all 3 were partners, is allocated among Ann, Beth, and Carl, $300,000 each. The remaining $800,000 of gain on the first parcel is allocated equally between Ann and Beth, the only partners while this much gain accrued, $400,000 each. As to the second parcel, no reverse Section 704(c) allocation is required, so that the $600,000 of taxable gain is divided equally between the 3 partners, $200,000 each. Thus, the total gain of $3.5 million is allocated: $1.3 million each to Ann and Beth and $900,000 to Carl. If the first parcel had been sold for less than $1 million, a ceiling rule problem would have been presented—but one readily solved with a curative or remedial allocation. (Why would a curative allocation work on these facts?)

The masochistic may want a more complicated example: Dave and Ellen form a partnership. Dave provides $100,000 of cash. Ellen contributes $900,000 of cash. They buy a piece of machinery that is 10–year property with the $1 million. (For a shred of simplicity, assume that all depreciation is straight-line and that a full year of depreciation is allowed in the year property is placed in service.) Their deal is that depreciation is allocated 10–90, and all other items are allocated 50–50, which deal has substantial economic effect. At the beginning of the 6th year, the property has an adjusted basis of $500,000 and is worth $800,000. The partnership has no other material assets or liabilities. Also, at the beginning of the 6th year, they admit Faye for $400,000 of cash. All of this cash is put in the bank. (For simplicity, ignore any interest earned.) Under the amended and restated partnership agreement, Faye is entitled to 1/3d of every partnership item, with the remaining 2/3ds allocated between David and Ellen based on their prior agreement. In the 6th year, the partnership has $100,000 of depreciation for tax purposes. Under a reverse Section 704(c) allocation, the property was rebooked to $800,000 at the beginning of the year. (Assume that the remedial method is not adopted for the property.) Thus, there is $160,000 of book depreciation, Faye's share is 1/3d: $53,333. Under the reverse Section 704(c) allocation she is allocated $53,333 of the tax depreciation. The remaining $46,667 is allocated 10–90: Dave getting $4,667, and Ellen getting $42,000. No ceiling rule problem is presented. The same result applies in each of the next 4 years.

Reverse Section 704(c) allocations are not explicitly required by the regulations. The last sentence of Section 1.704–1(b)(2)(iv)(*f*) (read it, including following all of the cross references) threatens awful things if the partnership does not make these allocations, however.[19] Thus, most tax lawyers include reverse Section 704(c) allocations in their partnership agreements.

This raises an interesting issue. Most law firms, when they admit a new partner, do not allocate all income from uncollected time (whether billed or unbilled) solely to the old partners. In other words, they do not make a reverse Section 704(c) allocation.[20] Yet the IRS does not pursue this. Why? Presumably, the results achieved are so close to those that would result under a more correct accounting that the IRS does not care (or, perhaps, does not understand).

REVIEW: Reg. § 1.704–1(b)(2)(iv)(*f*)

Problem Set VI.C

Brenda and Eric form a 50–50 partnership, each contributing $1 million. The $2 million is spent buying an office building: land $1 million and building $1 million, which are net leased. (Use the depreciation assumptions adopted in the previous problems in this chapter.) All cash received as rent is immediately distributed. At the beginning of the 11th year, when the land is worth $1.1 million and the building is worth $810,000, Dave is admitted as a 1/3d partner for $955,000. (Ignore what is done with Dave's cash.)

1. Prepare the book and tax accounts for the partnership after Dave's admission.

2. How is depreciation determined and allocated for tax and book purposes thereafter?

3. If, 2 years after Dave's admission, the land and building are sold for $1.2 million and $750,000, respectively, how is that treated for tax and book purposes?

D. SALES OF PARTNERSHIP INTERESTS AND THE SECTION 754 ELECTION

At common law, a partnership interest could not be transferred, per se. Under property law, the interest was not a thing separate from the underlying partnership assets. Moreover, under the law of agency, an agent—here, the transferor partner—does not have the power to substitute another in her place. Under the 1914 UPA, however, the economic rights (to profits, distributions, and the like) underlying partnership interests were treated as transferable personal property, even though the

---

19. For example, Section VII.E of this text shows how failure to include a reverse Section 704(c) allocation can cause problems under Section 751(b).

20. Note that Section 1.704–3(a)(4) of the regulations subjects such items to Section 704(c) treatment, the closest possible analogy.

transferee may not be treated as a substituted limited partner. The basic entity approach of the 1914 UPA is mirrored in Section 741 of the Code.[21]

Section III.E of this text introduced some of the problems presented when a partnership interest is transferred: The new partner gets a cost basis in her partnership interest that is different from her share of inside basis. This causes her share of partnership items to be measured inappropriately. Section 743(b) adjustments triggered by a Section 754 election considerably reduce any mismeasurement. The problems associated with a transfer of a partnership interest are closely related to those considered thus far in this chapter: transactions outside the partnership that impact the partnership's measurement and allocation of tax items. This section analyzes the taxation of the sale or exchange of a partnership interest in more detail.[22]

An example illustrates what is at stake here: Gary, Helen, and Fred form a pro-rata partnership, each contributing $100,000. The partnership buys a parcel of real estate for $300,000. At a time when the parcel is worth $1.2 million (and the partnership has not made a Section 754 election), Gary sells his interest to Greta for $400,000. Greta gets a $400,000 cost outside basis in her partnership interest. If the partnership were then to sell the property for $1.2 million, the partnership would have a $900,000 taxable gain. Section 704(c)(1)(A) and reverse Section 704(c) do not apply. Thus, the gain would be allocated $300,000 each. Thereafter, Greta would have an outside basis of $700,000 in a partnership interest worth only $400,000 (1/3d of $1.2 million of cash, the partnership's only asset). Something is wrong. Greta is being taxed on gain, even though economically she has not benefitted from her participation in the partnership.

Section 754 provides an election to a partnership.[23] The election is effective for the tax year in which made and all subsequent years until revoked. Under Section 1.754–1(c) of the regulations, a revocation will not be approved if it is made to avoid a basis reduction. The Section 754

---

21. Hence, Rev. Rul. 77–137, 1977–1 C.B. 178, held that a transfer of a partner's economic interest in a partnership was a transfer for tax purposes even if the transferee does not become a partner under state law.

22. Note that some of these rules also apply to transfers of partnership interests by gift or bequest. For example, a partner who inherits her interest is subject to Section 743(b) if the partnership has a Section 754 election in place at the time of the death of the decedent partner. Section 752(d) may cause a partial sale upon a gift or, less likely, bequest. If so, the amount realized would be the transferor partner's share of partnership liabilities. The portion of the total value of the interest represented by such amount would be the portion of

the interest deemed sold. It might be possible to use the entire basis in the partnership interest in determining gain, however. *See* Treas. Reg. § 1.1001–1(e). Alternatively, Section 752(b) may trigger a deemed distribution equal to the transferor partner's share of partnership liabilities when a partnership interest is transferred by gift or at death.

23. Because of the administrative burden associated with a Section 754 election, and because some partners may be hurt by an inside basis writedown, many partnership agreements authorize the managing partner to make such an election at her discretion so as to protect her from litigation with respect to her decision whether to make the election or not.

election not only triggers Section 743(b) adjustments with respect to all transfers of partnership interests, but, also, Section 734(b) adjustments with respect to distributions, which will be discussed in the next 2 chapters.

When a valid Section 754 election is in force, Section 743(b) gives a special basis adjustment in partnership assets to the transferee partner only in an amount equal to the difference between the new partner's outside basis and her share of inside basis. Then, Section 743(c) sends us to Section 755 to determine how the special inside basis adjustment is allocated among the assets. Read Section 755 of the Code and Sections 1.755–1(a) and (b) of the regulations, focusing on purchased interests. The basic idea of the regulations is that, after the special basis adjustment to each asset, each partner's share of the inside basis of an asset (after including the partner's special basis adjustment) should equal the asset's share of the partner's outside basis—the asset's contribution to the value of the partnership interest. Some assets get an increase in basis, while others get a decrease. In other words, a purchasing partner gets cost inside bases as well as a cost outside basis.

The current Section 755 regulations were promulgated in 1999. Importantly, they work differently from their predecessor. The old regulations were based on the notion that the transferee should get an inside basis adjustment that reflects the transferor's gain or loss. Thus, if the transferor had a gain, the transferee could only write up the basis of assets by the amount of gain, and vice versa. For example, consider a 1/3d–1/3d–1/3d partnership among the original partners, each of whom put in $1 million of cash. The partnership's only assets are (i) Whiteacre, which cost $1 million and has a fair market value of $1.6 million, and (ii) Blackacre, which cost $2 million and is worth $1.4 million. One partner sells her interest for $1 million, recognizing no gain or loss. The buyer's outside basis is $1 million, which equals her share of inside basis. Thus, under the old regulations, she would have been allowed no asset adjustment if a Section 754 election were in effect. If Whiteacre were sold for $1.6 million, the buyer would pay tax on $200,000, even though she paid for the unrealized gain when she paid $1 million, and even though the seller, in effect, was taxed on this gain by offsetting it against the loss on Blackacre. Under the new regulations, as discussed in more detail below, the buyer would be allowed a Section 743(b) adjustment in Whiteacre of $200,000 (and a minus $200,000 adjustment in Blackacre), so that the buyer would have no gain if Whiteacre is sold for $1.6 million.

In the face of complex special allocations, it can be quite difficult to determine a partner's share of her partnership's assets. The new Section 755 regulations take special allocations into account with a quite clever piece of reverse engineering. Section 1.755–1(b)(1)(ii) postulates a hypothetical sale of all of the partnership's assets for fair market value the instant after the interest is transferred. The transferee's share of the hypothetical gain or loss on each asset (including goodwill) is determined taking special allocations into account. Then, Section 1.755–1(b)(3) provides that the transferee's basis adjustment with respect to each asset is this share of the hypothetical gain or loss on that asset.

The Section 755 regulations must deal with the possibility that the price paid for a partnership interest may not equal the interest's share of partnership value. In theory, outside price should equal inside value. In fact, the interest sale price is the best evidence of value. Any difference usually arises as a consequence of the approach adopted by the asset appraiser. But, a real difference can arise if buyer or seller out-negotiates the other. So, Section 1.755–2T(b)(2) of the regulations allocates any excess payment for a partnership interest to goodwill or going concern value. Section 1.755–1(b)(3)(ii)(B) allocates any discount only to capital gain property, proportionately to their respective fair market values.[24]

Just as rules are required regarding depreciation of tax-book differences for Section 704(c)(1)(A) and reverse Section 704(c) purposes, rules are required regarding the depreciation effect of Section 743(b) special basis adjustments. Under Section 1.743–1(j)(4) of the regulations, an increase is treated as a new property of the same character as the underlying property, much as with remedial Section 704(c) allocations. A decrease reduces depreciation pro-rata.

The question then arises as to how the Section 704(b) regulations interact with Section 743(b) adjustments. Under Section 1.704–1(b)(2)(iv)(m)(2), the capital accounts do not reflect Section 743(b) amounts. Thus, Section 743(b) operates independently from Section 704(b).

This all can be illustrated with a surprisingly straightforward example: The Helen, Irving, and Jane equal partnership has 3 material assets: (i) gold, which is ordinary income property, with a basis of $150,000 and a value of $300,000, (ii) land, which is a capital asset, with a basis of $210,000 and a value of $180,000, and (iii) machinery, which is Section 1231 property, with a basis of $90,000 and a value of $120,000. Any gain on the machinery would be subject to Section 1245. Helen sells her interest to Karen for $200,000. The partnership has made a Section 754 election. Karen's situation prior to applying Section 743 is as follows:

	Inside Basis	Share of Gain
Gold	50,000	50,000
Land	70,000	–10,000
Machinery	30,000	10,000
	150,000	50,000

24. The last sentence of Section 1.755–1(b)(2)(i), working through Section 1.755–1(b)(3)(i)(B), provides that when the negative adjustment for one partner in capital gain property exceeds the partnership's total basis in such property, ordinary income property is written down.

In this case, since the price paid equals her share of inside value, the built-in gain exactly equals the difference between inside and outside basis. Under Section 743(b), Karen has a positive $50,000 special basis adjustment in the gold, which is recovered as the gold is sold. She has a negative $10,000 adjustment with respect to the land. As a consequence, when the land is sold, Karen will have an extra $10,000 of capital gain. The $10,000 write-up to the machinery is a new Section 168 asset of the same character as the machinery.[25]

Technically, Section 743(b) creates special inside basis, while Section 704(c)(1)(A) and reverse Section 704(c) allocations merely allocate existing items (except under remedial allocations), probably because Section 743(b) is connected to a taxable sale of an interest. Nevertheless, all these rules deal with the same basic economic problem and have similar tax effects. Note that, under Section 1.704–3(a)(7) of the regulations, a transferee of a partnership interest generally is subject to the same Section 704(c)(1)(A) allocations as the transferor would have, but that, under Section 1.743–1(d)(1)(iii), these are reduced or eliminated if a Section 754 election brings Section 743(b) into play.

REVIEW: Code §§ 741–3, 754, and 755 and Reg. §§ 1.704–1(b)(2)(iv)(*m*)(2), 1.743–1(j)(4), 1.754–1(c), 1.755–1(a) and (b) and –2T

Problem Set VI.D

Alice, Barry, and Chuck form a pro-rata partnership, each contributing $1 million. After 5 years, the books look as follows:

Fair Market Value

	Assets		Liabilities
Cash	$200,000		–0–
Machinery	3.1 million		Equity
Goodwill	900,000	Alice	$1.4 million
	4.2 million	Barry	1.4 million
		Chuck	1.4 million
			4.2 million

---

25. Note that, assuming that Helen had a $150,000 outside basis, she would have had $60,000 of ordinary income under Section 751(a), leaving a $10,000 capital loss, so that the new Sections 743(b) and 755 regulations give the buyer of a partnership interest inside basis adjustments that are consistent with the seller's tax treatment.

Tax

Assets		Liabilities	
Cash	$200,000	–0–	
Machinery	1.6 million	**Equity**	
Goodwill	–0–	Alice	$600,000
	1.8 million	Barry	600,000
		Chuck	600,000
			1.8 million

All gain on the machinery would be subject to Section 1245. Chuck sells his interest to Diedre for $1.4 million. How is he taxed? How would a Section 754 election impact future allocations to Diedre?

E.   PARTIAL REDEMPTIONS OF PARTNERSHIP INTERESTS

Ignoring taxes, a current partner should be indifferent between disposing of her interest to the partnership (a redemption) or to a third party (a sale). Subchapter K has problems treating redemption transactions similarly to sales. This is not surprising given that even the entity-approach rules of Subchapter C have a hard time treating sales and redemptions the same, witness Sections 302(b), 304, 305, and 306. Subchapter K's attempt to treat these similar transactions similarly is discussed primarily in Chapter VIII, which deals with complete redemptions of partnership interests. A partial redemption of a partner creates special allocation problems, however, which are the subject of this last section of this chapter.[26]

The basic problem can be illustrated with an example. Maxine and Norma are 50–50 partners, each investing $500,000. The partnership's only assets are (i) land with a basis of $500,000 and a value of $1.5 million and (ii) $500,000 of cash. Maxine and Norma agree that Norma will be distributed the cash and thereafter will be a 1/3d partner, while thereafter Maxine will be a 2/3d partner. If, later, the partnership sells the property for $1.5 million, how should the $1 million of gain be taxed? The partners' amended deal provides that Norma would own 1/3d of the sales proceeds and Maxine 2/3ds. This does not mean that profit should be shared 1/3d–2/3ds, however. The redemption was priced based (a) on the $1.5 million value of the land and (b) on 50–50 sharing of the gain up to that point. Thus, the gain priced into the redemption should be taxed 50–50.

Section 1.704–1(b)(2)(iv)(*f*)(5)(ii) of the regulations achieves this result by providing for another form of reverse Section 704(c) allocation.

---

26. Further problems with partial redemptions are discussed in Chapter VII, particularly Section VII.E.

When Norma is redeemed, the partnership's assets are marked to market for capital accounting purposes. As in any reverse Section 704(c) allocation, the tax-book difference is allocated based on the profit shares at the time of the rebooking. Thus, the first $1 million of gain, the gain that accrued while the deal was 50–50, is taxed 50–50, with any excess taxed 2/3ds–1/3d. Note that the reverse Section 704(c) rules here are the same basic rules that apply with regard to contributions and not the regime applicable to interest sales, Section 743(b), even though one can view a redemption as similar to a sale.

REVIEW: Reg. § 1.704–1(b)(2)(iv)(*f*)(5)(ii)

Problem Set VI.E

Modify the example so that the partnership's only assets are (i) $500,000 of cash, (ii) land with a basis of $300,000 and value of $300,000, and (iii) a leased commercial office building (worth $1.2 million). (Make the customary half-year convention simplifying assumptions.) The building cost $1.95 million, and, when Norma is partially redeemed, had been depreciated 19 years (leaving 20 years of its tax recovery period) so that its adjusted basis at that time was $1 million. After the partial redemption, how is depreciation on the building allocated?

Chapter VII

NONLIQUIDATING DISTRIBUTIONS

A. INTRODUCTION

Under an entity approach, like Subchapter C, most distributions from a business organization to its owners are taxable. The owners have no direct interest in the underlying assets, so that the distribution gives them something that they did not have before, which makes the distribution an appropriate time to impose a tax. In contrast, under a full aggregate approach, an owner of an equity interest in a business organization withdrawing her share of the organization's assets is, in effect, just moving property from one pocket to another, so that a tax is not appropriate. Such an owner receiving more than her share of a given asset, however, would be an exchange, which would be taxable to all owners involved (the distributee owner is exchanging some of her interest in some assets of the business organization for other partners' shares of the withdrawn asset) unless Section 1031 or some other nonrecognition provision applies. Subchapter K's hybrid approach is more generous than either: generally treating all withdrawals as tax-free. As a consequence, complicated rules are required to prevent taxpayers from exploiting this generosity to achieve excessively tax-advantaged results. The most important types of withdrawal that present problems involve (i) a distribution to a partner of more than her share of the total assets of a given character (capital or ordinary) or (ii) a non-pro-rata distribution of property with an inside basis that differs from the property's contribution to the distributee partner's outside basis. These 2 situations, in the context of distributions that do not terminate a partner's interest in the partnership, are the subject of this chapter. Distributions that completely terminate a partner's interest in the partnership are covered in the next chapter.

B. OVERVIEW

READ: Code §§ 168(i)(7), 707(a)(2)(B), 731(a) and (b), 732(a) and (c), 733, 735, 1221(2), 1245(a)(2)(A), (b)(3), and (b)(6), and 1250(b)(1), (d)(3), and (d)(6)

Before proceeding with a detailed analysis of the 2 problem situations, it is helpful to expand upon Chapter III's basic discussion of distributions. Section 731 provides tax-free treatment of distributions, to the partnership and the partner, except that the distributee partner is taxed to the extent that cash distributions exceed outside basis.[1] Further rules specify the basis and other consequences of a property distribution.

When non-cash property is distributed, Section 732(a) control's the distributee partner's basis in the distributed property. In the usual case, the property takes a transferred basis from the partnership under Section 732(a)(1). In the rare case where the distributed property's inside basis exceeds the distributee partner's outside basis, Section 732(a)(1) limits the distributee partner's basis in the asset to her basis in her partnership interest.[2]

Further rules work to treat the distribution as a mere change in form of the ownership of the distributed property that has no tax effect. The distributee partner gets a transferred holding period in the distributed property under Section 1221.[3] Distribution of depreciable property does not trigger any built-in recapture, but the property continues with the same built-in recapture to the distributee partner as in the partnership's hands.[4] Section 168(i)(7) requires the distributee to continue with the partnership's depreciation method. Section 735(a)(1) preserves the ordinary income taint of any distributed unrealized receivables, as broadly defined for Section 751 purposes. Similarly, inventory, as broadly defined for Section 751 purposes, continues its ordinary taint for 5 years under Section 735(a)(2). These rules prevent the use of distributions to effect character conversions.

Under Section 733, a distributee partner's basis in her partnership interest is reduced by the amount of cash distributions and by the basis of non-cash property received. The distributee now has a direct interest in the distributed property, so that the property need not be reflected in the distributee's basis in her partnership interest.

---

1. A cash distribution can exceed outside basis (i) if the partner is receiving more than her share of cash in a partnership with unrealized gain in other assets, (ii) if the distributee partner purchased the interest at a discount, or (iii) if the partner is receiving the proceeds of a borrowing in excess of her share of debt under Section 752. Further issues presented in the first 2 cases are discussed below, while the 3d was discussed in Chapter V.

2. If multiple properties are distributed and subject to adjustment under Section 732(a)(2), Section 732(c) controls how the outside basis is allocated among them. Since multiple property distributions are more common in the context of the liquidation of a partnership, Section 732(c) is discussed in the next chapter.

3. Section 735(b) assures this result even when a transferred basis is not allowed under Section 732.

4. I.R.C. §§ 1245(a)(2)(A), (b)(3), (b)(6), 1250(b)(1), (d)(3), (d)(6).

An example helps illustrate the interaction between Sections 732 and 733: Sue and Judy are the original 50–50 partners in a partnership that owns 3 parcels of real estate. Whiteacre has a basis and value of $1 million. Blackacre has a basis of $90,000 and a value of $100,000. Greenacre has a basis of $110,000 and a value of $100,000. Each partner has a $600,000 outside basis in a partnership interest worth $600,000. Blackacre is distributed to Sue at the same time that Greenacre is distributed to Judy. After the distribution, Sue's basis in Blackacre is $90,000 under Section 732(a), so that the $10,000 of previously unrealized gain is preserved. To compensate Sue, Section 733 gives Sue a basis of $510,000 in a partnership interest now worth only $500,000, which creates a $10,000 built-in loss in her partnership interest, which offsets the $10,000 of gain built into Blackacre. Similarly, Judy has a $110,000 basis in Greenacre and a $490,000 basis in her partnership interest, so as to have a loss built into her land and a gain built into her partnership interest.[5]

Not only does a distribution have tax consequences immediately, as just discussed, but the distribution also may impact the taxation of the partners in the future. For example, property with built-in gain or loss being distributed to a partner presents the true reverse of the Section 704(c)(1)(A) transaction. In a Section 704(c)(1)(A) transaction, the value of contributed property is priced into the partner's shares, and is not subject to the allocations in the partnership agreement when taxable, so that special tax rules that operate independently of the allocations in the partnership are required. Here, a property distribution's economics are controlled by the partnership agreement and should be accounted for thereunder even though any gain or loss on the distributed property is not recognized by the partnership, but by the distributee partner, for tax purposes.

The key provisions are Sections 1.704–1(b)(2)(iv)(b)(5) and (e) of the regulations. Read them. There is a deemed sale of the distributed asset. The associated gain or loss is allocated among all of the partners under Section 704(b). Then, the distributee partner's capital account is reduced by the fair market value of the distributed property. As a consequence, the net effect on the capital accounts will be a reduction by the distributed property's tax basis, so that no new overall tax-book difference is introduced. But, this accounting reflects the real economics. The distributee benefitted from receiving the value of the distributed property. All partners were impacted by the use of appreciated or depreciated property to reduce the interest of the distributee partner.[6] These rules assure that the partners are taxed in accordance with the economics.

---

5. Note the artificiality of building gain or loss into the partnership interests. After the distribution, the partnership owns property worth $1 million with a basis of $1 million, yet one partner has a built-in gain and the other a built-in loss. Sections 732 and 733 work to give assets other than partnership interests "right" bases, but at the cost of having partnership interests having "wrong" bases. The "wrong" partnership bases present problems when a distributee partner is later liquidated, as to be discussed in Chapter VIII of this text.

6. Note that adjustments are made only with respect to the distributed asset, unless the distribution is made in connection with

An example illustrates what is at stake here: Norma and Paula have been 50–50 partners for years. They each have an outside basis and a capital account of $50,000. The partnership owns 4 parcels of real estate: A (basis $15,000, value $30,000), B (basis $40,000, value $30,000), C (basis $20,000, value $50,000), and D (basis $25,000, value $40,000). Parcel A is distributed to Norma and Parcel B to Paula. For capital accounting purposes, the $15,000 of gain on parcel A and the $10,000 of loss on parcel B are booked and allocated 50–50. Further, Norma's capital account is reduced by the $30,000 value of parcel A. Paula's capital account is reduced by the $30,000 value of parcel B. Thus, after all of this accounting, each partner has a capital account of $32,500. Even though Norma took property with built-in gain, while Paula took built-in loss property, the 2 properties' equal values were priced into the distribution. The capital accounting regulations reflect this while creating no new overall tax-book difference.[7]

Distributed property can be subject to debt. For capital accounting purposes, the distribution is valued at the net (of the debt) value of the distribution.[8] In contrast, for tax purposes Section 752(c), treats the distributee as assuming the debt in her individual capacity. This increases her outside basis under Section 752(a). At the same time, partnership debt is reduced. This triggers deemed cash distributions to all of the partners who had been allocated a portion of the debt under Section 752, which triggers deemed cash distributions to them under Section 752(b). These distributions either reduce outside basis or, if there is inadequate outside basis, trigger gain under Section 731(a). As to the partner who received the debt-laden property, however, the deemed distribution is simply netted against the deemed contribution by operation of Section 1.752–1(f) of the regulations.

To do an example, assume a pro-rata partnership with 6 equal partners. Each partner has an outside basis of $1 million. The partnership has numerous parcels of real estate subject to nonrecourse debt. Each parcel cost $100,000, is subject to $60,0000 of purchase-money debt, and is worth $150,000. The partnership distributes one parcel to each of the 6 partners. Inside the partnership, each partner's capital account is reduced by a net $40,000 (increased by $50,000 of gain and reduced by the $90,000 net distributions). Outside, since Section 1.752–3 has allocated the nonrecourse debt on each parcel pro-rata among the partners, when the properties are distributed, each partner is treated as making a deemed cash contribution of $60,000 under Section 752(a) (for taking property subject to $60,000 of debt) and receives a distribution of $60,000 under Section 752(b) (for being relieved of her 1/6th share of the partnership's debt on all 6 properties that were distributed), which nets

a partial redemption of an interest in the partnership, in which case Section 1.704–1(b)(2)(iv)(*f*)(5)(ii) triggers the full reverse Section 704(c) allocation, as discussed at the end of the preceding chapter.

7. The outside basis consequences to the partners of receiving property with built-in gain or loss is controlled by Sections 732 and 733, just discussed, and analyzed further in Section VII.F of this text, below.

8. Treas. Reg. § 1.704–1(b)(2)(iv)(*b*)(5).

out to nothing under Section 1.752–1(f) of the regulations. This is right, as the transaction has not changed any partner's total effective liability for the nonrecourse debt burdening the parcels. Since there is no deemed cash distribution, account need be taken of only the actual distribution of land. Section 731(a) provides that each partner's distribution is tax-free. A partner takes her parcel with a transferred basis of $100,000 under Section 732(a)(1). Accordingly, her outside basis is reduced by $100,000 to $900,000 under Section 733(a)(2). In effect, her indirect, outside, basis in the property received has been converted into a direct, actual basis in property now owned outright. Thus, notwithstanding the gymnastics of Section 752, everything works as it should, as is generally the case.

Section 1.707–6 of the regulations addresses transactions where property is distributed subject to debt without an adequate business purpose. The regulation taxes such transactions as sales by the partnership to the distributee partner. Read it. The regulation was promulgated under Section 707(a)(2)(B), and was discussed in Chapter II. There, the issue was transferring property subject to debt to a partnership. Section 707(a)(2)(B) also applies to distributions of debt-laden property, the case here. Reread Section II.D, above, for the discussion of what constitutes debt without an adequate business purpose.

These rules, while complicated, are fairly generous. This tempts taxpayers to cast transactions so as to be treated as distributions. For example, in *Comsat*,[9] the taxpayer was a partner in INTELSAT. As new partners were admitted in exchange for cash contributions to the partnership, the cash received was distributed by the partnership to the old partners. The taxpayer treated its receipts of cash in such transactions as tax-free reductions in the basis of its partnership interest under Sections 731(a) and 733. Not surprisingly, the government argued that the transactions were disguised sales of portions of partnership interests, so that the taxpayer could use only a portion of its basis in its partnership interest against the cash received, which characterization would result in taxable gain. The old Court of Claims upheld distribution characterization. That the structure of the transactions was designed by a committee of the United Nations acting independently from the partners in INTELSAT heavily influenced the court. Nevertheless, Congress apparently intended for Section 707(a)(2)(B) to reverse *Comsat* and similar cases.[10] The Treasury has reserved the issue in regulations, however.[11] Hence, the scope of Section 707(a)(2)(B) with regard to recharacterizing distributions associated with contributions as interest sales is unclear.

9. *Communications Satellite Corp. v. U.S.*, 625 F.2d 997 (Ct.Cl.1980).

10. Only the Ways and Means Committee report expressly refers to *Comsat*. H.R. Rept. No. 98–432, 1218 (1984). The interest sale versus distribution distinction also arises when a partner leaves her partnership, as discussed in the next chapter of this text.

11. Treas. Reg. § 1.707–7.

NOTICE 2001–64
2001–41 I.R.B. 316.

The Internal Revenue Service and the Treasury Department are considering issuing proposed regulations under § 707(a)(2)(B) of the Internal Revenue Code relating to disguised sales of partnership interests. As part of this consideration, comments are being solicited concerning the scope and substance of this guidance.

Effective April 24, 1991, the Service and Treasury issued final regulations adding new regulations § 1.707–0 and § 1.707–2 through § 1.707–9 to the Income Tax Regulations (26 CFR part 1) under section 707(a)(2). These regulations apply to transfers described in § 707(a)(2)(A) and (B). Section 1.707–7 was reserved for rules on disguised sales of partnership interests.

The legislative history of § 707(a)(2) indicates that the provision was adopted as a result of Congress' concern that taxpayers were deferring or avoiding tax on sales of partnership property, including sales of partnership interests, by characterizing sales as contributions of property, including money, followed or preceded by a related partnership distribution. See H.R. Rep. No. 861, 98th Cong., 2nd Sess. 861 (1984), 1984–3 (Vol. 2) C.B. 115. Specifically, Congress was concerned about court decisions that allowed tax-free treatment in cases that were economically indistinguishable from sales of property to a partnership or another partner and believed that these transactions should be treated for tax purposes in a manner consistent with their underlying economic substance. See H.R. Rep. No. 432, 98th Cong., 2nd Sess. 1218 (1984), and S. Prt. No. 169 (Vol. I), 98th Cong., 2nd Sess. 225 (1984) (discussing *Communications Satellite Corp. v. United States,* 625 F.2d 997 (Ct.Cl. 1980), and *Jupiter Corp. v. United States,* 2 Cl.Ct. 58 (1983), both of which involved the disguised sale of a partnership interest).

Comments are requested on the scope and substance of guidance concerning disguised sales of partnership interests, including any applicable safe harbors or exceptions. Prior to the issuance of regulations, the determination of whether a transaction is a disguised sale of a partnership interest under § 707(a)(2)(B) is to be made on the basis of the statute and its legislative history.

REVIEW: Code §§ 168(i)(7), 707(a)(2)(B), 731(a) and (b), 732(a) and (c), 733, 735, 1221(2), 1245(a)(2)(A), (b)(3), and (b)(6), and 1250(b)(1), (d)(3), and (d)(6) and Reg. §§ 1.704–1(b)(2)(iv)(*b*)(5), (*e*), and (*f*)(5), 1.707–6 and –7, and 1.752–1(f)

Problem Set VII.B

1. Mary and Nick are the original 50–50 partners of a general partnership. The partnership uses the accrual method for tax purposes. After years, the accounts look as follows:

Fair Market Value

Assets		Liabilities	
Cash	$560,000	Payables	$160,000
Receivables	150,000		
Inventory	400,000	Equity	
Machinery	850,000		
Buildings	700,000	Mary	2,000,000
Land	1,000,000	Nick	2,000,000
Goodwill	500,000		4,000,000
	4,160,000		

Tax

Assets		Liabilities	
Cash	$560,000	Payables	$160,000
Receivables	150,000		
Inventory	200,000	Equity	
Machinery	500,000		
Buildings	600,000	Mary	1,200,000
Land	550,000	Nick	1,200,000
Goodwill	–0–		2,400,000
	2,560,000		

All gain on the machinery and buildings is subject to recapture under Sections 1245 and 1250, respectively. If Mary were to sell her interest for $2 million (plus the buyer taking over Mary's share of the partnership's debt), how would the total gain be taxed? What if the partnership were to distribute $250,000 cash to each partner prior to an interest sale for $1.75 million (plus taking over her share of the debt)? What if, rather than distributing cash, the partnership distributed $150,000 of inventory to each partner prior to Mary selling her interest for $1.85 million (plus taking over her share of the partnership debt)? What if she sold the inventory for $150,000?

2. Sue and Tom are 50–50 partners. The partnership's only assets are 3 parcels of land held for investment. Parcel A has a cost basis of $1 million, is subject to $700,000 of debt, and is worth $1.7 million. Parcel B also has a cost basis of $1 million, is subject to $300,000 of debt, and is worth $1.3 million. Parcel C has a cost basis of $2 million, is subject to $1 million of debt, and is worth $2 million. Each partner has a capital account of $1 million and an outside basis of $2 million. Parcel A is distributed to Sue at the same time that Parcel B is distributed to Tom. What are the tax consequences?

C. DISTRIBUTIONS OF MARKETABLE SECURITIES

READ: Code § 731(c)

Section 731(c) provides that a distribution of marketable securities is treated as a distribution of an amount of cash equal to the fair market value of the distributed securities for purposes of taxing gain on the distribution under Section 731. This provision is not particularly important. What is interesting is that, when Section 731(c) was enacted in 1994, the legislative staff[12] wrote legislative history that gives a rare glimpse into their thinking about property distributions by partnerships. An excerpt from the Ways and Means Committee report follows:

HOUSE WAYS AND MEANS COMMITTEE REPORT ON THE URUGUAY ROUND AGREEMENTS BILL, H.R. 5110

H.R. Rept. No. 103–826, 187–93, 1994.

PARTNERSHIP DISTRIBUTIONS OF MARKETABLE SECURITIES (SEC. 741 OF THE BILL AND SECS. 731 AND 737 OF THE CODE)

Present law

Neither a partnership nor its partners generally recognize gain upon a distribution of partnership property to a partner (sec. 731(a)(1) and (b)). A partner is required to recognize gain, however, to the extent that the amount of money distributed exceeds the partner's basis in its partnership interest immediately before the distribution (sec. 731(a)(1)). Thus, in general, if a partnership distributes cash to a partner in an amount that exceeds the adjusted basis of the partner's interest in the partnership, the partner must recognize gain; but if the partnership distributes marketable securities to the partner in lieu of cash, the partner can defer recognizing gain.

A partner's basis in property distributed in a nonliquidating distribution is the lesser of the partnership's adjusted basis in the distributed property or the partner's adjusted basis in partnership interest (reduced by money distributed in the transaction) (sec. 732(a)). A partner's adjusted basis in its partnership interest is reduced by the amount of money and the basis of property distributed to him in a non-liquidating distribution (sec. 733).

A partner that contributes appreciated property to a partnership is required to include pre-contribution gain in income to the extent that the value of other property distributed by the partnership to that

---

12. Customarily, tax reports of both the House Ways and Means Committee and the Senate Finance Committee are drafted by the Staff of the Joint Committee on Taxation, subject both to the review of the majority and minority staffs of the relevant committee and to the comments of Treasury.

partner exceeds its adjusted basis in its partnership interest (sec. 737) [to be discussed later in this chapter]. This rule applies if the distribution is made within 5 years [now 7 years] after the contribution of the appreciated property.

Reasons for change

Concern has arisen that taxpayers can exchange interests in appreciated assets for marketable securities while deferring or avoiding tax on the appreciation, by using the present-law rules relating to partnership distributions. The present-law rules permit a partner to exchange, tax-free, his share of appreciated partnership assets for an increased share of the partnership's marketable securities. [Note that Congress is concerned only about non-pro-rata distributions. The problems illustrate this.] This transaction is the virtual economic equivalent of a sale of a partner's share of the partnership's assets. If the taxpayer were to exchange an interest in an appreciated asset for cash, he generally would recognize gain on the appreciated asset; yet if the taxpayer receives a partnership distribution of marketable securities, which are nearly as easily valued and as liquid as cash, he can avoid gain recognition.

This distinction in tax treatment between cash and marketable securities elevates form over substance, causes taxpayers to choose the form of transactions for tax reasons rather than economic reasons, and may not promote accurate income measurement. Rather, the present-law rule merely permits taxpayers to defer or avoid tax.

To limit the deferral or avoidance of taxation upon the receipt of marketable securities by a partner with unrealized appreciation in his partnership interest, the bill provides that the receipt of marketable securities in a partnership distribution causes the partner to recognize gain from the disposition of its partnership interest, to the extent that the value of the securities exceeds that partner's adjusted basis in its partnership interest. Thus, gain is recognized in the same manner, as if the partner had received money in lieu of securities.

[I]t is not intended that a partner be taxed under the provision on the partnership's gain attributable to his share of the partnership's marketable securities distributed to him, because he has not exchanged his share of any other partnership asset for an increased share of the partnership's marketable securities. Thus, an exception (structured as a limitation on gain recognized under the provision) applies, to the extent that the gain that would otherwise be recognized under the provision does not exceed the distributee partner's share of the partnership's built-in gain (if any) with respect to securities of the type distributed to him. Further, the bill provides an exception for a distribution of marketable securities if the distributed security was contributed by the distributee partner (except to the extent that the value of the distributed security arises from marketable securities or money contributed to an entity to which the distributed security relates).

Because the partnership tax rules provide a great deal of flexibility, and taxpayers can arrange their affairs so as to take advantage of this flexibility, the bill grants to the Treasury Department regulatory authority to prescribe rules that effectively prevent taxpayers from avoiding the intent of this provision (as well as to provide relief from the application of the provision, where appropriate).

Explanation of provision

In general.—The bill generally provides that, for purposes of determining the amount of gain that a partner recognizes upon the distribution of marketable securities by a partnership, the fair market value of the securities is treated as money. Thus, a partner generally recognizes gain under the provision to the extent that the sum of the fair market value of marketable securities and money received exceeds the partner's basis in its partnership interest.[13] The value of the marketable securities is their fair market value as of the date of the distribution.

Definition of marketable securities

In general.—Under the provision, marketable securities means financial instruments and foreign currencies that are, as of the date of the distribution, actively traded (within the meaning of section 1092(d)(1)). For purposes of the definition of marketable securities, a financial instrument includes financial products such as stocks and other equity interests, evidences of indebtedness, options, futures and forward contracts, notional principal contracts and derivatives.

Securities contributed by the distributee

The provision generally does not apply to the distribution of a marketable security to a partner if the security was contributed to the partnership by the partner. The provision does, however, apply, to the extent that the value of distributed security is attributable to marketable securities or money contributed (directly or indirectly) to the entity to which the distributed security relates. For example, if marketable securities are contributed by a partnership to a corporation (or lower tier subsidiary of a corporation) whose stock had been contributed to the partnership by a partner, the provision would apply to the distribution of stock of the corporation back to the contributing partner to the extent the value of such stock is attributable to the marketable securities or money contributed. The provision does not, however, apply (unless otherwise provided in regulations) to the extent that the value of an interest in an entity contributed by the distributee partner is attributable to marketable securities or money that the distributee also contributed to the partnership.

---

13. [Committee's Note 10:] Marketable securities are not treated as money under other provisions, for example, section 731(a)(2). Any loss on the distribution of marketable securities is not recognized under the provision, but rather is deferred to the same extent it is deferred under present law, by virtue of the present-law rules providing generally for carryover and substituted basis, respectively, of property distribution other than in liquidation (sec. 732(a)) and of property distributed in liquidation (sec. 732(b)).

Limitation on gain recognized

The bill permits a partner to receive a distribution of marketable securities without recognizing the gain that is attributable to his share of the partnership's net appreciation with respect to securities of the type distributed. For this purpose, a type of securities means a class of securities (for example, residual common stock) of a single issuer.

The bill provides that the amount of marketable securities treated as money is reduced by the excess of (1) the partner's distributive share of any net gain that he would take into account if all the securities (of the type distributed) held by the partnership immediately before the transaction were sold for their fair market value, over (2) the partner's distributive share of any net gain that he would take into account if all the securities (of that type) held by the partnership immediately after the transaction had been sold. In making this determination, the partner's share of net gain is determined immediately before and immediately after the transaction, using the same fair market value for the securities in each case. Thus, in the case of a transaction involving a series of distributions, the partner's share of net gain is unaffected by changes in the value of the distributed securities during the course of the distributions. In addition, the amount of gain allocated to a partner is determined with regard to any basis adjustment under section 743(b) with respect to that partner.

For example, assume that partnership ABC holds 300 shares of the common stock of X corporation, a marketable security, and other assets. A holds a 1/3 interest in the capital and profits of the partnership. Each share of stock held by the partnership has a basis of $10 and a value of $100. A's adjusted basis in its partnership interest is $5,000. Assume that the partnership distributes all the shares of X corporation to A in liquidation of his partnership interest. Under the general rule of new section 731(c), the $30,000 value of the X stock would be treated as money for purposes of determining A's gain. Under this gain limitation rule, however, the $30,000 amount is reduced by $9,000, the amount of gain that A would have taken into account if the partnership had sold all 300 shares of X stock for a total of $30,000. Thus, A recognizes a gain of $16,000 ($30,000 reduced by $9,000 (or $21,000), further reduced by A's $5,000 basis in his partnership interest).

Other rules

Basis of securities distributed.—The bill provides that the adjusted basis of the distributed marketable securities is increased (over the basis as determined under present-law section 732) by the amount of gain recognized by reason of this provision. The amount of gain so recognized is allocated among the distributed marketable securities in proportion to the amounts of unrealized appreciation (determined before the increase in basis under the provision).

For example, assume that a partnership distributes to a partner, in a nonliquidating distribution, marketable security A with a value of $100 and a basis of $60, and marketable security B with a value of $100 and a basis of $40. The distributee partner's basis in his partnership interest is

$120. Under present law, no gain is recognized, the partner's basis in security A is $60 and in security B is $40, and his adjusted basis in his partnership interest is $20. Assume that the partner will recognize gain of $40 under the provisions of the bill.[14] Under the bill, 40 percent of the gain (i.e., $16) is allocated to security A, and 60 percent of the gain (i.e., $24) is allocated to security B. Thus, the partner's basis in security A is $76 (i.e., $60 basis plus $16 gain allocated), and in security B is $64 (i.e., $40 basis plus $24 gain allocated). This result is the same whether security A and security B are securities of different issuers, of different classes of the same issuer, or blocks of securities of the same class and issuer but with different adjusted bases in the hands of the partnership.

Other basis rules

The adjusted basis of the partner's partnership interest and the partnership's adjusted basis in its remaining assets are determined without regard to this provision. The bill provides that rules for determining the distributee partner's basis in his partnership interest (sec. 733) are applied as if no gain were recognized, and no adjustment were made to the basis of property, under this provision. Thus, as under present law,[15] the distributee partner's basis in his partnership interest is reduced (in a nonliquidating distribution) by the basis of the distributed securities, as determined under section 732 and without regard to the provisions of the bill. Therefore, in the foregoing example, the distributee's basis in his partnership interest, initially $120, is reduced by the sum of the bases (in the hands of the partnership) of security A ($60) and security B ($40), for a total reduction of $100. After the distribution, his basis in his partnership interest is $20.

REVIEW: Code § 731(c)

Problem Set VII.C

1. Bunker and Lamar are 50–50 partners. They are the original partners, each with an outside basis of $10 million. The partnership owns a parcel of real estate with a basis of $10 million and a value of $100 million. (This means that the partnership is not an "investment partnership" within the meaning of Section 731(c)(3)(C)(i).) Also, the partnership owns blocks of stock in 10 publicly-traded companies. Each block has a basis of $1 million and a value of $10 million. What are the tax consequences if the partnership distributes one of the blocks of stock to Bunker and reduces his interest to 9/19ths (and increases Lamar's to 10/19ths)?

2. What would be the result in Problem 1, above, if, rather than the non-pro-rata distribution of 5 blocks, the partnership distributed 2 entire separate blocks to each of the partners?

---

14. [Committee's Note 15:] The amount of gain recognized under the provision depends on the partner's share of partnership appreciation in securities of the same type (class and issuer) as securities A and B, as discussed above.

15. [Committee's Note 16:] The distribution of marketable securities continues, as under present law, to be treated as a distribution of property for purposes of determining basis.

3. If all of the blocks of stock were in the same class of the same company, how would Section 731(c)(3)(B) impact the analysis in Question 2?

4. Based on the analysis of the problems above, does Section 731(c) achieve its purposes as articulated in the legislative history above?

D. NIXING MIXING BOWLS

The most obvious problem presented by current law's hybrid approach to distributions is so-called "mixing bowl" transactions. In such a transaction, the taxpayer's goal is to use Sections 721 and 731 to effect a tax-free exchange (that otherwise would not be). For example, Quincy and Ralph may want to swap Quincy's real estate for Bob's gold bullion. A direct exchange would be taxable. Instead, they form a partnership with their respective properties and then withdraw the property contributed by the other. Under the literal words of Subchapter K, the contributions and distributions would be tax-free. If this worked, however it would be quite a hole in the general tax principle that gain or loss is recognized on exchanges of property. Thus, Section 1.731–1(c)(3) of the regulations has long nixed obvious mixing bowl transactions. Read it.[16]

Tax-free treatment is so attractive, however, that taxpayers are tempted to try less obvious mixing bowls. One rule that limits opportunities here has been discussed already, Section 704(c). It assures that property contributions do not shift the taxation of any built-in gain or loss on contributed property. But, Section 704(c) only operates as long as the contributed property stays in partnership solution. What if property is contributed to a partnership, left there long enough to avoid Section 1.731–1(c)(3), and then distributed before Section 704(c) has had any real bite? Congress responded to this possibility by enacting Section 704(c)(1)(B) in 1989 and tightening it in 1997. Read Section 704(c)(1)(B). Under the current rule, if Section 704(c) property is distributed to a partner other than the partner who contributed the property within 7 years of the day of the contribution, the contributing partner is taxed on the portion of the built-in gain or loss on the property at the time of contribution that has not been recaptured already by Section 704(c)(1)(A).[17] This gain or loss has the same character as would have been recognized if Section 721 had not provided tax-free treatment on the contribution. Then, under Section 704(c)(1)(B)(iii), the contributing partner increases her basis in her partnership interest, and the distributee partner increases her basis in the distributed property (and reduces her basis in her partnership interest), as if the partnership (i) had purchased the property with cash provided by the contributing partner

16. Section 707(a)(2)(B) also taxes a straightforward property swap that is effected through a partnership.

17. Interestingly, Section 704(c)(2) authorizes regulations, yet to be issued, that do not tax the contributing partner when

her property is distributed to another partner if the contributing partner receives property which would be like-kind under Section 1031, so that, under a full aggregate regime, the transaction would have been tax-free to the contributing partner.

(triggering gain and creating basis) and, (ii) then, distributed the purchased property to the distributee partner (with a cost basis).[18] Read Sections 1.704–4(e)(1) and (2) of the regulations.

Congress addressed another spin on the mixing bowl in 1992. In this transaction, the contributing partner separates herself from her former property, not by the partnership distributing the contributed property to a partner other than the contributing partner, the Section 704(c)(1)(B) transaction, but by the partnership distributing non-cash property to the contributing partner. A nonliquidating distribution to a contributing partner alone would not present a problem, however, as Section 704(c) would tax the contributing partner on any built-in gain or loss on the contributed property as long as the contributor remains a partner.[19] Nevertheless, Congress apparently was concerned about near liquidations setting up a later abuse transaction and did not want to define what is a near liquidation.[20] Section 737, Congress' response, therefore, applies to all distributions of non-cash property to a partner who contributed other property, but only in a limited fashion. (Since cash distribution in excess of basis trigger gain, Congress did not see them as providing sufficient abuse potential to merit statutory attention.)

When a partner who contributed property to her partnership receives a distribution of non-cash property that she did not contribute, Section 737 taxes the partner on non-recaptured Section 704(c) gain (including reflecting this gain's tax character) only to the extent that the value of the distributed property exceeds the partner's outside basis. Read Section 737.[21] Note that it does not apply to cash distributions (including, under the language of Section 731(c)(1), deemed cash distributions that result from the operation of Section 731(c)); but that, as to cash distributions, Section 731(a)(1) picks up the same amount of gain.[22] For basis determination purposes, the transaction is taxed as if, before the real distribution, the partnership had distributed a portion of the contributed property (with no basis) back to the contributor and then purchased the portion back for cash (that was contributed by contributor) in an amount equal to the taxable gain triggered by Section 737.[23]

18. Compare this to the paradigm underlying Section 731(c): the distributee partner receiving the marketable securities and then selling and buying back the portion of the distribution taxable under Section 731(c).

19. The rules with regard to liquidating distributions are reviewed in the next chapter of this text.

20. Note 27, below, examines why Section 751(b) might not address all concerns here in the non-liquidating distribution context.

21. Both Section 704(c)(1)(B) and Section 737 apply at the same time to the same contributor partner when contributed property is distributed to a non-contributor partner at the same time that the contribu-

tor receives a distribution of other partnership property. In this case, Section 1.737–1(c)(2)(iv) of the regulations provides that the more comprehensive Section 704(c)(1)(B) applies first, which reduces the untaxed precontribution gain potentially taxable under Section 737.

22. Section 731 only creates capital gain, however, while Section 704(c)(1)(B) can create items of varying tax character. Section 751(b), discussed in the next section of this text, deals with converting ordinary income into capital gain in the Section 731 context, but with a mechanism much different from Section 704(c)(1)(B)'s.

23. Treas. Reg. § 1.737–3. The deemed Section 737 transaction is treated occurring before the actual distribution of non-cash

Thus, the distributee partner increases her basis in her partnership interest for the Section 737 gain (the deemed cash contribution) under Section 737(c)(1). Similarly, the partnership gets an increased basis in the contributed property, which increase is treated as new property for depreciation purposes under Section 737(c)(2).

REVIEW: Code §§ 704(c)(1)(B) and 737 and Reg. §§ 1.704–3(a)(7) and –4(e)(1) and (2) and 1.737–1,–3(a), and –3(b)(1)

Problem Set VII.D

Ralph has a parcel of (debt-free) real estate with a basis of $600,000 and a value of $1 million. Quincy owns gold bullion for investment with a basis of $750,000 and a value of $1 million. Ralph and Quincy form a 50–50 partnership, each contributing their respective properties plus $500,000 in cash. The $1 million cash is invested in silver. Assume that Section 707(a)(2)(B) and Section 1.731–1(c)(3) of the regulations do not apply to any distributions. If the partnership distributed the gold to Ralph and the silver to Quincy (each now having a value of $1.5 million), what would be the tax consequences?

E. SHIFTING SHARES IN ORDINARY INCOME ASSETS: SECTION 751(b)

READ: Code § 751(b)

Subchapter K's basis rules applicable to distributions, Sections 732 and 733, assure that a tax-free distribution under Section 731 does not facilitate tax avoidance, but merely defers tax. But, because assets come in different flavors, the basis rules alone do not prevent abuse. Section 751(b), the topic of this section of this text, addresses 2 situations (which are the mirror images of each other) where partnership distributions could be used to convert ordinary income (or loss) to capital gain (or loss): (i) a partner withdrawing more than her share of property other than ordinary income property so as to avoid future tax on the partnership's ordinary income and (ii) a partner withdrawing more than her share of ordinary income property so that the other partners are avoiding the associated ordinary income tax.[24] Remember that Section 751(a), which contains the collapsible partnership rules discussed in Chapter III, addresses similar conversion problems with regard to the transfer of a partnership interest.

The language of Section 751(b) is straightforward. It addresses a distribution that effects a shift in a partner's interest in "hot" assets:

property so as to increase the Section 732(a)(2) ceiling on the distributed property's basis, which is discussed later in this chapter.

24. The closest analogy in Subchapter C is Section 304. Section 304 is directed at a purchase (an **exchange** of stock for cash) that has the effect of a distribution. Here, there is a distribution that has the effect of an exchange. In Subchapter C exchanges (basis recovery and capital gain) are taxed more favorably than distributions (100% ordinary income if out of earnings and profits), while here an exchange triggers tax, some ordinary income, while a distribution is tax free. Hence, the distribution versus exchange issue is reversed in Subchapter K from Subchapter C.

unrealized receivables and/or **substantially-appreciated** inventory. "Unrealized receivables" and "inventory" have the same broad definitions here as for Section 751(a) purposes, which were discussed in Chapter III. The substantial appreciation requirement applicable to inventory applies only for purposes of Section 751(b), and not for purposes of Section 751(a). Presumably, Congress was reluctant to apply the rather draconian Section 751(b) too broadly. Section 751(b)(3) defines "substantial appreciation" of inventory as the partnership's total inventory being worth 20% more than its adjusted basis.[25] Bizarrely, for purposes of determining if inventory is so substantially appreciated, real unrealized receivables (not recapture property) are treated as inventory.[26] When a distribution effects a swap of the total amount of these 2 types of hot property for other property of a different tax character, there is a taxable sale between the distributee partner and the partnership.[27] This taxable exchange usually results in tax consequences for all partners, as the gain recognized by the partnership passes through to the non-distributee partners.[28] A cash distribution taxable under Section 751(b), however, only has consequences to the distributee partner since the partnership has no gain on the disposition of cash.

Before analyzing the application of Section 751(b) to nonliquidating distributions in detail, it is helpful to note how all of the provisions that impact the taxation of the distributee partner relate to each other. As to a given distribution, first, Section 704(c)(1)(B) comes into play to tax the distributee if, in connection with the distribution, another partner receives property that had been contributed by the distributee to the partnership in the 7 years prior to the distribution. Any gain or loss under Section 704(c)(1)(B) adjusts the distributee's outside basis for purposes of applying all of the other relevant provisions.[29]

Next, Section 751(b) applies so as to potentially recharacterize a distribution into a different distribution (taxed under the regular rules applicable to distributions) followed by an exchange, as soon to be discussed.[30] Then, the basic rules, Sections 731 and 732, apply to the distribution as so recharacterized.[31] Section 737 may tax the distributee if she contributed property to the partnership within the previous 7 years.[32] Finally, Section 731(c) potentially taxes the distributee on gain if she receives marketable securities.

While the idea underlying Section 751(b) is straightforward, its application is quite involved because of the complexity inherent in

---

25. Treas. Reg. § 1.751–1(d)(1).

26. Treas. Reg. § 1.751–1(d)(2)(ii).

27. Because Section 751(b) looks at shifting interests in all hot assets, rather than in specific properties, it was not adequate to deal with the shifting interests in specific contributed property to which Section 737 is directed.

28. Blessedly, Congress did not adopt a regime under Sections 704(c)(1)(B), 731(c), or 737 that taxes all partners, even though

there, as here, the problem is a non-prorata distribution, so that a deemed swap more naturally applies than the artificial deemed transactions created by these later-enacted provisions.

29. Treas. Reg. § 1.704–4(e).

30. I.R.C. §§ 731(d), 737(d)(2).

31. Treas. Reg. § 1.732–1(e).

32. I.R.C. § 731(d).

determining what is being exchanged for what in connection with a nonliquidating distribution. Consider an example: Olive and Paula form a partnership with cash contributions. Olive has a 45% pro-rata share, Paula the remaining 55%. The partnership uses the accrual method of accounting for tax purposes. After years, the partnership's accounts look as follows:

Fair Market Value

Assets		Liabilities	
Cash	$560,000	Payables	$160,000
Receivables	150,000		
Inventory	400,000	Equity	
Machinery	850,000		
Buildings	700,000	Olive	1,800,000
Land	1,000,000	Paula	2,200,000
Goodwill	500,000		4,000,000
	4,160,000		

Tax

Assets		Liabilities	
Cash	$560,000	Payables	$160,000
Receivables	150,000		
Inventory	200,000	Equity	
Machinery	500,000		
Buildings	600,000	Olive	1,080,000
Land	550,000	Paula	1,320,000
Goodwill	–0–		2,400,000
	2,560,000		

All gain on the machinery would be recaptured as ordinary income under Section 1245.[33]

While the partnership's receivables are not Section 751(c) unrealized receivables, the built-in gain on the machinery is. A careful lawyer would worry that some of the value attributed to goodwill relates to contracts to provide goods or services, and therefore constitutes a Section 751 unrealized receivable, but, in the interests of simplicity, we do not here. As a whole, the inventory (which, for that purpose, includes the receivables) is substantially appreciated for Section 751(b) purposes.

The partnership distributes $400,000 of cash to Paula. In connection with this distribution, her interest (in assets and liabilities) is decreased to 1/2 (with Olive's increased to 1/2).[34] If Section 751(b) did not apply,

33. Unrecaptured Section 1250 gain for purposes of Section 1(h) is not an unrealized receivable for Section 751 purposes, since, by definition, this income is not ordinary income.

34. Note that, in the interests of simplicity, this deal does not make a reverse Section 704(c) allocation, which, if made, could avoid the Section 751(b) problem by

Paula would pay no tax under Section 731,[35] and would reduce her outside basis to $1 million.[36] To determine the impact of Section 751(b), it is necessary to figure out what, if anything, is being exchanged for what. Before the distribution, Paula owned (indirectly) the following, at fair market value (subject to her share of the debt):

Before (55% of Partnership)

Cash	$308,000
Receivables	82,500
Inventory	220,000
Machinery	467,500
Buildings	385,000
Land	550,000
Goodwill	275,000
	2,288,000

After reflecting her 55% of the debt, $88,000, the net value of her interest is $2.2 million.

After the transaction, Paula owns, directly and indirectly:

After ($400,000 Cash + 1/2 of Partnership)

Cash	$480,000
Receivables	75,000
Inventory	200,000
Machinery	425,000
Buildings	350,000
Land	500,000
Goodwill	250,000
	2,280,000

After reflecting her 1/2 of the debt, $80,000, the value of her ownership stays at $2.2 million.[37]

In this light, Paula's interest in cash has increased, and her interest in each of the other partnership properties has decreased by 5% of their respective values (from 55% to 50%). Cash, the only property that she now has more of, is not Section 751(b) ordinary income property. Thus, she has increased her interest in non-Section 751(b) property in ex-

---

preventing an immediate reduction in Paula's share of Section 751 assets (although also changing the economics somewhat).

35. Note that, unlike a redemption of corporate stock that is taxed under Section 302(a), a redemption of a partnership interest is treated as an operating distribution and not as a sale of part of the interest.

36. Because Paula is an original partner, her pre-distribution outside basis equaled his capital account before the distri-

bution, $1,320,000, plus her 55% share of debt, $88,000, before the distribution. It is assumed that Paula's share of the debt under Section 752 goes down to 1/2 as a consequence of the instant transaction, so as to trigger, in addition to the $400,000 of cash actually distributed, a deemed distribution of (55%–50%) x $160,000 = 8,000.

37. Olive gets a bigger piece of a smaller pie. Paula gets cash and a smaller piece of a smaller pie.

change for a reduced interest in some hot property. This exchange, but not any exchange of non-Section 751(b) property for cash, is taxable under Section 751(b). As noted above, the Section 751(b) property here consists of the inventory and the built-in recapture gain on the machinery. Accordingly, Paula would pay tax on $10,000 of inventory ordinary income and $17,500 of Section 1245 ordinary income. The partnership would increase its basis in the respective properties accordingly.[38] Paula's basis in her partnership interest would be $1,027,500.

Believe it or not, in the wacky world of Section 751(b), the example above is relatively simple, because the distribution consisted solely of cash. If the distribution had been of capital gain property, the partnership also would have had a taxable gain, which gain would have been allocated only to Olive.[39] Additionally, when multiple types of property are distributed, the underlying exchanges are pro-rata unless the partners specify otherwise.[40] For purposes of applying Section 732 to determine the basis in property distributed, the deemed distribution created by Section 751(b) occurs separately from, and prior to, the actual distribution.[41]

REVIEW: Code §§ 731(d), 737(d)(2), and 751(b) and Reg. §§ 1.704–4(e), 1.732–1(e), and 1.751–1(b), (c), (d), and (g)

Problem Set VII.E

1. What would be the result with regard to the Mary and Nick partnership in Problem 1 of Problem Set VII.B if, rather than any of the transactions there, the partnership distributed $300,000 of cash to Nick and $300,000 worth of inventory (basis $150,000) to Mary?

2. Compare the results in Problem 1 to an alternate transaction in which each partner gets a distribution of $150,000 of Cash and $150,000 of inventory, and, then, Nick sells his inventory to Mary for $150,000 cash.

F. FURTHER PROBLEMS ASSOCIATED WITH NON–PRO–RATA DISTRIBUTIONS

Thus far, this chapter's analysis has looked at the taxation of non-pro-rata distributions. The remainder of this chapter deals with the basis consequences of distributions and related concerns. This section deals with the most common situations. Later sections look at more obscure problems.

---

38. The Section 751(b) write-ups to partnership inventory, machinery, and buildings are treated as new assets of the same character.

39. Treas. Reg. § 1.751–1(b)(3)(ii). The reverse is also true. Treas. Reg. § 1.751–1(b)(2)(ii).

40. Treas. Reg. § 1.751–1(g) (Examples 3, 4).

41. Treas. Reg. §§ 1.732–1(e); 1.751–1(b)(1)(iii), (2)(iii), (3)(iii).

Consider this example: Max and Maxine form a 50–50 partnership, each putting in $1 million in cash. They buy a parcel of real estate for $500,000. (For simplicity, assume that the left-over $1.5 million of cash is put in the bank and earns no interest.) After a few years, the land has appreciated in value to $4.5 million. The $1.5 million in cash is distributed to Max. His interest is reduced to 1/3d, while Maxine's is now 2/3ds. Max is taxed on $500,000 of gain under Section 731 because the cash distribution exceeds his outside basis.[42] There are further tax consequences of the distribution, however. The reverse Section 704(c) allocation triggered by the partial redemption, as discussed at the end of the preceding chapter, assures that Max still will be taxed on 1/2 of the first $4 million of gain on the asset, even though he already has paid tax with regard to $500,000 of that gain. This seems like double taxation.[43]

Current law provides some relief. The basis problem here, where, in effect, a partnership acquires a partnership interest from a partner, is analogous to the basis problem created when a partnership interest is purchased by a third party, as discussed in Chapter VII. There, if a Section 754 election has been made, Section 743(b) goes a long way toward harmonizing inside and outside basis. Here, dissonance between inside and outside basis also creates problems. Congress recognized the similarity of the problems and opted for parallel fixes: A Section 754 election also triggers the operation of Section 734(b). Read it. Section 734(b)(1)(A) adjusts the partnership's basis in its assets, in contrast to Section 743(b), which gives a transferee partner a personal special basis adjustment. In the example here, the partnership gets a $500,000 basis adjustment in its assets.[44] This relief looks to give the partnership basis because a partner paid tax.

Here, as with Section 743(b), Section 755 and its regulations prescribe how the basis of the specific assets of the partnership are to be adjusted. (In the example here, there is only one non-cash asset, however). Read Section 1.755–1(c)(1)(ii) of the regulations. Since the partner probably paid only a capital gains tax, the partnership only adjusts the bases of capital gain property. While Section 743(b) can simultaneously increase and decrease the basis of assets, here there can only be an increase. Any basis increase to an asset is treated as a new tax asset that has the same character as the underlying real asset under Section 1.734–1(e). For capital accounting purposes, these adjustments duplicate the write-up triggered by the partial redemption, however, so that, under

---

42. In effect, he has managed to realize his share of the unrealized gain in the partnership's assets as a consequence of Maxine allowing him to withdraw more than his share of cash. Some might ask why Max is taxed on borrowing from Maxine when he would not be taxed if the partnership borrowed and distributed to Max his share of the proceeds.

43. Of course, this extra gain creates basis that gives Max a loss when the partnership liquidates, as discussed in the next chapter. But, that can be cold comfort today.

44. In the pro-rata cash distribution followed by a sale example, Maxine would get a $625,000 special adjustment under Section 743(b) if a Section 754 election were in place.

Section 1.704–1(b)(2)(iv)(m)(5) of the regulations, these adjustments have no independent capital account impact.

Matters can get even more complicated. A different inside versus outside problem can arise from non-pro-rata distributions of property other than cash. An example illustrates the concerns: Olivia and Paul form a 50–50 partnership, each contributing $500,000. They buy 3 undeveloped parcels of land for investment: Parcel A for $250,000, Parcel B for $550,000, and Parcel C for $200,000. Otherwise, the partnership does nothing. After a few years, Parcels A, B, and C are each worth $1 million. The partnership distributes Parcel A to Olivia and Parcel B to Paul. These distributions are completely tax-free under Sections 731 and 751(b). Then, under the general rules discussed earlier in this chapter, (i) each property would have a transferred basis to the respective distributee under Section 732(a)(1) and (ii) the partners' outside bases would be reduced accordingly under Section 733. This presents problems, however. Parcel B's inside basis is $550,000, but Paul's outside basis is only $500,000. Does he end up with a negative basis in his partnership interest? If not, he would be getting $50,000 of basis for nothing. In this case, Section 732(a)(2) steps in and limits the transferred basis of Parcel B to Paul's otherwise-available outside basis. Under this rule, Parcel B has a $500,000 outside basis and his basis in his partnership interest is reduced to zero. In effect, his $1 million of built-in gain is allocated 1/2 to Parcel B ($1 million value and $500,000 basis) and 1/2 to his partnership interest ($500,000 value and no basis). Thus, Section 732(a)(2) has assured that, as to Paul, no built-in gain or loss is created or eliminated by the distribution. Things are still a little off, however, as the zero basis partnership interest is associated with inside basis of $100,000 (1/2 of Parcel C's $200,000 cost basis.)

What is wrong? Paul has received more than his 1/2 share of inside basis, so that, if Paul is not to receive a windfall, either Parcel B's basis or Paul's basis in his partnership interest must be mismeasured. Before the transaction, Paul had a partnership interest worth $1.5 million with a basis of $500,000. After, he has property worth $1 million with a basis of $500,000 and a partnership interest worth $500,000 with a zero basis. The basis rules of Sections 732 and 733 reflect a decision to maintain the built-in gain or loss on distributed property rather than (i) to achieve symmetry between inside and outside basis with respect to the partnership interest,[45] or (ii) to allocate the distributee partner's total gain pro-rata (by value) between the distributed property and the distributee partner's partnership interest[46] This happens in any non-pro-rata distribution (where not all properties have appreciated or depreciated by the exact same percentage of their adjusted bases), but creates particular

45. Symmetry would give Parcel B a $400,000 basis and Paul's partnership interest a $100,000 basis. This result makes sense from the point of view of the interest, but is arbitrary as to the Parcel B.

46. This result would give Parcel B a $333,333 basis and the partnership interest a $166,667 basis. Each property gets its share of the total built-in gain. But, there is still an inside basis versus outside basis problem as to the partnership interest, and artificial gain on Parcel B has been manufactured.

problems in circumstances similar to those here with Paul, where the distributed property's inside basis exceeds outside basis, so that the Section 732(a)(2) limitation applies.

It is important to remember that, in a sense, this is only a timing problem. In the example, before the transaction, there was a total basis in the parcels of $1 million. Because of Section 732(a)(2), after the distribution, the total basis in the parcels is only $950,000 even though no partner got the benefit of the $50,000 of disappearing basis. This does not mean permanent overtaxation, however, as the partners' total outside basis (including former partnership assets now outside the partnership) remains $1 million, so that any overtaxation of a partner when the parcels are sold will be offset by a loss when the partner's partnership interest is liquidated, as discussed in the next chapter. In other words, the partnership's total inside basis is $200,000, while the partners' total outside basis in their interests is $250,000 (Olivia's $250,000 [her original cash contribution less the basis of Parcel A received)] plus Paul's zero). The outside basis ultimately controls the partners' tax outcomes, but the insufficient inside basis can create problems until the outside basis comes into play.

Here, with a non-cash property distribution, as above with a cash distribution, a Section 754 election triggers rules designed to mitigate any odd basis consequences of a non-pro-rata distribution. In the example, Section 734(b)(1)(B) gives the partnership $50,000 of asset basis to offset the $50,000 of asset basis eliminated by Section 732(a)(2), which basis is allocated among the partnership's remaining assets under the Section 755 regulations.[47] Under Section 1.755–1(c)(i), since Paul took capital gain property, only the bases of capital gain property are adjusted. Section 1.704–1(b)(2)(iv)(*l*)(3) provides the capital accounting. Read the second sentence.

It now is possible to analyze the tax consequences of our non-cash property distribution transaction to the partnership. After the distributions, the partnership's accounts look as follows:

Tax

Assets		Liabilities	
Parcel C	$200,000	–0–	
		Equity	
		Olivia	$200,000
		Paul	–0–
			200,000

---

47. If a liquidating partner recognizes a loss under Section 731(a)(2), Section 734(b) requires the partnership to write the bases of its assets down. I.R.C. § 704(b)(2)(A).

Book

	Assets		Liabilities
Parcel C	$200,000		–0–

			Equity	
		Olivia	$100,000[48]	
		Paul	100,000	
			200,000	

With a Section 754 election in place, the accounts look as follows:

Tax

	Assets		Liabilities
Parcel C	$250,000		–0–

			Equity
		Olivia	$225,000
		Paul	25,000
			250,000

Book

	Assets		Liabilities
Parcel C	$250,000		–0–

			Equity
		Olivia	$125,000
		Paul	125,000
			250,000

Note that, regardless of whether a Section 754 election is in place, there is no tax-book difference as to assets, but there is a tax-book difference in the partners' capital accounts. Some practitioners believe a special tax-only allocation should be available to eliminate the discrepancy. This allocation would increase Paul's tax on income from inside of the partnership because he took high-basis property outside of the partnership.[49] Others believe that, since the difference will have no tax or economic consequences per se (because it does not arise from a tax-book

48. 500,000 original basis plus $600,000 share of book gain triggered by distributing both properties less the $1 million value of the property received.

49. Note that this is not a Section 704(c) or a reverse Section 704(c) allocation as these allocations deal with allocating a tax-book difference on assets among the partners. Specifically, here a reverse Section 704(c) allocation would still allocate all gain on Parcel C 50–50.

difference with respect to an asset), a special allocation would not be appropriate. It is not obvious that Paul should be taxed on phantom income just because he took high-basis property. (This is the reverse of the previous example in many ways.)

Note the similarity in the 2 situations that trigger an inside basis adjustment under Section 734(b) (i.e., (i) when gain is taxed under Section 731(a)(1) because a cash distribution exceeds outside basis and (ii) when 732(a)(2) applies to limit basis in a distributed asset because the distributee lacks sufficient outside basis. Section 731(a)(1) taxes the cash distribution because otherwise there would be a negative basis in the partnership interest under Section 733. Section 732(a)(2) cuts back the basis of distributed property to avoid a negative partnership interest basis. In both cases, a partner is taking more than her share of inside basis, so that Section 734(b), when activated, steps in to create appropriate inside basis.

When multiple properties are distributed in a transaction subject to Section 732(a)(2), Section 732(c) prescribes how the total outside basis is to be allocated among the distributed properties. Read Section 732(c). The basic ideas are (i) to avoid tampering with the basis of ordinary income property as much as possible, and (ii) to write down assets with an unrealized loss before writing down other assets.[50] These rules are discussed in more detail in the next chapter, which deals with the liquidation of a partnership interest, where the distribution of multiple properties is more common than here with nonliquidating distributions.

REVIEW: Code § 732 and Reg. §§ 1.704–1(b)(2)(iv)(*l*)(4) and (*m*)(5), 1.734–1(e), and 1.755–1(c)

Problem Set VII.F

1. Zelda and Xavier are 50–50 partners in a debt-free partnership that has made a Section 754 election. The partnership's only material asset is a parcel of investment real estate with a basis of $200,000 and a value of $2.5 million. Each partner has an outside basis of $100,000. The partnership borrows $1 million dollars, using the land as security. Under the terms of the borrowing, Zelda is not liable on the debt. [Note that this is an unusual transaction.] The $1 million of borrowed cash is distributed—$500,000 to each partner. What are the tax consequences to each partner and the partnership?

2. Barb and Bob have been 50–50 partners for years. Each has a basis in her partnership interest of $500,000. The partnership has 2 assets: parcels of investment real estate. Parcel A has a basis of $100,000 and is worth $1.5 million. Parcel B has a basis of $900,000 and is worth $500,000. The partnership distributes Parcel B to Bob, reducing his

---

50. Section 731(c) also contains rules for basis write-ups, but these rules only come into play with regard to a liquidation of a partnership interest that is subject to Section 732(b), discussed in the next chapter, and not here, with regard to nonliquidating distributions subject to Section 732(a)(1).

interest to 1/3d and increasing Barb's to 2/3ds. What are the tax consequences to all parties?

G. DISTRIBUTIONS OF PROPERTY TO A TRANSFEREE OF A PARTNERSHIP INTEREST

Basis can present further problems, even in a pro-rata distribution, if the distributee acquired her interest from a partner and not from the partnership. Consider the pro-rata partnership between Ellen, Liz, and Eric, the original partners, all of whom contributed cash only. The partnership owns 6 properties, each with a basis of $50 and a value of $80. Ellen sells her interest to Emil for $160. Shortly thereafter, the partnership distributes one property to Emil, reducing his interest to 1/5th and increasing the interests of Liz and Eric to 2/5ths each. The distribution is tax-free. Emil's basis in the property is $50 and his outside basis is reduced $110. Thus, Emil owns property worth $80 with a basis of $50 and a partnership interest worth $80 with a basis of $110. Artificial built-in gain and loss has been manufactured by Sections 732 and 733.

Unfortunately, a Section 754 election does not solve the problem completely. Under Sections 743(b) and 755, Emil would have a $10 special basis adjustment in each of the partnership's 6 assets. Then, Sections 1.743–1(g)(1)(i) and (2)(i) of the regulations provide that, when an asset is distributed to a partner who has a special Section 743(b) basis adjustment with regard to that asset, that inside adjustment is reflected in determining the partner's basis in the asset under Section 732. Thus, if a Section 754 election is in place, Emil has property with a value of $80 and a basis of $60 and a partnership interest with a value of $80 and a basis of $100. Better, but still a problem.[51]

Finally, Section 732(d) can give a distributee a special basis adjustment with regard to the distributed property even if the partnership does not make a Section 754 election. Read Section 732(d). Congress, perhaps out of sympathy for a partnership not willing to commit to all of the complexities of a Section 754 election, or perhaps out of sympathy for a purchaser of a minority partnership interest who cannot get her partnership to make a Section 754 election, allows a purchaser of a partnership interest to elect treatment similar to that afforded by a partnership Section 754 election with regard to distributions made within 2 years of the interest purchase.[52]

In contrast to the pro-taxpayer election afforded by the first sentence of Section 732(d), the second sentence of Section 732(d) prevents taxpayer abuse (by the partnership not making a Section 754 election).

51. The regulations do provide a perfect fix if the distributee is completely liquidated, as to be discussed in the next chapter.

52. Section 743(b) can create basis that may be depreciated prior to the distribution, while Section 732(d) cannot. Treas. Reg. § 1.732–1(d)(1)(iv).

The second sentence of Section 732(d) authorizes Section 1.732–1(d)(4) of the regulations. Read it. Basically, Section 732(d)'s Section 743(b)-like basis adjustments apply for purposes of determining the bases of property distributed to a transferee of a partnership interest (regardless of how long after the transfer the distribution occurs) in a partnership with appreciated assets if the Section 743(b) basis adjustment would have had the effect that the depreciable property later distributed would have had a smaller basis to the distributee under Section 732. This mandatory feature of Section 732(d) was aimed at problems under an old version of Section 732(c), but can still apply today. It is most likely to come up in liquidating distributions, however. Thus, it is examined in more detail in the next chapter of this text.

REVIEW: Code § 732(d) and Reg. §§ 1.732–1(d)(1), –1(d)(4), and –2(b) and 1.743–1(g)

Problem Set VII.G

What would be the result for Emil in the example in the text if, right after Emil purchased his interest, the partnership distributed one property to each of the 3 partners?

Chapter VIII

LIQUIDATING DISTRIBUTIONS

A. INTRODUCTION

This chapter concludes the analysis of the basic provisions of Subchapter K with a review of the rules that apply with regard to distributions in complete liquidation of a partner.[1] There are 2 issues present in complete liquidation of a partner that are not presented in non-liquidating distributions. First, special rules are needed to properly tax the liquidated partner with regard to partnership income since (i) the liquidated partner will not be a partner at the end of the partnership's tax year, when normally its income flows out to the partners under Section 706(a), and (ii) a liquidating distribution may reflect payment for partnership income to be accounted for in the future under the partnership's accounting method, but the liquidated partner will not be a partner at the time that the partnership earns the income. Sections 706(c) and 736 deal with when and how a liquidated partner is taxed on partnership income. Second, any difference between the liquidated partner's inside and outside basis must be addressed at liquidation, if ever, since the liquidated partnership interest is disappearing. Sections 731 and 732 contain special rules for liquidating distributions that deal with this concern.

The same basic issues arise, and the same basic rules apply, regardless of whether the liquidated partner's involvement in the partnership is ending because she is leaving an ongoing enterprise or because the entire partnership is terminating. In this regard, Subchapter K is different from Subchapter C, which has separate rules for complete redemptions and corporate liquidations, although the separate corporate rules achieve similar results in the 2 contexts.

---

1. As noted above, Subchapter K generally treats a partner's interest as a unified whole. Here, Section 761(d) makes clear that a "liquidation" of a partnership interest is only its complete liquidation. For this reason, there is little tax difference between a partial redemption and an ordinary distribution. The principal difference is, as noted above in Chapter VI, that the Section 704(b) regulations "require" that, upon a partial redemption, the capital accounts be marked to market so that the built-in gain or loss at that time thereafter is allocated according to the reverse Section 704(c) methodology. Treas. Reg. § 1.704–1(b)(2)(iv)(*f*).

Subchapter K's partner liquidation rules have an aggregate-approach feature: the treatment of the liquidated partners depends upon both what is received and the composition of the partnership's other assets. Thus, these rules are quite complicated. To avoid having complexity in application distract from the simplicity of the underlying rules, it is best to develop the rules by examining their application, first, in the simplest context, and, then, in increasingly involved situations.

B. BACKGROUND: INTEREST SALE v. LIQUIDATION

READ: Code § 736

A partner can dispose of an entire interest in 2 ways, by having it liquidated or by transferring it to a third party. Ideally, there would be no tax difference between the two. But, under current law, there can be. Thus, there needs to be a way of distinguishing the two in hard cases. The trial court and appellate opinions in the same case below set out the basic tax concerns:

FOXMAN v. COMMISSIONER

United States Tax Court, 1964.
41 T.C. 535.

The principal issue is whether an agreement dated May 21, 1957, between petitioner Jacobowitz and petitioners Foxman and Grenell resulted in a "sale" of Jacobowitz's interest in a partnership to the two remaining partners under section 741, I.R.C. 1954, or whether the transaction must be considered a "liquidation" of Jacobowitz's partnership interest under sections 736 and 761(d).

FINDINGS OF FACT

Prior to 1954, Abbey Record Manufacturing Co. was a partnership composed of petitioner Jacobowitz and two associates named Zayde and Brody, engaged in the business of custom manufacturing of phonograph records. The enterprise had been founded about 1948, with Jacobowitz as the active principal. Prior to 1954 the partnership, hereinafter referred to as Abbey, manufactured primarily 10–inch 78 r.p.m. records on contract for various companies. Petitioner Grenell purchased the interests of Zayde and Brody on December 31, 1953, and became an equal partner with Jacobowitz on January 2, 1954. Early in 1954 the partners agreed to enter the business of manufacturing 12–inch long playing records, known as LPs. Petitioner Foxman, who had been a consultant to the business when it was originally formed in 1948, was hired as a salaried employee in June 1954 to provide the necessary technical assistance for the changeover in machinery and production methods. Thereafter, as a result of certain agreements dated February 1, 1955, and January 26, 1956, Foxman, Grenell, and Jacobowitz became equal partners in Abbey, each with a one-third interest.

A related venture commenced by Jacobowitz, Foxman, and Grenell, individually, was represented by Sound Plastics, Inc., a corporation in which each owned one-third of the stock; it was engaged in the business of manufacturing "biscuits" or vinyl forms used in the making of records.

During the early period of the changeover to LPs, Abbey faced many problems in production and quality control. However, with Foxman and Jacobowitz in charge of production and with Grenell responsible for much of the selling, Abbey's fortunes were on the upswing. Its net income for the fiscal year ending February 29, 1956, was approximately $108,000, and for the fiscal year ending February 28, 1957, was approximately $218,000. Grenell, who acted as consultant and repertory director for two mail-order record companies, Music Treasures of the World and Children's Record Guild, was able to get these companies as customers of Abbey and they accounted for approximately 50–75 percent of Abbey's business.

Notwithstanding Abbey's success there was considerable disharmony among and between the partners. As a result there were discussions during the spring of 1956 relating to the withdrawal of Jacobowitz from Abbey. These negotiations did not lead to any agreement and the partners continued to work and to quarrel. Early in 1957, Foxman and Grenell decided to resolve the conflict by continuing the partnership without Jacobowitz and discussions were resumed again in March 1957. It was at about this time that Foxman offered Jacobowitz $225,000 in cash, an automobile which was in Abbey's name, and Foxman's and Grenell's interest in Sound Plastics, Inc. for Jacobowitz's interest in Abbey. Jacobowitz prepared a draft of an option agreement providing for Foxman's purchase of his one-third interest in the partnership and sent it to Foxman. Foxman never signed the option agreement. During the latter part of March or early April 1957, the negotiations of the three partners led to a tentative agreement whereby Jacobowitz's partnership interest would be purchased for $225,000 plus the aforementioned auto and stock in Sound Plastics, Inc. Jacobowitz, who did not trust either Foxman or Grenell, initially desired cash. Foxman and Grenell explored the possibilities of a $200,000 bank loan from the First National Bank of Jersey City, hereinafter referred to as First National, and informed First National of their tentative agreement to buy Jacobowitz's interest for $225,000; they had further discussions with First National concerning a possible loan on May 1, 1957, and on May 3, 1957. First National indicated, on the basis of an examination of the financial assets of Abbey, that it would consider a loan of approximately only $50,000.

The negotiations of the three partners culminated in an agreement dated May 21, 1957, for the "sale" of Jacobowitz's partnership interest; the terms of this agreement were essentially the same terms as the terms of the option agreement which Foxman did not execute.

Relevant portions of the May 21, 1957, agreement are as follows:

Agreement, made this 21st day of May 1957, between Norman B. Jacobowitz, hereinafter referred to as the "First Party", and Horace W. Grenell, and David A. Foxman, individually, jointly and severally, hereinafter referred to as the "Second Parties" and Abbey Record Mfg. Co., hereinafter referred to as the "Third Party", Witnesseth:

Whereas, the parties hereto are equal owners and the sole partners of Abbey Record Mfg. Co., a partnership, hereinafter referred to as "Abbey", and are also the sole stockholders, officers and directors of Sound Plastics Inc., a corporation organized under the laws of the State of New York; and

Whereas, the first party is desirous of selling, conveying, transferring and assigning all of his right, title and interest in and to his one-third share and interest in the said Abbey to the second parties; and

Whereas, the second parties are desirous of conveying, transferring and assigning all of their right, title and interest in and to their combined two-thirds shares and interest in Sound Plastics, Inc. to the first party;

Now, Therefore, it is Mutually Agreed as Follows:

First: The second parties hereby purchase all the right, title, share and interest of the first party in Abbey and the first party does hereby sell, transfer, convey and assign all of his right, title, interest and share in Abbey and in the moneys in banks, trade names, accounts due, or to become due, and in all other assets of any kind whatsoever, belonging to said Abbey, for and in consideration of the following:

A) The payment of the sum of two hundred forty two thousand five hundred & fifty ($242,550.00) dollars, payable as follows:

$67,500.00, on the signing of this agreement, the receipt of which is hereby acknowledged;

$67,500.00 on January 2nd, 1958;

$90,000.00 in eighteen (18) equal monthly installments of $5,000.00 each, commencing on February 1st, 1958 and continuing on the first day of each and every consecutive month thereafter for seventeen (17) months;

$17,550.00, for services as a consultant, payable in seventy-eight (78) equal weekly installments of $225.00 each, commencing on February 1st, 1958 and continuing weekly on the same day of each and every consecutive week thereafter for seventy-seven (77) weeks.

The balance set forth hereinabove is represented by a series of non-interest bearing promissory notes, bearing even date herewith, and contain an acceleration clause and a grace period of ten (10) days.

Said balance is further secured by a chattel mortgage, bearing even date herewith and contains a provision that same shall be cancelled and discharged upon the payment of the sum of $67,500.00 on or before January 2nd, 1958.

The right is hereby granted to the second parties to prepay all or part of the balance due to the first party. If prepayment is made of both of the sums of $67,500.00 and $90,000.00 set forth above, prior to February 1st, 1958, there shall be no further liability for the balance of $17,550.00 or any of the payments of $225.00 weekly required thereunder. If such prepayment is made after February 1st, 1958, the first party shall be entitled to retain payments made to date of payment of the full sums of $67,500.00 and $90,000.00 (plus any weekly payments as aforesaid to date of payment) and there shall be no further liability for any remaining weekly payments.

B) In addition to the payments required under paragraph "A" hereof, the second parties hereby transfer, convey and assign all of their right, title and interest in Sound Plastics, Inc. to the first party. Simultaneously herewith, the second parties have delivered duly executed transfers of certificates of stock, together with their resignations as officers and directors of said Sound Plastics, Inc. Receipt thereof by the first party is hereby acknowledged.

C) In addition to the payments required under paragraph "A" hereof and the transfer of stock referred to in paragraph "B" hereof, the second parties hereby transfer, convey and assign all of their right, title and interest in and to one, 1956 Chrysler New Yorker Sedan, as evidenced by the transfer of registration thereof, duly executed herewith, the receipt of which by the first party is hereby acknowledged.

Second: So long as a balance remains due to the first party, the second parties agree to continue the partnership of Abbey and each of the second parties agree to devote the same time, energy, effort, ability, endeavors and attention to furthering the business of said Abbey and to promote its success as heretofore and will not engage in any other business or effort, except that Horace W. Grenell shall be permitted to continue to create master records for other persons or companies.

The second parties further agree not to substantially change the form of business, engage in a new business, assign or transfer any of the assets or the lease of Abbey, without the written consent of the first party, unless such new business and/or assignee and/or transferee, by an agreement in writing, assumes all the obligations, terms, covenants and conditions of this agreement and delivers such assumption agreement to the first party in person or by registered mail, within five (5) days from the date of the commencement of such new business and/or assignment and/or transfer. It is expressly understood and agreed that such assumption agreement shall in no wise release the second parties from any of their obligations hereunder.

* * *

Fourth: All parties do hereby agree that the true and accurate status of Abbey and Sound Plastics, Inc. as to liabilities and assets are reflected in the balance sheets attached hereto and made a part hereof and represent the true condition of the companies as of March 1, 1957. *First party shall not be entitled to any further share of profits that may accrue since March 1, 1957 and may retain any sums received therefrom to date hereof.* [Italicized words inserted by hand.]

Fifth: Except as herein otherwise expressly provided, the second parties do hereby forever release and discharge the first party from any and all liability of whatsoever nature, description, character or kind arising out of any transaction or matter connected directly or indirectly between themselves or in connection with Abbey and/or Sound Plastics, Inc.

* * *

Eleventh: The second parties agree that they will forever indemnify and save the first party, free, clear and harmless of and from all debts, taxes (other than personal income taxes) claims, damages or expenses, upon, or in consequence of any debt, claim or liability, of whatsoever kind or nature due or claimed by any creditor to be due from Abbey and/or the first party, by reason of the first party having been a member of the partnership of Abbey, except as set forth in paragraphs "Eighth" and "Fourth" hereof. The first party likewise agrees that he will forever indemnify and save the second parties, free, clear and harmless of and from all debts, taxes (other than personal income taxes) claims, damages or expenses, upon, or in consequence of any debt, claim or liability of whatsoever kind or nature due or claimed by any creditor to be due from Sound Plastics, Inc., and/or the second parties, by reason of the second parties having been stockholders, officers and directors of said corporation, except as provided in paragraph "Fourth" hereof.

Paragraph Twelfth of the agreement provides that "The first party [Jacobowitz] hereby retires from the partnership." The part of the agreement designating payment of $17,550 in weekly installments of $225 per week found in paragraph "First: A)" was embodied in a separate document also dated May 21, 1957; it was signed by Abbey, Foxman, and Grenell, respectively.

The chattel mortgage mentioned in "First A)" of the agreement, in describing the translation provided for in the agreement of May 21, 1957, stated in part:

the party of the second part [Jacobowitz] has sold, transferred, assigned and conveyed all his right, title and interest as a partner

* * * to the parties of the first part [Foxman and Grenell, individually and trading as Abbey].

Samuel Feldman, a New York City attorney who represented Foxman and Grenell, drafted the agreement of May 21, 1957; at Feldman's suggestion, Abbey was added as a party to the agreement. An earlier draft of the proposed agreement did not include Abbey as a party. During the negotiations leading to the May 21, 1957, agreement, the words "retirement" or "liquidation of a partner's interest" were not mentioned. There was no specific undertaking by the third party (Abbey) any place in the instrument. A sale of a partnership interest was the only transaction ever discussed.

Jacobowitz unsuccessfully tried to obtain guarantees of payment of the notes he held from the wives of Foxman and Grenell; he was also unsuccessful in trying to obtain the homes of Foxman and Grenell as security on the notes.

The first $67,500 payment due on the signing of the agreement was made by cashier's check. On the promissory note due January 2, 1958, the name of Abbey appears as maker; the signatures of Foxman and Grenell appear on the face of the note as signatories in behalf of Abbey and on the back of it as indorsers. The 18 promissory notes, each in the amount of $5,000, also bear the signatures of Foxman and Grenell on the face of the instrument as signatories in behalf of Abbey, the maker, and on the back of the instrument as indorsers.

Payments to Jacobowitz pursuant to the May 21, 1957, agreement were timely made. Foxman and Grenell made an election to prepay pursuant to "First A)" of the May 21, 1957, agreement, and Jacobowitz returned the series of 18 promissory notes of Abbey, in the amount of $5,000 each, and the promissory note of Abbey in the amount of $17,550 payable in 78 weekly installments of $225. Jacobowitz was paid this $90,000 amount by check with Abbey's name appearing as drawer and the names of Foxman and Grenell appearing as signatories in behalf of Abbey; they did not indorse this check. Payments made to Jacobowitz for his interest were charged to Abbey's account. The parties did not contemplate any performance of services by Jacobowitz in order for him to receive the $17,550 under the May 21, 1957, agreement; this amount was considered by the parties either as a penalty or in lieu of interest if Foxman and Grenell failed to pay the $90,000 amount prior to February 1, 1958.

Just prior to May 21, 1957, Abbey borrowed $9,000 from each of four savings banks and also borrowed $9,000 from Foxman and Grenell. On December 27, 1957, Abbey borrowed $75,000 from First National.

Abbey had no adjusted basis for goodwill as of February 28, 1957, nor at any time subsequent thereto. The balance sheets of Abbey for its fiscal years ending February 28, 1957, and February 28, 1958, do not reflect an account for goodwill. The balance sheet of Abbey as of February 28, 1957, was as follows:

Assets

Cash	$63,702.30
Notes and accounts receivable	141,521.88
Inventories	16,630.73
Buildings and other fixed depreciable assets:	
(a) Less: Accumulated depreciation and amortization	73,803.91
Other assets	6,176.91
Total assets	301,835.73

Liabilities and Capital

Accounts and notes payable	97,365.55
Partners' capital accounts	204,470.18
Total liabilities and capital	301,835.73

On May 21, 1957, Foxman and Grenell entered into an agreement providing for a continuation of the Abbey partnership which recited that Abbey had purchased the interest of Jacobowitz in Abbey.

After May 21, 1957, the date of Jacobowitz's termination of his interest in Abbey, improvements were made at Abbey's plant.

The reported earnings of Abbey for the fiscal year ending February 28, 1958, without reduction for alleged payments to partners, were $303,221.52.

In its tax return for the fiscal year ending February 28, 1958, Abbey treated the sum of $159,656.09 as a distribution of partnership earnings to Jacobowitz in the nature of a guaranteed payment under section 736 of the Internal Revenue Code of 1954. This amount was computed as follows:

Cash payments	$225,000.00
Value of automobile	2,812.82
Share of Jacobowitz's liabilities	32,455.18
Total partnership payments	260,268.00
Less Jacobowitz's share of partnership property	100,611.91
Balance	159,656.09

Jacobowitz, on the other hand, treated the transaction as a sale in his return for 1957, reporting a long-term capital gain in the amount of $164,356.09.

OPINION

RAUM, *Judge*:

1. *Tax consequences of termination of Jacobowitz's interest in Abbey; the agreement of May 21, 1957.*—On May 21, 1957, Jacobowitz's

status as a partner in Abbey came to an end pursuant to an agreement executed on that day. The first issue before us is whether Jacobowitz thus made a "sale" of his partnership interest to Foxman and Grenell within section 741 of the 1954 Code, as contended by him, or whether the payments to him required by the agreement are to be regarded as "made in liquidation" of his interest within section 736, as contended by Foxman and Grenell. Jacobowitz treated the transaction as constituting a "sale," and reported a capital gain thereon in his return for 1957.[2] Foxman and Grenell, on the other hand, treated the payments as having been "made in liquidation" of Jacobowitz's interest under section 736, with the result that a substantial portion thereof reduced their distributive shares of partnership income for the fiscal year ending February 28, 1958.[3]

The Commissioner, in order to protect the revenues, took inconsistent positions. In Jacobowitz's case, his determination proceeded upon the assumption that there was a section 736 "liquidation," with the result that payments thereunder were charged to Jacobowitz for the partnership fiscal year ending February 28, 1958, thus not only attributing to Jacobowitz additional income for his calendar year 1958 but also treating it as ordinary income rather than capital gain. In the cases of Foxman and Grenell, the Commissioner adopted Jacobowitz's position that there was a section 741 "sale" on May 21, 1957, to Foxman and Grenell, thus disallowing the deductions in respect thereof from the partnership's income for its fiscal year ending February 28, 1958; as a consequence, there was a corresponding increase in the distributive partnership income of Foxman and Grenell for that fiscal year which was reflected in the deficiencies determined for the calendar year 1958 in respect of each of them.

As is obvious, the real controversy herein is not between the various petitioners and the Government, but rather between Jacobowitz and his two former partners. We hold, in favor of Jacobowitz, that the May 21, 1957, transaction was a "sale."

The provisions of sections 736 and 741 of the 1954 Code have no counterpart in prior law. They are contained in "Subchapter K" which for the first time, in 1954, undertook to deal comprehensively with the income tax problems of partners and partnerships.

That a partnership interest may be "sold" to one or more members of the partnership within section 741 is not disputed by any of the parties.

Did Jacobowitz *sell* his interest to Foxman and Grenell, or did he merely enter into an arrangement to receive "payments * * * in liqui-

---

2. [Editor's Note: At that time, Section 453 would not apply if more than 30% of the payments (including the stock and the car) were received in the first year.]

3. [Editor's Note: As discussed in Section VIII.D of this text, below, prior to 1993, Section 736 provided that many payments in liquidation were treated as guaranteed payments or as an allocation and distribution. The old law is summarized in the Tax Court's Note 7, reprinted below.]

dation of [his] * * * interest" from the partnership? We think the record establishes that he sold his interest.

At first blush, one may indeed wonder why Congress provided for such drastically different tax consequences, depending upon whether the amounts received by the withdrawing partner are to be classified as the proceeds of a "sale" or as "payments * * * in liquidation" of his interest.[4] For, there may be very little, if any, difference in ultimate economic effect between a "sale" of a partnership interest to the remaining partners and a "liquidation" of that interest. In the case of a sale the remaining partners may well obtain part or all of the needed cash to pay the purchase price from the partnership assets, funds borrowed by the partnership or future earnings of the partnership. Yet the practical difference between such transaction and one in which the withdrawing partner agrees merely to receive payments in liquidation directly from the partnership itself would hardly be a meaningful one in most circumstances.[5] Why then the enormous disparity in tax burden, turning upon what for practical purposes is merely the difference between Tweedledum and Tweedledee, and what criteria are we to apply in our effort to discover that difference in a particular case? The answer to the first part of this question is to be found in the legislative history of subchapter K, and it goes far towards supplying the answer to the second part.

In its report on the bill which became the 1954 Code the House Ways and Means Committee stated that the then "existing tax treatment of partners and partnerships is among the most confused in the entire tax field"; that "partners * * * cannot form, operate, or dissolve a partnership with any assurance as to tax consequences"; that the proposed statutory provisions [subchapter K] represented the "first comprehensive statutory treatment of partners and partnerships in the history of the income tax laws"; and that the "principal objectives have been simplicity, flexibility, and equity as between the partners." H. Rept.

---

4. [Court's note 7:] If the transaction were a "sale" under section 741, Jacobowitz's gain would be taxed as capital gain (there being no section 751 problem in respect of unrealized receivables or inventory items which have appreciated substantially in value), and would be reportable in 1957 rather than in 1958. On the other hand, if the transaction were a section 736 "liquidation," the amounts received by him (to the extent that they were not for his "interest * * * in partnership property" pursuant to section 736(b)(1)) would be taxable as ordinary income and would be reportable by him in 1958, rather than in 1957. [Editor's Note: This is explained in Section VIII.D of this text, below.] The tax liabilities of the remaining partners, Foxman and Grenell, would be affected accordingly, depending upon whether section 736 or 741 governed the transaction

5. [Court's Note 8:] The only difference suggested by counsel for Foxman and Grenell, for the first time in their reply brief, is that in the event of bankruptcy of the partnership the liability to the withdrawing partner might be subject to a different order of priority depending upon whether there is involved the liability of the partnership itself, as in the case of a "liquidation," or the liability of the purchasing partners, as in the case of a "sale." However, it stretches credulity to the breaking point to assume that any such consideration motivated the parties in determining to enter into a "sale" rather than a "liquidation," or vice versa, where the only immediate matter of economic consequence was the substantial difference in tax liability depending upon which course was followed.

No. 1337, 83d Cong., 2d Sess., p. 65. Like thoughts were expressed in virtually identical language by the Senate Finance Committee. S. Rept. No. 1622, 83d Cong., 2d Sess., p. 89.

Although there can be little doubt that the attempt to achieve "simplicity" has resulted in utter failure,[6] the new legislation was intended to and in fact did bring into play an element of "flexibility." Tax law in respect of partners may often involve a delicate mechanism, for a ruling in favor of one partner may automatically produce adverse consequences to the others. Accordingly, one of the underlying philosophic objectives of the 1954 Code was to permit the partners themselves to determine their tax burdens *inter sese* to a certain extent, and this is what the committee reports meant when they referred to "flexibility." The theory was that the partners would take their prospective tax liabilities into account in bargaining with one another.[7] Nor is this concept before us for the first time. We considered it in the interpretation of some related provisions of section 736 in *V. Zay Smith*, 37 T.C. 1033, affirmed 313 F.2d 16 (C.A. 10), involving payments in respect of goodwill in the liquidation of a partner's interest. We there said (37 T.C. at 1038):

> This interpretation will also make for the flexibility and equity between the partners stressed by Congress. It will allow the partners flexibility in that they may determine the tax consequences of a liquidation payment by the choice of words in the partnership agreement. * * *

Recurring to the problem immediately before us, this policy of "flexibility" is particularly pertinent in determining the tax consequences of the withdrawal of a partner. Where the practical differences between a "sale" and a "liquidation" are, at most, slight, if they exist at all, and where the tax consequences to the partners can vary greatly, it is in accord with the purpose of the statutory provisions to allow the partners themselves, through arm's-length negotiations, to determine whether to take the "sale" route or the "liquidation" route, thereby allocating the tax burden among themselves.[8] And in this case the record

6. [Court's Note 9:] The distressingly complex and confusing nature of the provisions of subchapter K present a formidable obstacle to the comprehension of these provisions without the expenditure of a disproportionate amount of time and effort even by one who is sophisticated in tax matters with many years of experience in the tax field. If there should be any lingering doubt on this matter one has only to reread section 736 in its entirety and give an honest answer to the question whether it is reasonably comprehensible to the average lawyer or even to the average tax expert who has not given special attention and extended study to the tax problems of partners. Surely, a statute has not achieved "simplicity" when its complex provisions may confidently be dealt with by at most only a compara-tively small number of specialists who have been initiated into its mysteries.

7. [Court's Note 10:] Whether this was a realistic assumption in view of the large number of small partnerships that may not have the benefit of the highly specialized tax advice required, or whether, in view of the almost incomprehensible character of some of the provisions in subchapter K, the parties could with confidence allocate the tax burden among themselves—these are matters on which we express no opinion. The point is that Congress did intend to provide a certain amount of "flexibility" in this respect.

8. [Court's Note 11:] See S. Rept. No. 1616, 86th Cong., 2d Sess., in respect of the proposed "Trust and Partnership Income Tax Revision Act of 1960" (H.R. 9662):

leaves no doubt that they intended to and in fact did adopt the "sale" route.[9]

The agreement of May 21, 1957, indicates a clear intention on the part of Jacobowitz to sell, and Foxman and Grenell to purchase, Jacobowitz's partnership interest. The second "whereas" clause refers to Jacobowitz as "selling" his interest and part "First" of the agreement explicitly states not only that the "second parties [Foxman and Grenell] hereby purchase * * * the * * * interest of * * * [Jacobowitz] * * * in Abbey," but also that "the first party [Jacobowitz] does hereby sell" his interest in Abbey. Thus, Foxman and Grenell obligated themselves *individually* to purchase Jacobowitz's interest. Nowhere in the agreement was there any obligation on the part of Abbey to compensate Jacobowitz for withdrawing from the partnership. Indeed, a portion of the consideration received by him was the Sound Plastics stock, not a partnership asset at all. That stock was owned by Foxman and Grenell as individuals and their undertaking to turn it over to Jacobowitz as part of the consideration for Jacobowitz's partnership interest reinforces the conclusion that *they as individuals* were buying his interest, and that the transaction represented a "sale" of his interest to them rather than a "liquidation" of that interest by the partnership. Moreover, the chattel mortgage referred to in part "First" of the agreement of May 21, 1957, states that Jacobowitz "has sold * * * his * * * interest as a partner."

In addition to the foregoing, we are satisfied from the evidence before us that Foxman and Grenell knew that Jacobowitz was interested only in a sale of his partnership interest. The record convincingly establishes that the bargaining between them was consistently upon the basis of a proposed sale. And the agreement of May 21, 1957, which represents the culmination of that bargaining, reflects that understanding with unambiguous precision. The subsequent position of Foxman and Grenell, disavowing a "sale," indicates nothing more than an attempt at hindsight tax planning to the disadvantage of Jacobowitz.

Foxman and Grenell argue that Jacobowitz looked only to Abbey for payment, that he was in fact paid by Abbey, that there was "in substance" a liquidation of his interest, and that these considerations should be controlling in determining whether section 736 or section 741 applies. But their contention is not well taken.

"under present law even though there is no economic difference it is possible for partners to arrange different tax effects for the disposition of the interest of a retiring or deceased partner, merely by casting the transaction as a sale rather than a liquidating distribution (p. 76).

" * * * Under present law, if the transaction is in the form of a sale of an interest, then section 741 (rather than section 730) would govern, even though the interest of the selling partner is transferred to the other member of a two-man partnership (p. 103)."

9. [Court's Note 12:] In *Bolling v. Patterson*, ___ F. Supp. ___ (N.D.Ala.), 7 A.F.T.R. 2d 1464, 1465, 61–1 U.S.T.C. par. 9417, the judge, in his charge to the jury, instructed it that the one question it must answer is did "the partners * * * intend to liquidate Ramsey's interest in the partnership or did the two partners * * * intend to buy and did Ramsey intend to sell * * * his partnership interest."

Jacobowitz distrusted Foxman and Grenell and wanted all the security he could get; he asked for, but did not receive, guarantees from their wives and mortgages on their homes. Obviously, the assets of Abbey and its future earnings were of the highest importance to Jacobowitz as security that Foxman and Grenell would carry out their part of the bargain. But the fact remains that the payments received by Jacobowitz were in discharge of their obligation under the agreement, and not that of Abbey. It was they who procured those payments in their own behalf from the assets of the partnership which they controlled. The use of Abbey to make payment was wholly within their discretion and of no concern to Jacobowitz; his only interest was payment. The terms of the May 21, 1957, agreement did not obligate Abbey to pay Jacobowitz.

Nor is their position measurably stronger by reason of the fact that Jacobowitz was given promissory notes signed in behalf of Abbey. These notes were endorsed by Foxman and Grenell individually, and the liability of Abbey thereon was merely in the nature of security for their primary obligation under the agreement of May 21, 1957. The fact that they utilized partnership resources to discharge their own individual liability in such manner can hardly convert into a section 736 "liquidation" what would otherwise qualify as a section 741 "sale." It is important to bear in mind the object of "flexibility" which Congress attempted to attain, and we should be slow to give a different meaning to the arrangement which the partners entered into among themselves than that which the words of their agreement fairly spell out. Otherwise, the reasonable expectations of the partners in arranging their tax burdens *inter sese* would come to naught, and the purpose of the statute would be defeated. While we do not suggest that it is never possible to look behind the words of an agreement in dealing with problems like the one before us, the considerations which Foxman and Grenell urge us to take into account here are at best of an ambiguous character and are in any event consistent with the words used. We hold that the Commissioner's determination in respect of this issue was in error in Jacobowitz's case but was correct in the cases involving Foxman and Grenell.

The "flexibility" notion in Judge Raum's opinion has given many tax planners considerable comfort. Even today, lawyers rely on this analysis to conclude that *Gregory v. Helvering*[10] does not apply to Subchapter K, and, therefore, that the anti-abuse regulations are invalid. With this in mind, it is useful to see what the appeals court in *Foxman* itself did with the flexibility notion.

10.   293 U.S. 465, 55 S.Ct. 266, 79 L.Ed. 596 (1935).

FOXMAN v. COMMISSIONER

United States Court of Appeals for the Third Circuit, 1965.
352 F.2d 466.

WILLIAM F. SMITH, Circuit Judge.

This matter is before the Court on petitions to review decisions of the Tax Court, 41 T.C. 535, in three related cases consolidated for the purpose of hearing. The petitions of Foxman and Grenell challenge the decision as erroneous only as it relates to them. The petition of the Commissioner seeks a review of the decision as it relates to Jacobowitz only if it is determined by us that the Tax Court erred in the other two cases.

The cases came before the Tax Court on stipulations of fact, numerous written exhibits and the conflicting testimony of several witnesses, including the taxpayers. The relevant and material facts found by the Tax Court are fully detailed in its opinion. We repeat only those which may contribute to an understanding of the narrow issue before us.

As the result of agreements reached in February of 1955, and January of 1956, Foxman, Grenell and Jacobowitz became equal partners in a commercial enterprise which was then trading under the name of Abbey Record Manufacturing Company, hereinafter identified as the Company. They also became equal shareholders in a corporation known as Sound Plastics, Inc. When differences of opinion arose in the spring of 1956, efforts were made to persuade Jacobowitz to withdraw from the partnership. These efforts failed at that time but were resumed in March of 1957. Thereafter the parties entered into negotiations which, on May 21, 1957, culminated in a contract for the acquisition of Jacobowitz's interest in the partnership of Foxman and Grenell. The terms and conditions, except one not here material, were substantially in accord with an option to purchase offered earlier to Foxman and Grenell. The relevant portions of the final contract are set forth in the Tax Court's opinion.

The contract, prepared by an attorney representing Foxman and Grenell, referred to them as the "Second Party," and to Jacobowitz as the "First Party." We regard as particularly pertinent to the issue before us the following clauses:

> "WHEREAS, the parties hereto are equal owners and the sole partners of ABBEY RECORD MFG. Co., a partnership, * * *, and are also the sole stockholders, officers and directors of SOUND PLASTICS, INC., a corporation organized under the laws of the State of New York; and

> "WHEREAS, the first party is desirous of selling, conveying, transferring and assigning all of his right, title and interest in and to his one-third share and interest in the said ABBEY to the second parties; and

> "WHEREAS, the second parties are desirous of conveying, transferring and assigning all of their right, title and interest in and to their combined two-thirds shares and interest in SOUND PLASTICS, INC., to the first party;

"NOW, THEREFORE, IT IS MUTUALLY AGREED AS FOLLOWS:

"First: The second parties hereby purchase all the right, title, share and interest of the first party in ABBEY and the first party does hereby sell, transfer, convey and assign all of his right, title, interest and share in ABBEY and in the moneys in banks, trade names, accounts due, or to become due, and in all other assets of any kind whatsoever, belonging to said ABBEY, for and in consideration of the following. * * * "

The stated consideration was cash in the sum of $242,500; the assignment by Foxman and Grenell of their stock in Sound Plastics; and the transfer of an automobile, title to which was held by the Company. The agreement provided for the payment of $67,500 upon consummation of the contract and payment of the balance as follows: $67,500 on January 2, 1958, and $90,000 in equal monthly installments, payable on the first of each month after January 30, 1958. This balance was evidenced by a series of promissory notes, payment of which was secured by a chattel mortgage on the assets of the Company. This mortgage, like the contract, referred to a sale by Jacobowitz of his partnership interest to Foxman and Grenell. The notes were executed in the name of the Company as the purported maker and were signed by Foxman and Grenell, who also endorsed them under a guarantee of payment.

The down payment of $67,500 was by a cashier's check which was issued in exchange for a check drawn on the account of the Company. The first note, in the amount of $67,500, which became due on January 2, 1958, was timely paid by a check drawn on the Company's account. Pursuant to the terms of an option reserved to Foxman and Grenell, they elected to prepay the balance of $90,000 on January 28, 1958, thereby relieving themselves of an obligation to pay Jacobowitz a further $17,550, designated in the contract as a consultant's fee. They delivered to Jacobowitz a cashier's check which was charged against the account of the Company.

In its partnership return for the fiscal year ending February 28, 1958, the Company treated the sum of $159,656.09, the consideration received by Jacobowitz less the value of his interest in partnership property, as a guaranteed payment made in liquidation of a retiring partner's interest under § 736(a)(2). This treatment resulted in a substantial reduction of the distributive shares of Foxman and Grenell and consequently a proportionate decrease in their possible tax liability. In his income tax return Jacobowitz treated the sum of $164,356.09, the consideration less the value of his partnership interest, as a long term capital gain realized upon the sale of his interest. This, of course, resulted in a tax advantage favorable to him. The Commissioner determined deficiencies against each of the taxpayers in amounts not relevant to the issue before us and each filed separate petitions for redetermination.

The critical issue before the Tax Court was raised by the antithetical positions maintained by Foxman and Grenell on one side and Jacobowitz on the other. The former, relying on § 736(a)(2), supra, contended that the transaction, evidenced by the contract, constituted a liquidation of a retiring partner's interest and that the consideration paid was accorded correct treatment in the partnership return. The latter contended that the transaction constituted a sale of his partnership interest and, under § 741 of the Code, the profit realized was correctly treated in his return as a capital gain. The Tax Court rejected the position of Foxman and Grenell and held that the deficiency determinations as to them were not erroneous; it sustained the position of Jacobowitz and held that the deficiency determination as to him was erroneous. The petitioners Foxman and Grenell challenge that decision as erroneous and not in accord with the law.

It appears from the evidence, which the Tax Court apparently found credible, that the negotiations which led to the consummation of the contract of May 21, 1957, related to a contemplated sale of Jacobowitz's partnership interest to Foxman and Grenell. The option offered to Foxman and Grenell early in May of 1957, referred to a sale and the execution of "a bill of sale" upon completion of the agreement. The relevant provisions of the contract were couched in terms of "purchase" and "sale." The contract was signed by Foxman and Grenell, individually, and by them on behalf of the Company, although the Company assumed no liability thereunder. The obligation to purchase Jacobowitz's interest was solely that of Foxman and Grenell. The chattel mortgage on the partnership assets was given to secure payment.

Notwithstanding these facts and the lack of any ambiguity in the contract, Foxman and Grenell argue that the factors unequivocally determinative of the substance of the transaction were: the initial payment of $67,500 by a cashier's check issued in exchange for a check drawn on the account of the Company; the second payment in a similar amount by check drawn on the Company's account; the execution of notes in the name of the Company as maker; and, the prepayment of the notes by cashier's check charged against the Company's account.

This argument unduly emphasizes form in preference to substance. While form may be relevant "the incidence of taxation depends upon the substance of a transaction." *Commissioner of Internal Revenue v. Court Holding Co.*, 324 U.S. 331, 334, 65 S. Ct. 707, 708, 89 L. Ed. 981 (1945); *United States v. Cumberland Pub. Serv. Co.*, 338 U.S. 451, 455, 70 S. Ct. 280, 94 L. Ed. 251 (1950). The "transaction must be viewed as a whole, and each step, from the commencement of negotiations" to consummation, is relevant. Ibid. Where, as here, there has been a transfer and an acquisition of property pursuant to a contract, the nature of the transaction does not depend solely on the means employed to effect payment. Ibid.

It is apparent from the opinion of the Tax Court that careful consideration was given to the factors relied upon by Foxman and Grenell. It is therein stated, 41 T.C. at page 553:

"These notes were endorsed by Foxman and Grenell individually, and the liability of [the Company] thereon was merely in the nature of security for their primary obligation under the agreement of May 21, 1957. The fact that they utilized partnership resources to discharge their own individual liability in such manner can hardly convert into a section 736 'liquidation' what would otherwise qualify as a section 741 'sale'."

* * * "* * * the payments received by Jacobowitz were in discharge of their [Foxman's and Grenell's] obligation under the agreement, and not that of [the Company.] It was they who procured those payments in their own behalf from the assets of the partnership which they controlled. The use of [the Company] to make payment was wholly within their discretion and of no concern to Jacobowitz; his only interest was payment."

We are of the opinion that the quoted statements represent a fair appraisal of the true significance of the notes and the means employed to effect payment.

When the members of the partnership decided that Jacobowitz would withdraw in the interest of harmony they had a choice of means by which his withdrawal could be effected. They could have agreed inter se on either liquidation or sale. On a consideration of the plain language of the contract, the negotiations which preceded its consummation, the intent of the parties as reflected by their conduct, and the circumstances surrounding the transaction, the Tax Court found that the transaction was in substance a sale and not a liquidation of a retiring partner's interest. This finding is amply supported by the evidence in the record. The partners having employed the sale method to achieve their objective, Foxman and Grenell cannot avoid the tax consequences by a hindsight application of principles they now find advantageous to them and disadvantageous to Jacobowitz.

The issue before the Tax Court was essentially one of fact and its decision thereon may not be reversed in the absence of a showing that its findings were not supported by substantial evidence or that its decision was not in accord with the law. There has been no such showing in this case.

The decisions of the Tax Court will be affirmed.

It is worth reflecting on the policy problem underlying *Foxman* for a moment. There are 3 related situations: (i) a partner continuing with her partnership, (ii) a partner selling her interest in her partnership, and (iii) a partner having her interest completely liquidated by her partnership. Ideally, the tax law should not favor one of the 3 over the other 2. Unfortunately, it is impossible to make matters work perfectly. The characterization of a transaction affects tax outcomes. How characterization is to be done—in general and, specifically, in Subchapter K—is not clear. At one extreme is Judge Raum's flexibility notion: The parties should be free to allocate the tax liabilities among themselves as long as total revenues are not impacted. At the other extreme is substance-over-form doctrine, which endeavors to discern the substance of a transaction, regardless of how cast by the parties, and tax the transaction accordingly, as discussed by the Third Circuit in *Foxman*. In between these 2 extreme ways of characterizing a transaction for tax purposes, the business purpose requirement respects form as long as supported by some requisite connection to a non-tax purpose. And, of course, shams are not respected for tax purposes. All of this is revisited below in Chapter XI's discussion of the anti-abuse regulations.

One situation where it seems that all of this doctrine failed the tax law was presented in *Comsat*, discussed in Section VII.B of this text, above. There, the parties were able to structure a partial disposition of a partnership interest so as to reduce the total taxes of all involved. Congress responded with Section 707(a)(2)(B). It is not clear if Section 707(a)(2)(B) has reversed *Foxman* on its facts.

C.　THE EASIEST CASE

READ: Code §§ 706(c), 731(a), 734, 752(b), and 761(d) and Reg. § 1.736–1(b)(6)

SKIM: Code §§ 732, 736, and 751(b)

With *Foxman* as background, it is time to begin the analysis of the complete liquidation of a partner. Most of the complexity here arises (i) from the rules in Section 732 for non-cash property distributions, (ii) from the rules in Section 736 for service partnerships (partnerships in which capital is not a material income-producing factor), and (iii) from the rules in Section 751(b) for non-pro-rata distributions by partnerships that own unrealized receivables and substantially appreciated inventory. Thus, it is best to start simply, by looking at a situation that does not involve these 3 sets of intricate rules: a complete liquidation of an interest in a non-service partnership that owns no unrealized receivables or inventory where any distributions are of cash (including deemed cash distributions under Section 752(b)).

The first question that arises when a partner leaves her partnership is how she is taxed on partnership operations with regard to the last year in which she was a partner. As discussed way back in Chapter IV, under Section 706(a), a partner includes partnership items for a partnership taxable year in her income for her tax year that includes the end of the partnership tax year. Under Section 706(c)(2)(A), a partnership's tax year terminates with regard to a liquidated partner at the time that the liquidation is completed. The partnership's income is attributed to the period prior to the complete interest liquidation using the same rules that apply when a partner sells her entire interest, which were discussed above in Chapter IV. Thus, for example, if a calendar-year partner in a partnership with a fiscal year that ends January 30 is liquidated on December 15, 2001, she includes in her taxable income for 2001 both (i) her share of the partnership's income for 2000 (which passed through at the end of the partnership's year on January 30, 2001) and (ii) her share of 10–1/2 months of partnership income (which passed through on December 15, 2001).

The next question that arises is how the liquidated partner is taxed with regard to any liquidating distributions that she received. Section 731 applies to liquidating distributions as well as to non-liquidating distributions, with the same rules for taxing gain, but with different rules for taxing losses: Gain is recognized to the extent that the cash received exceeds outside basis. As to loss, non-liquidating distributions do not generate a loss under Section 731(a)(2), because, in order to measure any loss, it would be necessary to value the partner's remaining partnership interest, and the Code resists valuations in the absence of a transaction that objectively demonstrates the value, such as a sale. In contrast, after a complete partnership interest liquidation, the partnership interest no longer exists and, thus, has no value, so that the loss is determined clearly. Further, with a cash-only liquidation (or a liquidation involving no distribution), the case here, it is now or never to deal with the difference between inside and outside basis by allowing her a loss, as it is not possible to adjust the basis of cash so that the partner is allowed the loss in the future. Under these circumstances, Section 731(a)(2) allows a loss to the extent that the partner's outside basis exceeds any cash received in liquidation. Note that the liquidated partner is treated as receiving a cash distribution in an amount that is equal to her share of partnership debt by Section 752(b).

When liquidating distributions are spread over more than one tax year, the normal rule for accounting for any taxable gain or loss under Section 731 is the "open transaction" method: In the case of gain, distributions first reduce basis, so that gain is taxed only after the cumulative distributions have offset the partner's outside basis. Loss is allowed only after the last distribution has been received. However, Section 1.736–1(b)(6) of the regulations allows liquidating partners to elect reporting that is similar to that provided for installment sales in Section 453. If the election is made, gain **and loss** (loss cannot be accounted for under Section 453) are pro-rated over the payments to be received.

The final question is how the liquidation affects the partnership. Section 731(b) provides a general rule that a distribution has no tax impact on the partnership. If a Section 754 election is in place, however, the basis of partnership assets is increased for any gain recognized by the distributee under Sections 734(b) and 755, as discussed in Chapter VII. Loss can be recognized on liquidating distributions, but not on non-liquidating distributions, however. Section 734(b)(2)(A) and Section 1.755–1(c)(1)(ii) of the regulations also provide that any such loss reduces the partnership's bases in its capital gain assets under Section 755.[11] Additionally, Section 1.704–1(b)(2)(iv)(f) of the regulations "re-

---

11. If there is insufficient basis in capital gain property to absorb the entire write-down, any excess is carried over to succeeding tax years to be applied when the part-

quires" that the interest liquidation trigger a reverse Section 704(c) allocation, as discussed in Chapter VI. When more than one partner is liquidated at the same time, say, as part of a termination of the partnership, it is not clear how adjustments triggered by one partner affect the other partners.

The rules discussed in this section of this text apply to all liquidating distributions, but, in the interests of simplicity, these rules are not reflected in the discussion of the more complicated transactions reviewed in the succeeding sections of this chapter, except when needed.

REVIEW: **Code §§ 706(c), 731(a) and (b), 734(b), 752(b), and 761(d) and Reg. §§ 1.704–1(b)(2)(iv)(f), 1.736–1(b)(6), and 1.755–1(c)**

Problem Set VIII.C

1.   Fred has a $600,000 basis in a partnership interest. The partnership's only assets are cash and real estate held for investment. He is completely redeemed out in exchange for 2 cash payments from the partnership, $500,000 in Year 1 and $500,000 in Year 2. How is he taxed?

2.   What if each payment is only $250,000?

3.   If the partnership had made a Section 754 election, what would be the effect on the partnership of the transactions in Problems 1 and 2?

D.   CONGRESS' FOCUS: A GENERAL PARTNER WITHDRAWING FROM A SERVICE PARTNERSHIP FOR CASH ONLY

READ: Code §§ 736, 751(c), and 753 and Reg. § 1.736–1

The next case to be examined is a partner withdrawing from a service partnership (that has no inventory or recapture property) for only cash (and, under Section 752(b), deemed cash) distributions.[12] Since most partnerships in 1954 were either service partnerships or small businesses, Congress gave a great deal of attention to service partnerships in Subchapter K, particularly in Section 736.[13]

When a partner retires from a partnership, matters may not be wound up immediately. For example, a partner may leave a law firm and still be entitled to some percentage of the uncollected receivables and unbilled time. It makes sense to tax this income the same regardless of whether the amounts are collected before or after a partner withdraws.

---

nership acquires such property. Treas. Reg. §§ 1.755–1(c)(3), (4).

12.   A partner can retire from a service partnership or die, thereby terminating her involvement by operation of law.

13.   While, Section 736's title refers to a "retiring" or "deceased" partner, which seems to imply that the provision only applies with regard to partners that are individuals, the provision itself applies to any liquidation of a partnership interest, including one held by a corporate partner.

Since service partnerships may have little in the way of tangible assets—leasing real estate, copying machines, and the like—much of the value of a withdrawing partner's interest may be attributable to goodwill. Payments to a retiring partner for her interest in partnership goodwill, present much the same tax issue as payments for uncollected and unbilled time. Goodwill, by definition, represents the extra value in a business that is not represented by other assets. The value of goodwill is demonstrated by the business earning profits in excess of those appropriate for just the business' other assets. Thus, for a service business, goodwill represents the present value of a portion of future fees. If those fees had been paid to the withdrawing partner, she, and not her partners, would have been taxed on them. Under this analysis, payments to a withdrawing partner for partnership goodwill should both carry out ordinary income to the withdrawing partner and draw that income away from the other partners.

Section 736 deals with all this. 2 separate regimes that apply simultaneously to the interest liquidation are provided by Sections 736(a) and 736(b), respectively. First, Section 736(a) applies to payments that are not treated as being for the liquidated partner's interest in the partnership's assets. These payments carry out income to the retiring partner (and away from the other partners). Second, Section 736(b) applies to payments for the liquidated partner's share of partnership assets. These payments are taxed under Section 731: (i) no income carry-out (or deduction) to the partnership and (ii) basis recovery and gain or loss to the liquidated partner.

Specifically, a payment subject to Section 736(a) is treated either (i) as a share of the partnership's profits (with an associated distribution) or (ii) as a guaranteed payment (as discussed in Chapter IV), depending upon whether the amount of the payment is determined with regard to the income of the partnership.[14] In the case of a successor in interest of a deceased partner, Section 753 provides that Section 736(a) amounts are taxable to the recipient as income in respect of a decedent.[15]

The scope of Section 736(a) is defined by negation: It applies to all liquidating payments that are not subject to Section 736(b). Section 736(b), by its terms, applies to payments for partnership property (with an exception, to be discussed shortly). It is hard to imagine what the withdrawing partner is being paid for if not her interest in partnership

---

14. As noted by the courts in *Foxman*, above, both a guaranteed payment and a distribution (with associated profit allocation) give the payee partner ordinary income which is not taxed to the other partners, however. Treas. Reg. § 1.736–1(a)(4). Section 1.736–1(a)(6) of the regulations treats the retired partner as still a member of the firm for purposes of applying Section 736. In the case of a deceased partner, the estate or other successor is treated as the partner. Thus, Section 1.736–1(a)(5) can tax the partner on Section 736(a) amounts at the end of the partnership's tax year, even if the amounts are guaranteed. This explains why Section 736 treatment would have deferred income for a year in *Foxman*.

15. Section 753, by its terms, does not provide that Section 736(a) distributions are the only partnership amounts treated as income in respect of a decedent. Under an aggregate approach, any items held by the partnership that would be income in respect of a decedent if held directly would be so treated.

property. As a consequence, Section 736(b) at first pass applies to most liquidating distributions and very little is covered by the general rule of Section 736(a). The only example in the regulations of a distribution that is not for property is a payment in the nature of mutual insurance.[16] Section 736(b)(2), however, limits Section 736(b) so as to extend the reach of Section 736(a) to additional payments of real significance. Section 736(b)(2) so provides Section 736(a) ordinary income carry out status to payments (i) for real unrealized receivables (not to recapture[17]) and (ii) for goodwill that are not so specified in the partnership agreement.[18]

Since 1993, Section 736(b)(3) has limited Section 736(b)(2) to payments to a general partner of a service partnership—a partnership in which capital is a material income-producing factor. It is unclear how the "general partner" requirement applies to LLC members.

All payments distributed in complete liquidation of a partner that are not subject to Section 736(a) are treated as Section 731 partnership distributions (with no associated further profit allocation) by operation of Section 736(b). These payments are tax-free to the withdrawing partner to the extent of basis, with the excess resulting in capital gain. The partnership gets no benefit except to the extent that any gain recognized by the withdrawing partner creates basis under Section 734(b), if applicable.

This regime achieves common-sense results in the liquidation of a general partner of a service partnership: The liquidated partner usually is getting paid for her share of uncollected or unbilled time (unrealized receivables) and goodwill. If she had stayed with the firm, she, not the other partners, would have been taxed thereon. Section 736(a) achieves the same result here. Any additional payments—for partnership assets— are taxed as are any other partnership distributions (except that a loss may be allowed here).

Because the tax interests of the withdrawing partner and the continuing partners usually are adverse,[19] the parties are afforded considerable flexibility in structuring the tax consequences of a partner's withdrawal. As already noted, the Code expressly provides the partners

16. Treas. Reg. § 1.736–1(a)(2)(3d sentence).

17. The 2d sentence of Section 751(c) specifically indicates that recapture is not an unrealized receivable for Section 736 purposes. Then, Section 1.751–1(b)(4)(ii) of the regulations makes clear that Section 751(b) does not apply to payments taxed under Section 736(a).

Note that ordinary income carry out treatment with regard to payments for unrealized receivables only applies to the extent that the payments for the receivables exceed the partner's share of the partnership's basis therein, including any special basis adjustment resulting from a Section 754 election. Treas. Reg. § 1.736–1(b)(2). In the usual case, however, the relevant inside basis will be zero.

18. Apparently, the idea is that, by specifying an amount for goodwill in the partnership agreement, the partners have treated goodwill as an asset. The regulations contemplate, however, that the amount paid for goodwill can be identified in a side valuation agreement and still be taxed under Section 736(a). Treas. Reg. § 1.736–1(b)(3).

19. To get the partnership an effective deduction, the withdrawing partner must bear an ordinary income tax.

flexibility in determining the tax treatment of payments for goodwill by providing different treatment depending upon the terms of the partnership agreement. Also, the Section 736 regulations generally respect an arm's length side allocation agreement between the withdrawing partner and the partnership that allocates the total cash paid among the various kinds of payments. The total amount treated as a Section 731 distribution cannot exceed the value of partnership property, however.[20]

REVIEW: Code §§ 736, 751(c), and 753 and Reg. § 1.736–1

Problem Set VIII.D

Sue is retiring from her law firm organized as a general partnership. All partners are in the same tax bracket. The partnership uses the cash method of accounting for tax purposes. All partners acquired their interests from the partnership in exchange for cash. The partnership has no material tangible assets. Its unbilled time is worth $10 million. Uncollected receivables (bills that have been sent out, but payment has not been received) are worth $15 million. There are no pertinent partnership liabilities. Sue is a 2% pro-rata general partner. She recently received a large distribution, so her basis in her interest is zero. The partnership is willing to pay her about $600,000 in cash for her partnership interest. What tax advice would you give her to leave her with the most after-tax?

E. CASH LIQUIDATING DISTRIBUTIONS OTHER THAN TO A GENERAL PARTNER OF A SERVICE PARTNERSHIP

READ: Reg. §§ 1.751–1(b)(3) and (g)(Example 2)

The next cases to be examined are distributions of cash (and, under Section 752(b), deemed cash) in complete liquidation (i) of a partner in a partnership in which capital is a material income-producing factor and (ii) of a non-general partner in a service partnership. In these cases, for all practical purposes,[21] Section 736(a) does not apply, so that Section 736(b) characterizes all payments as Section 731 distributions.

Section 731(a)'s application to cash liquidating distributions was described in Section VIII.C of this text and is quite straightforward. The source of the additional complexity here is our old nemesis: Section 751(b). As discussed in the preceding chapter, when a partner in a partnership that has Section 751 property receives a cash distribution not in liquidation, Section 751(b) applies only to the extent that the cash received is in exchange for the distributee's share of hot assets. For example, a pro-rata cash distribution does not reduce the partners' respective interest in other assets so as to trigger Section 751(b). In

---

20. *See* Treas. Reg. § 1.736–1(b)(5)(iii).

21. As noted in the preceding section, Section 736(a) by itself has limited scope,

mutual insurance being the only example in the regulations.

contrast, with a cash-only liquidating distribution (from a partnership with hot assets), almost always some of the cash must be in exchange for these hot assets, as the partner had an interest in hot assets before the distribution and has no interest after. Thus, almost all complete interest liquidations present a Section 751(b) concern.[22] Fortunately, the application of Section 751(b) is more straightforward with liquidating distributions than with non-liquidating distributions, as it is easier to determine what is being exchanged for what. Then, the regulations treat the transaction as involving (i) a deemed nonliquidating distribution of the assets that the withdrawing partner is deemed to have disposed of under Section 751(b) (ii) that is followed by a liquidating distribution (that is reduced to take account of the deemed distribution), (iii) which, in turn, is followed by a deemed asset exchange between the distributee and the partnership (not including the liquidated partner), in which exchange the partnership reacquires the assets deemed distributed for the assets viewed as exchanged therefor under Section 751(b).[23]

The mechanics of Section 751(b) are best illustrated with an example; specifically, a modified version of the example used in the preceding chapter. Mary, Nick, and Nora form a 1/3d–1/3d–1/3d partnership, which uses the accrual method for tax purposes. After years, the accounts look as follows:

Fair Market Value

Assets		Liabilities	
Cash	$2,580,000	Payables	$180,000
Receivables	150,000		
Inventory	390,000	**Equity**	
Machinery	870,000		
Buildings	690,000	Mary	$2,000,000
Land	900,000	Nick	2,000,000
Goodwill	600,000	Nora	2,000,000
	6,180,000		6,000,000

Tax

Assets		Liabilities	
Cash	$2,580,000	Payables	$180,000
Receivables	150,000		
Inventory	210,000	**Equity**	
Machinery	510,000		
Buildings	480,000	Mary	$1,400,000
Land	450,000	Nick	1,400,000
Goodwill	–0–	Nora	1,400,000
	4,380,000		4,200,000

22. It is possible that a partnership's special allocations have the effect that a liquidated partner has no interest in any unrealized Section 751 gain so that a cash liquidating distribution does not reduce the liquidated partner's interest in hot assets.

23. Treas. Reg. §§ 1.755–1(b)(2)(ii) and (3)(ii).

All gain on the machinery and the buildings would be recapture under Sections 1245 and 1250, respectively.

The partnership distributes $2,000,000 of cash to Nick in complete liquidation of his interest.

The partnership is not a service partnership. Thus, Section 736(a) does not apply. If Section 751(b) did not apply, Nick would have $600,000 of capital gain under Section 731.[24]

To determine the impact of Section 751(b), it is necessary to figure out what is being exchanged for what. Before the distribution, Nick owned (indirectly) the following, at fair market value (subject to his share of the debt):

Before (1/3d of Partnership)

Cash	$860,000
Receivables	50,000
Inventory	130,000
Machinery	290,000
Buildings	230,000
Land	300,000
Goodwill	200,000
	2,060,000

The net value of his interest is $2 million. After the transaction, Nick owns $2 million cash.

The Section 751 assets disposed of are his shares of the inventory (including the receivables) and of the built-in recapture on the machinery. Nick would have $60,000 of ordinary income with regard to the substantially appreciated inventory and $120,000 of Section 1245 ordinary income.[25] Nick reduces his outside basis for his share of the inside basis of these properties, $120,000. The Section 731 distribution now is reduced by $300,000 (the cash received (i) for his share of the inventory and (ii) for his share of the built-in recapture). Thus, Section 731 taxes $420,000 of capital gain. The total $600,000 of gain is bifurcated into $180,000 of ordinary income and $420,000 of capital gain. If the Section 751(b) gain had exceeded the gain otherwise realized, Section 731(a)(2) would allow a loss, applying similarly to the application of Section 751(a) to losses. Notice that the application of Section 751(b) here is much simpler than in a non-liquidating distribution.

---

24. Because Nick is an original partner, his outside basis equals his capital account, $1,400,000, plus his 1/3d share of debt, $60,000. The total Section 731 distribution is the $2 million cash plus his share of the debt, $60,000, which is deemed distributed under Section 752(b).

25. The partnership increases its inside basis in the inventory and machinery similarly to reflect its deemed repurchase for cash.

A small amount of tax planning may be possible in the example. The partners may wish to argue that some of the $2 million is not for property, but in the nature of mutual insurance. If upheld, this would give Nick ordinary income, but Mary and Nora would get ordinary deductions. Little other planning seems possible here.

Note that, if any of the property had been contributed by Nick, all recapture work still would have been done by Section 751(b), as Section 737 does not apply to cash distributions. Thus, only Section 751 property and not all ordinary income property is subject to recapture. In contrast, if, say, ordinary income property contributed by Nick was distributed to another partner as part of a liquidation of the entire partnership, Section 751(b) in effect would play a back-up role, as Section 704(c)(1)(B) would trigger all ordinary income built-in at the time of Nick's contribution, regardless.[26]

It is helpful to compare these Section 751(b) results to the results under Section 751(a) in a comparable partnership interest sale. Consider the consequences in the example if Nick, rather than being liquidated for a $2 million cash distribution from the partnership, sold his partnership interest to a third party for $2 million cash. His total gain would be $600,000. For purposes of Section 751(a), his share of Section 751 ordinary income is $190,000. This leaves $410,000 of capital gain. In short, taking Section 751 into account, a complete liquidation of a partner's entire interest for cash is taxed the same as a cash sale of the entire partnership interest provided (i) that Section 736(a) does not apply to the liquidation and (ii) that the partnership has no inventory that is not substantially appreciated so as to trigger ordinary income under Section 751(a) but not under Section 751(b).

REVIEW: Code §§ 704(c)(1)(B), 734(b), and 737 and Reg. §§ 1.751–1(b)(3), (b)(4)(ii), and (g)(Example 2)

Problem Set VIII.E

Redo Problem 1 in Problem Set VIII.D on the new assumptions (i) that capital is a material income-producing factor for the law firm, which now also owns personal property, equipment and a library, worth $10 million, but with a basis of $5 million (so that all gain would be Section 1245 recapture), and (ii) that the partnership is willing to pay Sue $800,000 in cash for her partnership interest.

F. NON–CASH PROPERTY DISTRIBUTIONS WHEN SECTION 736(a) DOES NOT APPLY

READ: Code §§ 731, 732(a) through (e), and 733

Next, we examine complete interest liquidations to which Section 736(a) does not apply that involve distributions of property other than cash.

---

26. Mechanically, Section 751(b) applies first. Treas. Reg. § 1.704 4(o)(?)

The first concern is the gain or loss of the liquidated partner. As discussed above in this chapter, when only cash is distributed in liquidation of a partner, Section 731(a) provides that any realized gain or loss is recognized. In contrast, here, where non-cash property is so distributed, gain or loss generally is not taxed under Section 731(a), as the gain or loss can be built into the distributed property by giving the distributed property a tax basis such that the gain or loss is taken into account later upon a subsequent realization transaction involving the property.

Next, rules are needed to deal with any difference between the liquidated partner's outside basis (adjusted for cash) and the inside basis of any non-cash property that she receives. With a non-liquidating distribution, any difference between a partner's outside basis and the distributed property's basis must be addressed only in the relatively unusual situation where the inside basis of the non-cash property distributed exceeds the outside basis, in which case the property's outside basis is limited to the distributee partner's outside basis under Section 732(a)(2).[27] Any other difference between inside and outside basis can be left built into the partnership interest. In contrast, upon liquidation of a partner, it is not possible to leave the difference between inside and outside basis built into the partnership interest, since that interest disappears.

Problems from a difference between inside and outside basis of a liquidated partner arise either (i) with regard to a partner who acquired her interest from another partner or (ii) with non-pro-rata distributions. As to the first problem, if a Section 754 election had been in place at all relevant times, there should be little problem.[28] Also Section 732(d) can apply so as to partially solve the problem when the distribution is within 2 years of the partner acquiring her interest.[29]

As to the 2d problem, non-pro-rata distributions, the only way to avoid all problems is to treat such distributions as taxable exchanges to the extent that the distributee partner reduces her interest in one partnership property as a consequence of receiving a distribution of other partnership property. Current law does not require an immediate tax, but tries to reduce problems (i) by preserving the unrealized gain or loss in the distributed assets that is reflected in the liquidated partner's **outside** basis, (ii) while not allowing taxpayers either to manufacture artificial losses, particularly ordinary losses, or to convert ordinary income to capital gain by misallocating basis.

---

27. With a cash distribution, since the basis of cash cannot be adjusted, when the amount of cash received exceeds the distributee partner's outside basis, gain is taxed under Section 731(a)(1), so that the partner does not get free basis.

28. Note that here, unlike with the non-liquidating distributions discussed above in Section VII.G, the special Section 743(b) adjustment in all partnership assets moves to the distributed assets so that the distributee partner gets the full benefit of these adjustments. Treas. Reg. § 1.743–1(g)(3).

29. The Section 732(d) adjustment reallocates to the distributed assets, much as with the Section 743(b) adjustment, as discussed in the preceding footnote. Treas. Reg. § 1.732–1(d)(1)(v).

Section 732(b) requires that the liquidated partner allocate her total outside basis (reduced by any cash received) among the non-cash properties received in liquidation. Then, Section 732(c) provides how that allocation is to be done:

First, Section 751 unrealized receivables (including recapture) and inventory keep their inside basis (reflecting any special basis adjustment with respect to the partner[30]).[31] If only Section 751 assets are received and any outside basis remains unallocated, Section 731(a)(2) allows a loss. This loss usually is capital under the second sentence of Section 731(a)(2) so that conversion of ordinary income into capital gain is avoided, yet outside basis is conserved.

Second, if non-Section 751 assets are received, any outside basis not allocated to Section 751 assets is spread among the remaining assets: Again, Section 732(c) starts by allocating to each asset its inside basis (reflecting any special basis adjustment with respect to the partner[32]). If the total inside basis exceeds the outside basis to be so allocated, the bases of the assets is reduced until the excess is eliminated: First, assets with unrealized depreciation have their bases reduced proportionately to their unrealized depreciation until the unrealized amount is eliminated (i.e., until their basis equals their value). If, after such reduction, the total basis of these assets still exceeds the outside basis to be allocated, the assets are written down proportionately to their bases as just determined until the excess is finally eliminated.

If the total inside basis of the non-Section 751, non-cash, assets received is less than the outside basis to be so allocated (i.e., the outside basis as reduced by cash and by the bases of inventory and unrealized receivables), write-ups are required: First, assets with unrealized appreciation are written up proportionately thereto until their basis equals their value, and, then, if necessary, all such assets are written up proportionately to their value until the total asset basis equals the outside basis to be allocated.[33]

As already noted, in applying Section 732 to determine the bases of the distributed assets, one takes into account any special basis adjustments in the distributed assets to which the partner is entitled under Section 732(d) or 743(b). Also, the mandatory (on the taxpayer and the Commissioner) application of Section 732(d), as implemented by Section 1.732–1(d)(4) of the regulations, may come into play. Read Section 1.732–1(d)(4).

---

30. Treas. Reg. § 1.743–1(g)(1)(i). Similar rules apply if Section 732(d) applies to the distributee, either by election or because of the anti-abuse feature. Treas. Reg. § 1.732–1(d)(1)(iii).

31. In the rare case where the outside basis is less than the total inside basis of unrealized receivables and inventory, the basis of these assets is reduced to eliminate this discrepancy under Section 732(c)(3).

32. See Note 30, above.

33. Note that the residual allocation of write-downs is proportionate to the assets' respective bases, while the residual allocation of write-ups is proportionate to the assets' respective values.

An example illustrates the mandatory application of Section 732(d): Kevin buys a 10% pro-rata interest in a partnership from an original partner for $3 million. At the time, the partnership owned (i) inventory worth $10 million with a tax basis of $1 million, (ii) 10 identical buildings, one on each parcel, each worth $1 million with a basis of $500,000, and (iii) 10 identical parcels of land, each worth $1 million with a basis of $1 million.[34] The partnership distributes all cash as received, so that the partnership's only material assets are the land and buildings. Years later, (i) the partnership has inventory with the same basis and value, (ii) each of the buildings is worth $600,000 with a basis of zero, and (iii) each of the parcels is worth $1.2 million each. Kevin, and no other partner, is completely liquidated in exchange for one parcel with a building on it and a 10% share of the inventory (with 10% of the basis). At that time, his outside basis is $2.5 million.

When Kevin bought his interest, the total partnership assets were worth $30 million and had a basis of $16 million. So, the requirement of Section 1.732–1(d)(4)(i) was satisfied. If Kevin's interest had been liquidated at that time pro-rata, his basis in the assets received would have been (i) $100,000 in inventory, (ii) $1.45 million in buildings, and (iii) $1.45 million in land.[35] Thus, the buildings would have had a basis in excess of their value by operation of Section 732(c). This apparently is the kind of shift contemplated by Section 1.732–1(d)(4)(ii) of the regulations.[36] If no Section 754 election is made, upon liquidation, Kevin's bases in the assets received would be (a) inventory $100,000, (b) buildings, $800,000, and (c) land, $1.6 million.[37] If a Section 743(b)-like rule[38]

34. Assuming that all gain on the buildings would be subject to Section 1250, the seller would have recognized $500,000 of Section 1250 gain under Section 1.1(h)–1 of the regulations and $900,000 of ordinary income under Section 751(b). Note that Section 1250 gain is no longer ordinary income (it once was), so that it is not an unrealizable receivable as defined in Section 751(c).

35. The total of $3 million of outside basis is allocated first under Section 732(c)(1)(A)(i) ($100,000 to the inventory), then under Section 732(c)(1)(B)(i) ($500,000 to the buildings and $1 million to the land), and next under Sections 732(c)(1)(B)(ii) and 732(c)(2)(A) ($500,000 to the buildings), and finally under Sections 732(c)(1)(B)(ii) and 732(c)(2)(B) ($450,000 each to the land and buildings).

36. The provision can be read to require that the inside basis of non-depreciable property is reduced upon the deemed distribution under Section 732(c). At least in a pro-rata partnership, Section 732(c) does not so reduce these assets' basis from their inside basis when there is basis available under Section 732(c)(1)(B)(ii) to allocate to depreciable property. Thus, if the Section 732(d) regulations were read to require a

write-down in non-depreciable assets, the regulations never would apply to a pro-rata partnership. Prior to 1999, the regulations contained examples that adopted the analysis in the text, that the shift required is outside basis attributable to the **value** (not basis) of nondepreciable property being allocated to depreciable property by Section 732(c)—but, when the regulations were amended in 1999 to conform with the legislative changes in Section 732(c), the examples were omitted. There is no evidence, however, that the omission was intended to change the interpretation. T.D. 8847, 64 F.R. 69903, 69904 (1999).

37. The total of $2.5 million of outside basis is allocated first under Section 732(c)(1)(A)(i) ($100,000 to the inventory), then under Section 732(c)(1)(B)(i) ($1 million to the land), next under Sections 732(c)(1)(B)(ii) and 732(c)(2)(A) ($600,000 to the buildings and $200,000 to the land), and finally under Sections 732(c)(1)(B)(ii) and 732(c)(2)(B) ($200,000 [$600,000 excess basis x ($600,000 building value/$1.8 million total FMV of Section 732(c)(1)(B)(ii) property)] to the buildings and $400,000 [$600,000 excess basis x ($1.2 million land value/$1.8 million total FMV of Section 732(c)(1)(B)(ii) property)] to the land).

is applied, these bases would be (I) inventory, $1 million, (II) buildings, $500,000, and (III) land, $1 million.[39] The requirement of Section 1.732–1(d)(4)(iii) is satisfied. Accordingly, this later allocation is required by Section 732(d). This is a better outcome, but it is not clear why the Treasury is concerned about just this one situation where there is no Section 754 election in place and not any of the numerous others. Nevertheless, Treasury reviewed this rule and reblessed it in 1999.[40]

Of course, Sections 704(c)(1)(B), 731(c), 737, 751(b), and 752 must be taken into account. Their priority here is the same as with non-liquidating distributions, which was examined above in Sections VII.B and VII.D of this text. Under Section 752, taking property subject to debt is treated as a contribution, which is offset against any partnership debt that the liquidated partner is no longer economically liable for, with the net increase (decrease) treated as a cash contribution (distribution) prior to the remainder of the transaction.[41] Under the Section 707(a)(2)(B) regulations, special rules apply if there is a tax avoidance purpose.[42]

The Section 751(b) analysis here, even though now we are looking at non-cash property liquidating distributions, still is simpler than with non-liquidating distributions, as it is easier to determine what is being exchanged for what in an interest liquidation. To the extent a partner does not receive her exact share of Section 751 property, she has gain or loss. If she gets more than her share of Section 751 property, the transaction is treated as if she had received and then exchanged non-Section 751 property with the partnership for the excess Section 751 property. If she gets less, there is a taxable exchange of her share of Section 751 property for non-Section 751 property.

Sections 704(c)(1)(B) and 737 can apply here if property contributed by a partner is involved. Of particular importance here is that both provisions have exceptions that apply when a partner receives back property that she contributed to the partnership.

Section 731(c) applies to liquidating distributions, as to non-liquidating distributions, so as to increase the potential gain under Section 731(a) when marketable securities are distributed, as discussed in the preceding chapter. Note here, however, that, under Section 731(c), since

---

38. An allocation under Section 732(d), which apparently is the idea in Section 1.732–1(d)(4)(iii). Section 743(b) adjustments would have impacted outside basis through depreciation and other effects on the partnership's profit and loss passed through to the partner.

39. Section 743(b) would have given inside basis adjustments of $900,000 in the inventory and $500,000 in the buildings. Thus, at the time of the liquidating distribution, Kevin's share of inside basis is $500,000 in the buildings (just the Section 743(b) adjustment, as the underlying partnership basis was eliminated by deprecia-

tion) and $1 million. Treas. Reg. § 1.732–1(d)(1)(iv). There is no clear rule for the inventory. The text assumes that one also does not take into account any reduction in the special basis adjustment to inventory as the inventory is sold, so that Kevin's share is $1 million. Then, these inside bases just carry out under Section 732(c)(1).

40. T. D. 8847, 64 F.R. 69904, 69904 (1999).

41. Treas. Reg. § 1.752–1(f).

42. Treas. Reg. § 1.707–6; Rev. Rul. 87–120, 1987–2 C.B. 161.

marketable securities are treated as "money" for purposes of Section 731(a)(1), but not for purposes of Section 731(a)(2), a distribution containing marketable securities cannot trigger a loss.

If a Section 754 election is in place, Sections 734(b)(1)(B) and (b)(2)(B) provide that the total Section 732 adjustment to the basis of distributed assets is mirrored in the basis of partnership assets. Under Section 1.755–1(c)(1)(i) of the regulations, If the distributee partner writes up the basis of capital gain (ordinary income) assets from their inside basis to the partnership, the partnership writes down its bases in retained capital gain (ordinary income) assets. The reverse applies if the distributee partner writes assets up.[43] These rules assure that the total basis in all capital gain and ordinary income assets (other than partnership interests) stays unchanged.

Except for different basis rules under Section 732, property distributed in liquidation of a partnership interest is treated similarly to other distributed property. Sections 1245 and 1250 recapture taint follows the property as does the depreciation method.[44] Most partnership ordinary income assets keep their character under Section 735.

REVIEW: Code §§ 168(i)(7), 731, 732(a) through (e), 734(b), 735, 752, 1245(b)(6), and 1250(d)(6) and Reg. §§ 1.707–6, 1.732–1(d)(1)(v) and (4), 1.743–1(g)(1)(i) and (3), 1.752–1(f), and 1.755–1(c)

Problem Set VIII.F

1.   The partnership in Problem 1 of Problem Set VII.B, rather than making the distributions described there, liquidates. Cash is used to pay off the payables. Mary takes the land and buildings and $300,000 of cash. Nick gets all of the remaining partnership property. Capital was a material income-producing factor to the partnership. How are the partners taxed, on the assumption that neither contributed non-cash property to the partnership.

2.   Assume the basic facts of Problem 1 of Problem Set VII.B. Prior to any distributions, Mary sells 1/2 of her interest (1/4 of the partnership) to Leann for $1 million. Shortly thereafter, but in a separate transaction for tax purposes, Leann is liquidated in exchange for $500,000 in cash, all $150,000 of receivables and $350,000 in value of the inventory (with a tax basis of $175,000).

43. As above, Section 734(b) adjustments, unlike Section 743(b) adjustments, are in one direction only. Treas. Reg. §§ 1.755–1(b), (c). For example, when a write-up is triggered, that cannot result in a write-down to some assets and a bigger write-up to others. Unused write-ups and write-downs carry forward to be applied when the partnership acquires appropriate property. Treas. Reg. § 1.755–1(c)(4).

44. Section 168(i)(7) provides that the distributee is treated the same as the partnership except to the extent the former partner gets an increase in basis under Section 732.

G. GENERAL PARTNERS OF SERVICE PARTNERSHIPS: THE GENERAL CASE

This chapter concludes with a crescendo of complexity: non-cash liquidating distributions to general partners in partnerships in which capital is not a material income-producing factor that own Section 751 property.[45] This case requires application of all of the rules reviewed in this chapter. Fortunately, the analysis only requires putting the analyses in Sections VIII.C through VIII.F together. Thus, this section also serves as a review of the rules applicable to all liquidating distributions.

The analysis of the distributee starts with Section 736.[46] The portion of the distribution taxed under Section 736(a) must be determined.[47] Payments for real unrealized receivables (not recapture) and payments for goodwill that are not so provided in the partnership agreement are treated as income carry-outs by Section 736(a).

Next, Section 704(c)(1)(B) comes in.[48] The distributee is taxed (on gain or loss) if any property she contributed is distributed to another partner in connection with the distribution to her. Her outside basis is adjusted accordingly.

Section 751(b) must be applied to the portion of the transaction not controlled by Section 736(a) in order to potentially recharacterize the distribution into a current distribution (of the property deemed distributed), followed by an exchange, followed by a (smaller) liquidating distribution. The Section 751(b) analysis here is the same as above.

Next, Section 731, including Section 731(c), applies. Gain is recognized only in a cash-only (including marketable securities) distribution in an amount that is in excess of the distributee partner's outside basis. Loss is recognized only in a distribution of only cash, receivables, and/or inventory that have an aggregate inside basis that is less than the distributee's outside basis.

Then, Section 737 applies. The distributee is taxed on any untaxed built-in gain on assets that she contributed to the partnership to the extent that the value of the distribution exceeds the partners's outside basis. Her outside basis is adjusted accordingly.

The basis in the respective assets received in the Section 731 portion of the distribution is determined under Section 732 (subject to Section 731(c)(4)). Basically, the distributed assets have a transferred basis. Any excess outside basis is allocated among assets other than cash, receiv-

45. This text does not discuss cash-only liquidating distributions from a service partnership that has inventory or recapture property. It is very unlikely that capital is not a material income-producing factor in a partnership with inventory. Issues presented by service partnerships with recapture property are considered in this section of this text.

46. I.R.C. §§ 731(d), 737(d)(2); Treas. Reg. §§ 1.704–4(e)(2), 1.736–1(a)(2), 1.737–1(a)(2), 1.751–1(b)(1), (4).

47. Remember that Section 736(a) applies almost exclusively to service partnerships.

48. After Section 736 is applied, the priority rules here are the same as with nonliquidating distributions, as discussed in Section VII.E, above.

ables, and inventory in proportion to the remaining built-in gain. Any shortfall is allocated among all the assets other than cash, receivables, and inventory in proportion to their respective unrealized losses. For these purposes, any special basis adjustments under Section 743(b) of the distributee partner (because she is a transferee of her partnership interest) are taken into account. Section 732(d), when applicable, can provide similar results for a transferee partner if a Section 754 election is not in effect. Any property treated as distributed for purposes of Section 731 keeps various tax attributes, as discussed in the preceding section of this text.

The distribution has no effect on the partnership, per se, under Section 731(b). But, Section 751(b) can create gain or loss to the partnership. Also, Sections 704(c)(1)(B), 737, and 751(b) can impact the partnership's basis in its assets. Section 1.704–1(b)(2)(iv)(*f*) "requires" that the capital accounts be marked to market. If a Section 754 election is in place, Section 734(b) can trigger adjustments to the basis of partnership assets that mirror the adjustments to distributed assets under Section 732, as discussed in the preceding section of this text.

REVIEW: Code §§ 731, 732(a) through (e), 734(b), 736, 737, and 751 and Reg. §§ 1.704–1(b)(2)(iv)(*f*) and –4(e)(2), 1.732–1(d)(1)(v), 1.736–1, 1.737–1(a)(2), 1.743–1(g)(1)(i) and (3), 1.751–1(b), and 1.755–1(c)

Problem Set VIII.G

Jeri is a 0.05% pro-rata partner in a cash-basis accounting firm in which capital (invested in computers) is a material income-producing factor. Her basis in her partnership interest is $50,000. All partners acquired their interests from the firm in exchange for cash only. The partnership's only material tangible assets are $500 million of computers, furniture, and office equipment. The total basis of these assets is $100 million. All gain would be Section 1245 recapture. The partnership also has a total of $100 million of Section 751 unrealized receivables representing uncollected or unbilled amounts for services already provided to customers. These amounts have a zero basis. There are no other Section 751 items or any partnership liabilities.

Jeri wants to start her own firm. Her current partnership interest is retired for $300,000 of cash and $50,000 worth of computers, furniture, and office equipment (with a total basis of $10,000.) What are the tax consequences?

Chapter IX

PARTNERSHIP M & A

A. INTRODUCTION

Much of the law relating to corporate taxation deals with corporate amalgamations and divisions. In contrast, there is little law regarding the taxation of similar partnership transactions. This is not surprising, however, given Subchapter K's respect for the historic state common-law view of partnership matters. At common law, a partnership was not an entity. Consequently, a partnership could not acquire another or be divided into other partnerships, per se. A partnership amalgamation was viewed as the partners of 2 or more former partnerships forming a brand new partnership to continue the businesses previously conducted by the old partnerships (which had discontinued) using assets previously used by the old partnerships. A division was viewed as the liquidation of the old partnership followed by the formation of new partnerships.

This state-law heritage is reflected in Subchapter K. The central issue regarding the taxation of a partnership amalgamation or division is whether the transaction constitutes a continuation of an old partnership (as it would not at common law). Thus, Section 708, entitled "Continuation of Partnership," is the most important statutory provision dealing with the taxation of such transactions. This chapter examines Section 708 and related provisions that deal with partnership amalgamations and divisions. Partnership incorporations and tiered partnership structures present tax concerns similar to those involved in amalgamations and divisions and, for this reason, also are examined here.

B. INCORPORATING A PARTNERSHIP

The basic notions involved in the taxation of partnership amalgamations and divisions were developed in a related context: the incorporation of a partnership. Hence, it is helpful to study partnership incorporations, not only because such transactions are important in their own right, but also because of their historical role in the development of the tax rules for partnership M & A. The tax concerns in incorporating a partnership are examined in the following Revenue Ruling:

174

REVENUE RULING 84–111
1984–2 C.B. 88.

ISSUE

Does Rev. Rul. 70–239, 1970 C.B. 74, still represent the Service's position with respect to the three situations described therein?

FACTS

The three situations described in Rev. Rul. 70–239 involve partnerships X, Y, and Z, respectively. Each partnership used the accrual method of accounting and had assets and liabilities consisting of cash, equipment, and accounts payable. The liabilities of each partnership did not exceed the adjusted basis of its assets. The three situations are as follows:

Situation 1

X transferred all of its assets to newly-formed corporation R in exchange for all the outstanding stock of R and the assumption by R of X's liabilities. X then terminated by distributing all the stock of R to X's partners in proportion to their partnership interests.

Situation 2

Y distributed all of its assets and liabilities to its partners in proportion to their partnership interests in a transaction that constituted a termination of Y under section 708(b)(1)(A) of the Code. The partners then transferred all the assets received from Y to newly-formed corporation S in exchange for all the outstanding stock of S and the assumption by S of Y's liabilities that had been assumed by the partners.

Situation 3

The partners of Z transferred their partnership interests in Z to newly-formed corporation T in exchange for all the outstanding stock of T. This exchange terminated Z and all of its assets and liabilities became assets and liabilities of T.

In each situation, the steps taken by X, Y, and Z, and the partners of X, Y, and Z, were parts of a plan to transfer the partnership operations to a corporation organized for valid business reasons in exchange for its stock and were not devices to avoid or evade recognition of gain. Rev. Rul. 70–239 holds that because the federal income tax consequences of the three situations are the same, each partnership is considered to have transferred its assets and liabilities to a corporation in exchange for its stock under section 351 of the Internal Revenue Code, followed by a distribution of the stock to the partners in liquidation of the partnership.

LAW AND ANALYSIS

Section 351(a) of the Code provides that no gain or loss will be recognized if property is transferred to a corporation by one or more persons solely in exchange for stock or securities in such corporation and immediately after the exchange such person or persons are in control (as defined in section 368(c)) of the corporation.

Section 1.351–1(a)(1) of the Income Tax Regulations provides that, as used in section 351 of the Code, the phrase "one or more persons" includes individuals, trusts, estates, partnerships, associations, companies, or corporations. To be in control of the transferee corporation, such person or persons must own immediately after the transfer stock possessing at least 80 percent of the total combined voting power of all classes of stock entitled to vote and at least 80 percent of the total number of shares of all other classes of stock of such corporation.

Section 358(a) of the Code provides that in the case of an exchange to which section 351 applies, the basis of the property permitted to be received under such section without the recognition of gain or loss will be the same as that of the property exchanged, decreased by the amount of any money received by the taxpayer.

Section 358(d) of the Code provides that where, as part of the consideration to the taxpayer, another party to the exchange assumed a liability of the taxpayer or acquired from the taxpayer property subject to a liability, such assumption or acquisition (in the amount of the liability) will, for purposes of section 358, be treated as money received by the taxpayer on the exchange.

Section 362(a) of the Code provides that a corporation's basis in property acquired in a transaction to which section 351 applies will be the same as it would be in the hands of the transferor.

Under section 708(b)(1)(A) of the Code, a partnership is terminated if no part of any business, financial operation, or venture of the partnership continues to be carried on by any of its partners in a partnership. Under section 708(b)(1)(B), a partnership terminates if within a 12–month period there is a sale or exchange of 50 percent or more of the total interest in partnership capital and profits.

Section 732(b) of the Code provides that the basis of property other than money distributed by a partnership in a liquidation of a partner's interest shall be an amount equal to the adjusted basis of the partner's interest in the partnership reduced by any money distributed. Section 732(c) of the Code provides rules for the allocation of a partner's basis in a partnership interest among the assets received in a liquidating distribution.

Section 735(b) of the Code provides that a partner's holding period for property received in a distribution from a partnership (other than with respect to certain inventory items defined in section 751(d)(2)) includes the partnership's holding period, as determined under section 1223, with respect to such property.

Section 1223(1) of the Code provides that where property received in an exchange acquires the same basis, in whole or in part, as the property surrendered in the exchange, the holding period of the property received includes the holding period of the property surrendered to the extent such surrendered property was a capital asset or property described in section 1231. Under section 1223(2), the holding period of a taxpayer's property, however acquired, includes the period during which the property was held by any other person if that property has the same basis, in whole or in part, in the taxpayer's hands as it would have in the hands of such other person.

Section 741 of the Code provides that in the case of a sale or exchange of an interest in a partnership, gain or loss shall be recognized to the transferor partner. Such gain or loss shall be considered as a gain or loss from the sale or exchange of a capital asset, except as otherwise provided in section 751.

Section 751(a) of the Code provides that the amount of money or the fair value of property received by a transferor partner in exchange for all or part of such partner's interest in the partnership attributable to unrealized receivables of the partnership, or to inventory items of the partnership that have appreciated substantially in value, shall be considered as an amount realized from the sale or exchange of property other than a capital asset.

Section 752(a) of the Code provides that any increase in a partner's share of the liabilities of a partnership, or any increase in a partner's individual liabilities by reason of the assumption by the partner of partnership liabilities, will be considered as a contribution of money by such partner to the partnership.

Section 752(b) of the Code provides that any decrease in a partner's share of the liabilities of a partnership, or any decrease in a partner's individual liabilities by reason of the assumption by the partnership of such individual liabilities, will be considered as a distribution of money to the partner by the partnership. Under section 733(1) of the Code, the basis of a partner's interest in the partnership is reduced by the amount of money received in a distribution that is not in liquidation of the partnership.

Section 752(d) of the Code provides that in the case of a sale or exchange of an interest in a partnership, liabilities shall be treated in the same manner as liabilities in connection with the sale or exchange of property not associated with partnerships.

The premise in Rev. Rul. 70–239 that the federal income tax consequences of the three situations described therein would be the same, without regard to which of the three transactions was entered into, is incorrect. As described below, depending on the format chosen for the transfer to a controlled corporation, the basis and holding periods of the various assets received by the corporation and the basis and holding periods of the stock received by the former partners can vary.

Additionally, Rev. Rul. 70–239 raises questions about potential adverse tax consequences to taxpayers in certain cases involving collapsible corporations defined in section 341 of the Code, personal holding companies described in section 542, small business corporations defined in section 1244, and electing small business corporations defined in section 1371. Recognition of the three possible methods to incorporate a partnership will enable taxpayers to avoid the above potential pitfalls and will facilitate flexibility with respect to the basis and holding periods of the assets received in the exchange.

HOLDING

Rev. Rul. 70–239 no longer represents the Service's position. The Service's current position is set forth below, and for each situation, the methods described and the underlying assumptions and purposes must be satisfied for the conclusions of this revenue ruling to be applicable.

Situation 1

Under section 351 of the Code, gain or loss is not recognized by X on the transfer by X of all of its assets to R in exchange for R's stock and the assumption by R of X's liabilities.

Under section 362(a) of the Code, R's basis in the assets received from X equals their basis to X immediately before their transfer to R. Under section 358(a), the basis to X of the stock received from R is the same as the basis to X of the assets transferred to R, reduced by the liabilities assumed by R, which assumption is treated as a payment of money to X under section 358(d). In addition, the assumption by R of X's liabilities decreased each partner's share of the partnership liabilities, thus, decreasing the basis of each partner's partnership interest pursuant to sections 752 and 733.

On distribution of the stock to X's partners, X terminated under section 708(b)(1)(A) of the Code. Pursuant to section 732(b), the basis of the stock distributed to the partners in liquidation of their partnership interests is, with respect to each partner, equal to the adjusted basis of the partner's interest in the partnership.

Under section 1223(1) of the Code, X's holding period for the stock received in the exchange includes its holding period in the capital assets and section 1231 assets transferred (to the extent that the stock was received in exchange for such assets). To the extent the stock was received in exchange for neither capital nor section 1231 assets, X's holding period for such stock begins on the day following the date of the exchange. Under section 1223(2), R's holding period in the assets transferred to it includes X's holding period. When X distributed the R stock to its partners, under sections 735(b) and 1223, the partners' holding periods included X's holding period of the stock. Furthermore, such distribution will not violate the control requirement of section 368(c) of the Code.

Situation 2

On the transfer of all of Y's assets to its partners, Y terminated under section 708(b)(1)(A) of the Code, and, pursuant to section 732(b), the basis of the assets (other than money) distributed to the partners in liquidation of their partnership interests in Y was, with respect to each partner, equal to the adjusted basis of the partner's interest in Y, reduced by the money distributed. Under section 752, the decrease in Y's liabilities resulting from the transfer to Y's partners was offset by the partners' corresponding assumption of such liabilities so that the net effect on the basis of each partner's interest in Y, with respect to the liabilities transferred, was zero.

Under section 351 of the Code, gain or loss is not recognized by Y's former partners on the transfer to S in exchange for its stock and the assumption of Y's liabilities, of the assets of Y received by Y's partners in liquidation of Y.

Under section 358(a) of the Code, the basis to the former partners of Y in the stock received from S is the same as the section 732(b) basis to the former partners of Y in the assets received in liquidation of Y and transferred to S, reduced by the liabilities assumed by S, which assumption is treated as a payment of money to the partners under section 358(d).

Under section 362(a) of the Code, S's basis in the assets received from Y's former partners equals their basis to the former partners as determined under section 732(c) immediately before the transfer to S.

Under section 735(b) of the Code, the partners' holding periods for the assets distributed to them by Y includes Y's holding period. Under section 1223(1), the partners' holding periods for the stock received in the exchange includes the partners' holding periods in the capital assets and section 1231 assets transferred to S (to the extent that the stock was received in exchange for such assets). However, to the extent that the stock received was in exchange for neither capital nor section 1231 assets, the holding period of the stock began on the day following the date of the exchange. Under section 1223(2), S's holding period of the Y assets received in the exchange includes the partner's holding periods.

Situation 3

Under section 351 of the Code, gain or loss is not recognized by Z's partners on the transfer of the partnership interests to T in exchange for T's stock.

On the transfer of the partnership interests to the corporation, Z terminated under section 708(b)(1)(A) of the Code.

Under section 358(a) of the Code, the basis to the partners of Z of the stock received from T in exchange for their partnership interests equals the basis of their partnership interests transferred to T, reduced by Z's liabilities assumed by T, the release from which is treated as a payment of money to Z's partners under sections 752(d) and 358(d).

T's basis for the assets received in the exchange equals the basis of the partners in their partnership interests allocated in accordance with section 732(c). T's holding period includes Z's holding period in the assets.

Under section 1223(1) of the Code, the holding period of the T stock received by the former partners of Z includes each respective partner's holding period for the partnership interest transferred, except that the holding period of the T stock that was received by the partners of Z in exchange for their interests in section 751 assets of Z that are neither capital assets nor section 1231 assets begins on the day following the date of the exchange.

READ: Code § 7704

In addition to an incorporation of a tax partnership under state law, the tax consequences of which are described in Revenue Ruling 84–111, there are 2 additional situations that, for tax purposes, also are treated as involving the incorporation of a partnership: (i) a tax partnership changing its tax character and becoming an association that is taxed as a corporation under the check-the-box regulations and (ii) a partnership becoming publicly traded so as to be taxed as a corporation under Section 7704.[1] Section 301.7701–3(g)(1)(i) of the regulations provides that a partnership that checks the box to be taxed as a corporation is treated as if it had used the state-law form that was used in Situation 1 of Revenue Ruling 84–111: the partnership incorporating its assets for stock and then liquidating by distributing the stock to its partners.[2] Section 7704(f) provides the same regime for an existing tax partnership that changes status to become a corporation for tax purposes by operation of Section 7704.

REVIEW: Code § 7704 and Reg. § 301.7701–3(g)(1)

Problem Set IX.B

1. Do the bases of the operating assets of the business change in any of the 3 forms for incorporating a partnership? If there is a difference between the forms, under what circumstances is one or more to be preferred to the others?

2. Is Section 357(c) more likely to apply under one or more of the forms than under the others.

C. CONTINUATION OF A PARTNERSHIP

READ: Code § 708 and Reg. § 1.708–1(b)

Before looking at the taxation of partnership amalgamations, one more background topic merits review. As already noted, the core issue in

---

1. For non-tax reasons, a partnership business about to go public may chose to incorporate under state law.

2. Interestingly, if an entity taxed as a corporation properly checks the box to be taxed as a partnership, Section 301.7701–3(g)(1)(ii) does not treat the old entity as transferring assets to the new entity, as when a partnership becomes a corporation, but rather treats the old entity as distributing its assets in liquidation: The tax corporation liquidates and its owners transfer the assets received in liquidation to the new tax partnership.

partnership M & A is whether a given transaction effects a termination of any of the partnerships involved. This section of this text sets out the basic tax rules that control the continuation of a partnership for tax purposes. The underlying questions here are (i) what circumstances, in addition to a formal liquidation of a partner or an entire partnership, draw the basic tax rules applicable to partnership liquidations, which were discussed in the preceding chapter of this text, into play and, (ii) if these rules are drawn into play, how they apply.

The central provision is Section 708. It provides that a partnership (with ongoing operations[3]) is treated as continuing so long as less than 1/2 of the partnership interests in capital **and** profits change hands by sale or exchange in any 12–month period.[4] Thus, for example, if a 49% pro-rata partner sells her interest, the partnership will terminate if all other sales or exchanges within 12 months before, or within 12 months after, the current sale involve an additional, different, 1% or more of the partnership's capital **and** profits. Conversely, a single 1% pro-rata interest can change hands every business day of a year without the partnership terminating as long as other transfers 12 months before, or after, each such transfer involve less than an aggregate 49% of the partnership's capital **and** profits.[5]

If 50% or more of the profits and capital interests are transferred in a 12–month period, there are tax consequences: The partnership's tax year ends,[6] which could accelerate the partners' income. There is a deemed liquidation of the partnership.[7] The liquidation occurs on the day of the sale or exchange that, when added to all sales or exchanges in the 12 months preceding that day (as to that tax partnership[8]), causes 50% of capital and profits to have changed hands.[9]

The consequences of such a deemed liquidation under Section 708(b)(1)(B) are not as bad as they could be, however. Since 1997, the regulations have labored mightily to reduce the tax consequences of a Section 708(b))(1)(B) termination. Section 1.708–1(b)(4) treats such a deemed liquidation as if the old partnership contributed its assets to a new partnership[10] and distributed the interests in the new partnership in liquidation.[11] Under this regime, there is no deemed distribution of the old partnership's assets, which could trigger gain or loss or change the bases of the assets (which was the result under the pre–1997 regulations).

---

3. I.R.C. § 708(b)(1)(A).

4. I.R.C. §§ 708(a), (b)(1)(B).

5. Treas. Reg. § 1.708–1(b)(2).

6. Treas. Reg. §§ 1.706–1(c)(1), 1.708–1(b)(3).

7. Treas. Reg. § 1.708–1(b)(2), (4).

8. Transfers of interests in a predecessor partnership are not taken into account.

9. Treas. Reg. § 1.708–1(b)(3)(ii).

10. Any Section 743(b) adjustments with regard to the sale that caused the deemed termination are made prior to the deemed contribution. Treas. Reg. § 1.708–1(b)(5).

11. Note that an approach where assets are transferred to the new entity first is adopted here, as in the check-the-box regulations and Section 7704, which were discussed in the preceding section of this text.

Conforming rules elsewhere also minimize the impact of a deemed liquidation. The capital accounts carry over from the old partnership to the new partnership.[12] Pre-termination Section 704(c) taint follows property over, but no new Section 704(c) property is created, and the 7–year periods under Sections 704(c)(1)(B) and 737 do not start anew.[13] Section 743(b) special basis carries over.[14] The new partnership must make its own Section 754 election, however.

**REVIEW: Code   § 708   and   Reg.   §§ 1.704–1(b)(2)(iv)(*l*),
            –3(a)(3)(i), –4(a)(4)(ii), and –4(c)(3), 1.708–1(b),
            and 1.737–2(a)**

Problem Set IX.D

1.   When a partnership terminates under Section 708 because of a sale or exchange of 50% or more of the capital and profits interests within a 12–month period, what is the holding period of the continuing partners in their partnership interests in the new tax partnership?

2.   What are the new partnership's holding periods in its assets?

3.   What is the effect of the Section 708 deemed termination on the depreciation of the old partnership's assets?

4.   As to partners with losses deferred under Section 704(d), does a deemed termination under Section 708 impact the utilization of those loses in the future?

5.   Can the buyer of 50% of a partnership (capital and profits interests) get the benefits of Section 743(b)?

D.   SECTION 708(b)(1)(A) TERMINATIONS

READ: Code § 708(b)

The new regulations that minimize the tax consequences of a Section 708(b)(1)(B) termination do not apply to a Section 708(b)(1)(A) liquidation.[15] A Section 708(b)(1)(A) termination usually is taxed as one would expect, as if the liquidating partnership distributes its assets to its partners. The end of a tax partnership by one partner buying the partnership interests of all of the others presents special problems, however. The issue is whether the buying partner is buying assets or partnership interests (and whether the selling partners are selling assets or interests). The IRS' analysis here is contained in the following Revenue Ruling:

---

12.   Treas. Reg. § 1.704–1(b)(2)(iv)(*l*).
13.   Treas.   Reg.   §§ 1.704–3(a)(3)(i), –4(a)(4)(ii), –4(c)(3); 1.737–2(a). Subsequent sales and distributions by the new partnership have the same effect under Sections

704(c)(1)(B) and 737 as if made by the old partnership.

14.   Treas. Reg. § 1.743–1(h)(1).
15.   Treas. Reg. § 1.708–1(b)(4).

REVENUE RULING 99-6
1999-1 C.B. 432.

ISSUE

What are the federal income tax consequences if one person purchases all of the ownership interests in a domestic limited liability company (LLC) that is classified as a partnership under § 301.7701–3 of the Regulations, causing the LLC's status as a partnership to terminate under § 708(b)(1)(A) of the Internal Revenue Code?

FACTS

[A]n LLC is formed and operates in a state which permits an LLC to have a single owner. Each LLC is classified as a partnership under § 301.7701–3. Neither of the LLCs holds any unrealized receivables or substantially appreciated inventory for purposes of § 751(b). For the sake of simplicity, it is assumed that neither LLC is liable for any indebtedness, nor are the assets of the LLCs subject to any indebtedness.

A and B are equal partners in AB, an LLC. A sells A's entire interest in AB to B for $10,000. After the sale, the business is continued by the LLC, which is owned solely by B.

After the sale, no entity classification election is made under § 301.7701–3(c) to treat the LLC as an association for federal tax purposes.

LAW

Section 708(b)(1)(A) and § 1.708–1(b)(1) of the Income Tax Regulations provide that a partnership shall terminate when the operations of the partnership are discontinued and no part of any business, financial operation, or venture of the partnership continues to be carried on by any of its partners in a partnership.

Section 731(a)(1) provides that, in the case of a distribution by a partnership to a partner, gain is not recognized to the partner except to the extent that any money distributed exceeds the adjusted basis of the partner's interest in the partnership immediately before the distribution.

Section 731(a)(2) provides that, in the case of a distribution by a partnership in liquidation of a partner's interest in a partnership where no property other than money, unrealized receivables (as defined in § 751(c)), and inventory (as defined in § 751(d)(2)) is distributed to the partner, loss is recognized to the extent of the excess of the adjusted basis of the partner's interest in the partnership over the sum of (A) any money distributed, and (B) the basis to the distributee, as determined under § 732, of any unrealized receivables and inventory.

Section 732(b) provides that the basis of property (other than money) distributed by a partnership to a partner in liquidation of the partner's interest shall be an amount equal to the adjusted basis of the partner's interest in the partnership, reduced by any money distributed in the same transaction.

Section 735(b) provides that, in determining the period for which a partner has held property received in a distribution from a partnership (other than for purposes of § 735(a)(2)), there shall be included the holding period of the partnership, as determined under § 1223, with respect to the property.

Section 741 provides that gain or loss resulting from the sale or exchange of an interest in a partnership shall be recognized by the transferor partner, and that the gain or loss shall be considered as gain or loss from a capital asset, except as provided in § 751 (relating to unrealized receivables and inventory items).

Section 1.741–1(b) provides that § 741 applies to the transferor partner in a two-person partnership when one partner sells a partnership interest to the other partner, and to all the members of a partnership when they sell their interests to one or more persons outside the partnership.

Section 301.7701–2(c)(1) provides that, for federal tax purposes, the term "partnership" means a business entity (as the term is defined in § 301.7701–2(a)) that is not a corporation and that has at least two members.

In *Edwin E. McCauslen v. Commissioner*, 45 T.C. 588 (1966), one partner in an equal, two-person partnership died, and his partnership interest was purchased from his estate by the remaining partner. The purchase caused a termination of the partnership under § 708(b)(1)(A). The Tax Court held that the surviving partner did not purchase the deceased partner's interest in the partnership, but that the surviving partner purchased the partnership assets attributable to the interest. As a result, the surviving partner was not permitted to succeed to the partnership's holding period with respect to these assets.

Rev. Rul. 67–65, 1967–1 C.B. 168, also considered the purchase of a deceased partner's interest by the other partner in a two-person partnership. The Service ruled that, for the purpose of determining the purchaser's holding period in the assets attributable to the deceased partner's interest, the purchaser should treat the transaction as a purchase of the assets attributable to the interest. Accordingly, the purchaser was not permitted to succeed to the partnership's holding period with respect to these assets.

ANALYSIS AND HOLDINGS

The AB partnership terminates under § 708(b)(1)(A) when B purchases A's entire interest in AB. Accordingly, A must treat the transaction as the sale of a partnership interest. Reg. § 1.741–1(b). A must report gain or loss, if any, resulting from the sale of A's partnership interest in accordance with § 741.

Under the analysis of *McCauslen* and Rev. Rul. 67–65, for purposes of determining the tax treatment of B, the AB partnership is deemed to make a liquidating distribution of all of its assets to A and B, and following this distribution, B is treated as acquiring the assets deemed to have been distributed to A in liquidation of A's partnership interest.

B's basis in the assets attributable to A's one-half interest in the partnership is $10,000, the purchase price for A's partnership interest. Section 1012. Section 735(b) does not apply with respect to the assets B is deemed to have purchased from A. Therefore, B's holding period for these assets begins on the day immediately following the date of the sale. See Rev. Rul. 66–7, 1966–1 C.B. 188, which provides that the holding period of an asset is computed by excluding the date on which the asset is acquired.

Upon the termination of AB, B is considered to receive a distribution of those assets attributable to B's former interest in AB, B must recognize gain or loss, if any, on the deemed distribution of the assets to the extent required by § 731(a). B's basis in the assets received in the deemed liquidation of B's partnership interest is determined under § 732(b). Under § 735(b), B's holding period for the assets attributable to B's one-half interest in AB includes the partnership's holding period for such assets (except for purposes of § 735(a)(2)).

Problem Set IX.D

Sue and Sally are the original equal partners in a partnership that owns (i) inventory with a value of $50,000 and a basis of $100,000 and (ii) investment real estate with a value of $150,000 and a basis of 100,000. Each has a $100,000 outside basis. Sue buys Sally's entire interest for $100,000 in cash. What are the tax consequences to Sue and Sally (including Sue's basis in the former partnership assets).

E. PARTNERSHIP AMALGAMATIONS

READ: Reg. § 1.708–1(c)

With the background above, it finally is time to consider partnership amalgamations (mergers and combinations). The rules here are provided by regulations adopted in 2001. Basically, at most one of the amalgamating partnerships is treated as the predecessor to the amalgamated partnership. This partnership, if any, has no tax consequences, per se.[16] All of the other partnerships are treated as liquidating, with the liquidation[s] taxed according to the state-law form utilized to effect the amalgamation.

A prior partnership continues if over 50% of the partnership interests in capital and profits of the amalgamated partnership are held by partners of the prior partnership.[17] Thus, none of the prior partnerships

---

16. If the amalgamation transaction shifts the obligation on debt under Section 752, the associated **net** deemed contributions and distributions also must be taken into account. Treas. Reg. § 1.752–1(f).

17. Compare this with Section 1.368–1(e) of the regulations, which looks to continuing stock interests, rather than continuing shareholders, in determining the continuity of proprietary interest required in a tax-free corporate reorganization.

may continue. When the amalgamated partnership continues more than one prior partnership under this ownership test, the continuing partnership that contributes the most assets (by net value) to the amalgamated partnership, is the predecessor of the amalgamated partnership.[18]

Next, the tax consequences with regard to the partnerships deemed terminated must be appraised. For this purpose, Subchapter K must determine how to view the amalgamation transaction. Under the regulations, in the spirit of Revenue Ruling 84–111, above, much deference is given to the state-law form.[19] For example, the amalgamation may be done under state law by one or all of the discontinued partnerships formally liquidating and then the former partners contributing their partnerships' assets to the amalgamated partnership. This is called the "assets-up" form in the regulations.[20] The regulations respect the state-law assets-up form for purposes of taxing the transaction:[21] The partners of the discontinued partnerships are treated as receiving their partnerships' assets as actually distributed under state law. This can trigger gain or loss under Sections 731 and 751(b). The bases of the assets are redetermined under Section 732. These bases and other tax characteristics follow the assets into the amalgamated partnership under Section 723 and other provisions. Built-in gain and loss (determined at this time) in assets transferred to the amalgamated partnership are subject to Sections 704(c)(1) and 737.

If the state-law assets-up form is not used, each discontinued partnership is treated as if it contributed assets to the amalgamated partnership in exchange for interests in the new partnership, which then are distributed in liquidation of the discontinued partnership.[22] This default form, referred to as the "assets-over" form in the regulations, resembles the treatment when a tax partnership checks the box to be taxed as a corporation, as discussed above. There are fewer tax consequences to this assets-over form than to the assets-up form: The discontinued partnership's tax year ends.[23] Assets transferred to the amalgamated partnership carry with them their bases and other tax characteristics. There are Section 704(c) allocations (and associated problems under Sections 704(c)(1)(B) and 737) to the partners in the discontinued partnership as they continue as partners in the amalgamated partnership. The partners are taxed under the rules examined in the preceding chapter. Partners

---

18. Treas. Reg. § 1.708–1(c)(1). Interestingly, these rules parallel the corporate tax rules regarding continuity of proprietary interest and continuity of business enterprise. Partnership tax law, however, does not defer to state partnership law in determining the surviving entity.

19. This deference is not absolute, however. There is an anti-abuse rule, Section 1.708–1(c)(6).

20. A transaction conforms to the assets-up form regardless of whether the amalgamated partnership continues a prior partnership for tax purposes.

21. Treas. Reg. § 1.708–1(c)(3)(ii).

22. Treas. Reg. § 1.708–1(c)(3)(i). In the spirit of *Foxman*, examined in the preceding chapter, an actual sale of an interest in the discontinued partnership to the resulting partnership as part of the merger will be respected as such for tax purposes and, inter alia, taxed under Sections 741 and 751(a). Treas. Reg. § 1.708–1(c)(4).

23. Treas. Reg. § 1.706–1(c)(1).

who receive no boot pay no tax on the deemed distribution (including under Section 751(b)) and continue with the same outside bases.[24]

It is helpful to compare and contrast the rules for corporate and partnership acquisitions. First, consider the acquirer: A corporation can acquire anything (property or services) with its own stock and the transaction is tax-free to the corporation.[25] As discussed in Chapter II, a partnership has no gain if it pays for property with a partnership interest, but has gain if it pays for services with a partnership interest.

Then, consider the other party to the transaction: A corporation can acquire stock in another corporation for its own stock in a transaction that is tax-free to the transferor to the corporation in a Section 351 transaction, in a B reorganization, or in a reverse triangular reorganization.[26] Assets (other than stock) can be acquired by a corporation for its own stock in a tax-free transaction in a Section 351 transaction, in a qualified merger or combination, or in a C reorganization.[27] In contrast, a partnership can acquire any property (but not services) for a partnership interest in a transaction that is tax-free to the other party.

In light of this analysis, note that (i) a corporation or partnership can always acquire a corporation or its assets tax-free to both parties (as long as the corporation does not liquidate) provided that only the acquirer's stock or partnership interests are paid, while (ii) the only way a corporation can acquire a partnership tax-free is in a Section 351 transaction. As a consequence, one reason for incorporating a business is that the incorporation sets the stage for a future tax-free disposition to an acquiring corporation (in exchange for stock in the acquiring corporation).

REVIEW: Reg. §§ 1.706–1(c)(1), 1.708–1(c), and 1.752–1(f)

Problem Set IX.E

Two law firms organized as partnerships have agreed to merge. Is there a tax advantage to one state-law form over another?

F. PARTNERSHIP DIVISIONS

READ: Reg. § 1.708–1(d)

The 2001 Section 708 regulations also contain rules for corporate divisions, which resemble the rules for amalgamations. Again, there are both continuing and terminated partnerships, with differing tax regimes for each. The partnership division regulations refer (i) to the old partnership that was divided as the "prior" partnership, (ii) to the partnership resulting from the division transaction that is treated under the regula-

---

24. As above, if the transaction shifts the debt under Section 752, the associated deemed contributions and distributions impact.

25. I.R.C. § 1032; Treas. Reg. § 1.1032–1(b).

26. I.R.C. §§ 354, 361, 368(a)(1).

27. *Id.*

tions as the one successor to the prior partnership, if any, as the "divided" partnership, and (iii) to the one or more resulting partnerships whose partners owned over 50% of the capital and profits of the prior partnership, if any, as "continuing" partnerships.[28]

The tax analysis gives state-law form considerable deference, as with amalgamations:[29] If the parties effect their transaction by using the assets-up form under state law, that form will be respected for tax purposes. Under the assets-up form, the prior partnership distributes some or all of its assets to its partners under state law. These distributions may be in complete liquidation of some or all of the historic partners of the prior partnership. The distributee partners then contribute some or all of the assets received to one or more resulting partnerships.[30] If the assets-up state-law form is not used, Subchapter K views the division transaction as having been effected using the assets-over form, even if that form, or no form, was used under state law. The transaction is taxed as if the prior partnership contributed some or all of its assets to one or more resulting partnerships and then distributes its interests in these partnerships to its partners. These distributions may be in complete liquidation of some or all of the historic partners of the prior partnership.[31]

The question then arises as to which continuing partnership, if any, is treated as the divided (successor) partnership for tax purposes. (If there is no continuing partnership, there is no divided partnership.) If (i) either the assets-up or assets-over form is used under state law (rather than, say, no form) and (ii) the prior partnership is continuing, it is treated as the divided partnership. Otherwise, if exactly one partnership resulting from division is continuing (i.e., its partners owned over 50% of the capital and profits of the prior partnership), that partnership is the divided partnership. If 2 or more resulting partnerships are continuing, the one of them that received the greatest net value of the assets of the prior partnership is the divided partnership.[32]

Once the division transaction has been characterized and the roles of the various partnerships identified for tax purposes, the actual tax consequences of the transaction must be determined: All partnerships (continuing or not) have new tax years that begin on the date of the division except the divided (successor) partnership, if any.[33] In contrast, all continuing partnerships are held to the prior partnership's tax elections.[34] Otherwise, as with amalgamations, the taxation rules apply in accordance with the tax form. Basically, the assets-up form triggers some gain and loss and changes the bases of the assets not retained by

---

28. Treas. Reg. §§ 1.708–1(d)(1), (4). For example, in a split-up of a partnership, none of the resulting partnerships may be "continuing" in the regulation's sense.

29. The division regulations, like the amalgamation regulations, do not respect state-law form absolutely. Treas. Reg. § 1.708–1(d)(6).

30. Treas. Reg. § 1.708–1(d)(3)(ii).

31. Treas. Reg. § 1.708–1(d)(3)(i).

32. Treas. Reg. § 1.708–1(d)(1), (4)(i).

33. Treas. Reg. § 1.708–1(d)(2)(i).

34. Treas. Reg. § 1.708–1(d)(2)(ii).

the divided corporation, if any, while the assets-over form has far fewer tax ramifications.

An example helps illustrate the basic approach of the partnership division regulations. A partnership has 5 equal partners: A, B, C, D and E. They each have an outside basis of $200,000 in a partnership interest worth $300,000. The partnership owns 4 parcels of investment real estate:

	Basis	FMV
Parcel 1	$200,000	$450,000
Parcel 2	400,000	450,000
Parcel 3	100,000	300,000
Parcel 4	300,000	300,000

A, B, and C want to develop Parcels 1, 2, and 3. (But this example assumes that the parcels are not ordinary income property, yet.) D and E want to own Parcels 3 and 4 separate from the development operations. Hence, a split-up is effected: The old partnership redeems the partnership interests of D and E in exchange for Parcels 3 and 4, respectively. D and E form a new 50–50 partnership, contributing Parcels 3 and 4.

The ABC partnership is a continuing partnership, as its partners owned more than 50% of the prior ABCDE partnership. ABC is the divided partnership. Since the assets-up form is used, ABCDE is treated as distributing the Parcels 3 and 4 in complete liquidation of D and E. The ABCDE partnership's tax year closes with regard to D and E, but not with regard to A, B, and C. Under Section 732(b), D and E get a basis of $200,000 in their respective parcels. Thus, the newly-formed DE partnership gets a basis of $200,000 in each parcel under Section 723. There is no change in the bases of Parcels 1 and 2 to the ABC partnership unless a Section 754 election is in place. The DE partnership is not bound to any tax elections that were made by the ABCDE partnership, since DE does not continue ABCDE. If the assets-up form had not been used, the bases of Parcels 3 and 4 would not have changed.[35]

REVIEW: Reg. § 1.708–1(d)

Problem Set IX.E

The MEGA law firm is organized as a partnership. Civil war has broken out between the tax lawyers and the remainder of the firm. The tax lawyers desire to leave the firm and form their own boutique (also to

---

35. If the DE partnership made a Section 754 election, the bases of Parcels 3 and 4 would be adjusted. I.R.C. § 761(e).

be organized as a partnership). Is there a tax advantage to one state-law form over another? What other facts do you need to know?

F. TIERED PARTNERSHIPS

A partnership can be a partner in another partnership. Such partnership tiering presents numerous issues under Subchapter K, the most important of which are reviewed in this section of this text.[36]

1. Partnership Operations

READ: Code §§ 706(a) and (d)(3) and 751(f) and Reg. §§ 1.704–2(k) and 1.752–2(i), –3(a)(1), and –4(a)

As a general proposition, when a partnership (the "upper partnership") is itself a partner in another partnership (the "lower partnership"), the upper partnership is treated as is any partner in the lower partnership. For example, the upper partnership is taxed on its share of the lower partnership's income in the upper partnership's tax year that includes the end of the lower partnership's tax year under Section 706(a).

Special rules are provided to deal with some special problems presented by such tiered partnerships, however. For example, Section 706(d)(3) looks through partnership veils to assure that a new partner in the upper partnership is not allocated items of the lower partnership that are attributable to the period prior to the admission of the new partner to the upper partnership. Similarly, Section 1.704–2(k) of the regulations applies the rules for nonrecourse deductions by looking through partnership tiers in determining shares of minimum gain and other relevant items. Section 751(f) looks through partnerships in determining whether an upper partnership has hot property for Section 751 purposes.

Section 1.752–4(a) of the regulations provides that debt flows through tiers of partnerships for Section 752 purposes. Recourse liabilities flow through in accordance with the economic risk of loss under Section 1.752–2(i). As to nonrecourse liabilities; under Section 1.752–3(a)(1), they first follow minimum gain (determined by looking through lower partnerships in accordance with Section 1.704–2(k), noted in the preceding paragraph), and then flow through under the general rules of Sections 1.752–3(a)(2) and (3).

---

36. Some topics are not covered. There is no consideration of interpartnership contributions and distributions of property specially treated under Subchapter K (say, under Sections 704(c) or 743(b)) or of the distribution by one partnership of an interest in another partnership.

REVIEW: Code §§ 706(a) and (d)(3) and 751(f) and Reg. §§ 1.704–2(k), 1.752–2(i), 1.752–3(a)(1), and 1.752–4(a)

2. Interest Transfers, Distributions, and Contributions

READ: Code §§ 708(b), 734(b) and 743(b) and Reg. § 1.708–1(b)(2).

Further issues are presented by adjustments to the ownership of the upper partnership. For example, Section 1.708–1(b)(2) of the regulations provides that if an upper partnership terminates under Section 708(b), that is treated as a sale or exchange of the upper partnership's interest in the lower partnership that counts toward the 50% of capital and profits in the lower partnership that, if exchanged in 12 months, terminates the lower partnership under Section 708(b)(1)(B). Thus, for example, if the upper partnership owns over 50% of the capital and profits interests of the lower partnership, a termination of the upper partnership also terminates the lower partnership.

The question also arises as to how Section 743(b) applies when an interest in the upper partnership is transferred. The following revenue ruling analyzes this issue. It is set out here in some detail, not only for its holdings, but also for how it uses the distinction between the aggregate and entity approaches to partnerships in the legal analysis.

REVENUE RULING 87–115
1987–2 C.B. 163.

Under section 743(b) of the Internal Revenue Code, does a sale of an interest in an upper-tier partnership [UTP] result in an adjustment to the basis of the property of a lower-tier partnership [LTP] in which UTP has an interest if:

> (1) both UTP and LTP have made an election under section 754?

> (2) only UTP has made the election under section 754?

> (3) only LTP has made the election under section 754?

FACTS

UTP is a partnership in which A, B, C, and D are equal partners. UTP is an equal partner in LTP, along with X and Y.

In 1985, A sold A's entire interest in UTP to E.

Situation 1

Both UTP and LTP have valid section 754 elections in effect.

Situation 2

UTP has a section 754 election in effect, but LTP does not.

Situation 3

UTP does not have a section 754 election in effect, but LTP does.

LAW AND ANALYSIS

In essence, if an election under section 754 is not in effect, the partnership is treated as an independent entity, separate from its partners. Thus, absent a section 754 election, even though the transferee receives a cost basis for the acquired partnership interest, the partnership does not adjust the transferee's share of the adjusted basis of partnership property. If, however, an election under section 754 is in effect, the partnership is treated more like an aggregate of its partners, and the transferee's overall basis in the assets of the partnership is generally the same as it would have been had the transferee acquired a direct interest in its share of those assets.

Situation 1

Because UTP made a section 754 election manifesting an intent to be treated as an aggregate for purposes of sections 754 and 743, it is appropriate, for purposes of section 743 and 754, to treat the sale of A's partnership interest in UTP as a deemed sale of an interest in LTP. Further, this deemed sale of an interest in LTP triggers the application of section 743(b) to LTP.

Situation 2

UTP has made a valid section 754 election. However, in this situation, LTP does not have a section 754 election in effect. That is, under section 743(a), LTP chose not to have the basis of its property adjusted as the result of the transfer of an interest in it. Thus, E's purchase of a partnership interest in UTP has no affect on LTP's adjusted basis in its property.

Situation 3

[B]y not making a section 754 election, UTP manifested an intent to be treated as an entity for purposes of sections 754 and 743. Thus, it is inappropriate, for purposes of sections 754 and 743, to treat A's sale of an interest in UTP as the sale of an interest in LTP. Consequently, UTP cannot increase E's share of the basis of LTP's property. Nevertheless, LTP's section 754 election is not meaningless. If UTP were to sell its partnership interest in LTP, the purchaser's share of the adjusted basis of LTP's assets would be adjusted.

HOLDINGS

Situation 1

Upon the sale of A's partnership interest in UTP, the transferee's (E's) share of UTP's adjusted basis in its assets is adjusted by the amount by which the basis in E's partnership interest differs from E's share of UTP's adjusted basis in its assets. In addition, E's share of LTP's adjusted basis in its assets is adjusted by the amount by which E's share of UTP's adjusted basis in LTP differs from E's share of the adjusted basis of LTP's property.

Situation 2

Upon the sale of A's partnership interest in UTP, E's share of UTP's adjusted basis in its assets is adjusted by the amount by which the basis in E's partnership interest differs from E's share of UTP's adjusted basis in its assets. However, because LTP did not make a section 754 election, the transfer does not affect LTP's adjusted basis in its property.

Situation 3

The sale of A's partnership interest in UTP does not affect either UTP's adjusted basis in its property or LTP's adjusted basis in its property.

Similarly, if the upper partnership makes a distribution while a Section 754 election is in place so as to trigger an adjustment to the bases of the assets of the upper partnership under Section 734(b), the basis of the upper partnership's interest in the lower partnership is adjusted. If the lower partnership has a Section 754 election in place, its assets also are adjusted.[37] There is no authority on how a reverse Section 704(c) allocation in the upper partnership applies to a lower partnership, but a look-through rule would make the most sense.

REVIEW: Code §§ 708(b), 734(b) and 743(b) and Reg. § 1.708–1(b)(2)

Problem Set IX.F

1.   Bert and Ernie are 50–50 partners. Their partnership has no material assets other than a 50% interest in a partnership with Donna. The lower partnership's only material asset is a parcel of real estate held for investment that is worth $1 million with a tax basis of $100,000. The Bert and Ernie partnership has a basis of $50,000 in its interest in the lower partnership. Bert and Ernie each have a $25,000 basis in their respective partnership interests.

Ernie sells 1/2 of his partnership interest (1/4th of the upper partnership) to Gladys for $125,000 cash. A year later, the lower partnership sells the real estate for $1 million (but does not cease business so as to terminate). How is Gladys taxed with regard to this sale?

2.   The facts are the same as in Problem 1 except that Gladys, rather than buy an interest from Ernie, buys a 1/5th interest in the upper partnership from that partnership (again for $125,000 cash). Bert and Ernie's interests are reduced to 2/5ths each. The cash is put in the bank by the upper partnership. Now, how is Gladys taxed when the lower partnership sells its real estate for $1 million cash?

---

37.   Rev. Rul. 92–15, 1992–1 C.B. 215.

Chapter X

FAMILY PARTNERSHIPS

A. INTRODUCTION

Chapter IV of this text discussed how Section 704(b) affords partners tremendous flexibility in allocating income. The assumption underlying Section 704(b) is that the partners are dealing at arms' length, except to the extent that they are trying to reduce their collective taxes. Thus, the focus of Section 704(b) is on assuring that tax consequences follow the arms'-length, pre-tax economics. Frequently, however, partners are members of the same family who are not dealing at arms' length. This Chapter examines how Subchapter K, particularly Section 704(e), deals with family partnerships.[1] Read the 3d sentence of Section 1.704–1(b)(1)(iii) of the regulations. Note that the basic problem in this Chapter, when should other tax rules override a partnership allocation that is valid under Section 704(b), arises in numerous other contexts. Most importantly, the Anti–Abuse Regulations, which are the subject of the next chapter, deal generally with when technical compliance with the Section 704(b) regulations is not respected for tax purposes.

REVIEW: Reg. § 1.704–1(b)(1)(iii)

B. BACKGROUND: ASSIGNMENT OF INCOME

READ: Code §§ 1(g) and 7872

Under the income tax, because of the progressive rate structure, who is taxed on income impacts the amount of tax on that income. Attempts to reduce the tax on the income of a family by assigning it to

---

1. Family partnerships also are popular because of claimed estate and gift advantages from their use, but these possibilities are beyond the scope of this text. In the professional literature, partnerships involving family members frequently are referred to as FLPs (Family Limited Partnerships), since limited partnerships were the state-law vehicle of choice for family partnerships until the check-the-box regulations made LLCs attractive. Even now, a limited partnership may be used for a family investment partnership, since general partner liability poses little real risk with regard to an investment partnership and the state-law limited partnership form simplifies the centralization of management in certain family members.

lower-taxed members of the family surfaced early in the history of the income tax. The courts were quick to respond by creating assignment-of-income doctrine out of inferred legislative intent. Consequently, Congress has not legislated expressly in the area much. The 2 principal legislative responses to assignment-of-income problems to date have been the "kiddie tax" of Section 1(g) and the gift interest-free loan rules in Section 7872. To understand how assignment-of-income problems are dealt with in the partnership context today, it is helpful to examine a few judicial opinions:

LUCAS v. EARL

Supreme Court of the United States, 1930.
281 U.S. 111, 50 S.Ct. 241, 74 L.Ed. 731.

MR. JUSTICE HOLMES delivered the opinion of the Court.

This case presents the question whether the respondent, Earl, could be taxed for the whole of the salary and attorney's fees earned by him in the years 1920 and 1921, or should be taxed for only a half of them in view of a contract with his wife which we shall mention.

By the contract, Earl and his wife agreed "that any property either of us now has or may hereafter acquire ... in any way, either by earnings (including salaries, fees, etc.), or any rights by contract or otherwise, during the existence of our marriage, or which we or either of us may receive by gift, bequest, devise, or inheritance, and all the proceeds, issues, and profits of any and all such property shall be treated and considered and hereby is declared to be received, held, taken, and owned by us as joint tenants, and not otherwise, with the right of survivorship." The validity of the contract is not questioned, and we assume it to be unquestionable under the law of the State of California, in which the parties lived.

The [relevant statutes] impose a tax upon the net income of every individual including "income derived from salaries, wages, or compensation for personal service ... of whatever kind and in whatever form paid." A very forcible argument is presented to the effect that the statute seeks to tax only income beneficially received, and that taking the question more technically the salary and fees became the joint property of Earl and his wife on the very first instant on which they were received. We well might hesitate upon the latter proposition, because however the matter might stand between husband and wife he was the only party to the contracts by which the salary and fees were earned, and it is somewhat hard to say that the last step in the performance of those contracts could be taken by anyone but himself alone. But this case is not to be decided by attenuated subtleties. It turns on the import and reasonable construction of the taxing act. There is no doubt that the statute could tax salaries to those who earned them and provide that the tax could not be escaped by anticipatory arrangements and contracts however skillfully devised to prevent the salary when paid from vesting even for a second in the man who earned it. That seems to us the import of the statute before us and we think that no distinction can be taken according to the motives leading to the arrangement by which the fruits are attributed to a different tree from that on which they grew.

HELVERING v. HORST

Supreme Court of the United States, 1940.
311 U.S. 112, 61 S.Ct. 144, 85 L.Ed. 75.

MR. JUSTICE STONE delivered the opinion of the Court.

The sole question for decision is whether the gift, during the donor's taxable year, of interest coupons detached from the bonds, delivered to the donee and later in the year paid at maturity, is the realization of income taxable to the donor.

The holder of a coupon bond is the owner of two independent and separable kinds of right. One is the right to demand and receive at maturity the principal amount of the bond representing capital investment. The other is the right to demand and receive interim payments of interest on the investment in the amounts and on the dates specified by the coupons. Together they are an obligation to pay principal and interest given in exchange for money or property which was presumably the consideration for the obligation of the bond. Here respondent, as owner of the bonds, had acquired the legal right to demand payment at maturity of the interest specified by the coupons and the power to command its payment to others, which constituted an economic gain to him.

The question here is, whether because one who in fact receives payment for services or interest payments is taxable only on his receipt of the payments, he can escape all tax by giving away his right to income in advance of payment. If the taxpayer procures payment directly to his creditors of the items of interest or earnings due him, he does not escape taxation because he did not actually receive the money.

Underlying the reasoning in [earlier assignment-of-income cases] cases is the thought that income is "realized" by the assignor because he, who owns or controls the source of the income, also controls the disposition of that which he could have received himself and diverts the payment from himself to others as the means of procuring the satisfaction of his wants. The taxpayer has equally enjoyed the fruits of his labor or investment and obtained the satisfaction of his desires whether he collects and uses the income to procure those satisfactions, or whether he disposes of his right to collect it as the means of procuring them.

Although the donor here, by the transfer of the coupons, has precluded any possibility of his collecting them himself, he has nevertheless, by his act, procured payment of the interest as a valuable gift to a member of his family. Such a use of his economic gain, the right to receive income, to procure a satisfaction which can be obtained only by the expenditure of money or property, would seem to be the enjoyment of the income whether the satisfaction is the purchase of goods at the corner grocery, the payment of his debt there, or such nonmaterial satisfactions as may result from the payment of a campaign or community chest contribution, or a gift to his favorite son. Even though he never receives the money, he derives money's worth from the disposition of the coupons which he has used as money or money's worth in the procuring of a satisfaction which is procurable only by the expenditure of money or money's worth. The enjoyment of the economic benefit accruing to him by virtue of his acquisition of the coupons is realized as completely as it would have been if he had collected the interest in dollars and expended them for any of the purposes named.

In a real sense he has enjoyed compensation for money loaned or services rendered, and not any the less so because it is his only reward for them. To say that one who has made a gift thus derived from interest or earnings paid to his donee has never enjoyed or realized the fruits of his investment or labor, because he has assigned them instead of collecting them himself and then paying them over to the donee, is to affront common understanding and to deny the facts of common experience. Common understanding and experience are the touchstones for the interpretation of the revenue laws.

The power to dispose of income is the equivalent of ownership of it. The exercise of that power to procure the payment of income to another is the enjoyment, and hence the realization, of the income by him who exercises it. We have had no difficulty in applying that proposition where the assignment preceded the rendition of the services, *Lucas v. Earl* [*supra*]. But it is the assignment by which the disposition of income is controlled when the service precedes the assignment, and in both cases it is the exercise of the power of disposition of the interest or compensation, with the resulting payment to the donee, which is the enjoyment by the donor of income derived from them.

This was emphasized in *Blair v. Commissioner*, 300 U.S. 5 [1937], on which respondent relies, where the distinction was taken between a gift of income derived from an obligation to pay compensation and a gift of income-producing property. In the circumstances of that case, the right to income from the trust property was thought to be so identified with the equitable ownership of the property, from which alone the beneficiary derived his right to receive the income and his power to command disposition of it, that a gift of the income by the beneficiary became effective only as a gift of his ownership of the property producing it. Since the gift was deemed to be a gift of the property, the income from it was held to be the income of the owner of the property, who was the donee, not the donor—a refinement which was unnecessary if respondent's contention here is right, but one clearly inapplicable to gifts of interest or wages. Unlike income thus derived from an obligation to pay interest or compensation, the income of the trust was regarded as no more the income of the donor than would be the rent from a lease or a crop raised on a farm after the leasehold or the farm had been given away.

The dominant purpose of the revenue laws is the taxation of income to those who earn or otherwise create the right to receive it and enjoy the benefit of it when paid. The tax laid upon income "derived from . . . wages, or compensation for personal service, of whatever kind and in whatever form paid, . . .; also from interest . . ." therefore cannot fairly be interpreted as not applying to income derived from interest or compensation when he who is entitled to receive it makes use of his power to dispose of it in procuring satisfactions which he would otherwise procure only by the use of the money when received.

Nor is it perceived that there is any adequate basis for distinguishing between the gift of interest coupons here and a gift of salary or commissions. The owner of a negotiable bond and of the investment which it represents, if not the lender, stands in the place of the lender. When, by the gift of the coupons, he has separated his right to interest payments from his investment and procured the payment of the interest to his donee, he has enjoyed the economic benefits of the income in the same manner and to the same extent as though the transfer were of earnings, and in both cases the import of the statute is that the fruit is not to be attributed to a different tree from that on which it grew.

COMMISSIONER v. CULBERTSON

Supreme Court of the United States, 1949.
337 U.S. 733, 69 S.Ct. 1210, 93 L.Ed. 1659.

MR. CHIEF JUSTICE VINSON delivered the opinion of the Court.

This case requires our further consideration of the family partnership problem. The Commissioner of Internal Revenue ruled that the entire income from a partnership allegedly entered into by respondent and his four sons must be taxed to respondent, and the Tax Court sustained that determination. The Court of Appeals for the Fifth Circuit reversed.

First. The Tax Court [applied] two essential tests of partnership for income-tax purposes: that each partner contribute to the partnership either vital services or capital originating with him. Its decision was based upon a finding that none of respondent's sons had satisfied those requirements during the tax years in question.

The Court of Appeals, on the other hand, was of the opinion that a family partnership entered into without thought of tax avoidance should be given recognition tax-wise whether or not it was intended that some of the partners contribute either capital or services during the tax year and whether or not they actually made such contributions, since it was formed "with the full expectation and purpose that the boys would, in the future, contribute their time and services to the partnership." We must consider, therefore, whether an intention to contribute capital or services sometime in the future is sufficient to satisfy ordinary concepts of partnership.

If it is conceded that some of the partners contributed neither capital nor services to the partnership during the tax years in question, as the Court of Appeals was apparently willing to do in the present case, it can hardly be contended that they are in any way responsible for the production of income during those years. The partnership sections of the Code are, of course, geared to the sections relating to taxation of individual income, since no tax is imposed upon partnership income as such. To hold that "Individuals carrying on business in partnership" includes persons who contribute nothing during the tax period would violate the first principle of income taxation: that income must be taxed to him who earns it. *Lucas v. Earl* [*supra*].

A partnership is an organization for the production of income to which each partner contributes one or both of the ingredients of income—capital or services. The intent to provide money, goods, labor, or skill sometime in the future cannot meet the demands of [the statute] that he who presently earns the income through his own labor and skill and the utilization of his own capital be taxed therefor. The vagaries of human experience preclude reliance upon even good faith intent as to future conduct as a basis for the present taxation of income.[2]

Second. We turn next to a consideration of the Tax Court's approach to the family partnership problem. It treated as essential to membership in a family partnership for tax purposes the contribution of either "vital services" or "original capital." Use of these "tests" of partnership indicates, at best, an error in emphasis.

The question is not whether the services or capital contributed by a partner are of sufficient importance to meet some objective, but whether, considering all the facts—the agreement, the conduct of the parties in execution of its provisions, their statements, the testimony of disinterested persons, the relationship of the parties, their respective abilities and capital contributions, the actual control of income and the purposes for which it is used, and any other facts throwing light on their true intent—the parties in good faith and acting with a business purpose intended to join together in the present conduct of the enterprise. There is nothing new or particularly difficult about such a test. Triers of fact are constantly called upon to determine the intent with which a person acted. Whether the parties really intended to carry on business as partners is not, we think, any more difficult of determination or the manifestations of such intent any less perceptible than is ordinarily true of inquiries into the subjective.

Unquestionably a court's determination that the services contributed by a partner are not "vital" and that he has not participated in "management and control of the business" or contributed "original capital" has the effect of placing a heavy burden on the taxpayer to show

2. [Court's Note 8:] The *reductio ad absurdum* of the theory that children may be partners with their parents before they are capable of being entrusted with the disposition of partnership funds or of contributing substantial services occurred in *Tinkoff v. Commissioner*, 120 F.2d 564 [7th Cir. 1941], where a taxpayer made his son a partner in his accounting firm the day the son was born.

the bona fide intent of the parties to join together as partners. But such a determination is not conclusive, and that is the vice in the "tests" adopted by the Tax Court. It assumes that there is no room for an honest difference of opinion as to whether the services or capital furnished by the alleged partner are of sufficient importance to justify his inclusion in the partnership. If, upon a consideration of all the facts, it is found that the partners joined together in good faith to conduct a business, having agreed that the services or capital to be contributed presently by each is of such value to the partnership that the contributor should participate in the distribution of profits, that is sufficient.

Third. The Tax Court's isolation of "original capital" as an essential of membership in a family partnership also indicates an erroneous reading of [an earlier] opinion. We did not say that the donee of an intra-family gift could never become a partner through investment of the capital in the family partnership. The facts may indicate, on the contrary, that the amount thus contributed and the income therefrom should be considered the property of the donee for tax, as well as general law, purposes. [A]pplying the principles of *Lucas v. Earl, supra;* and *Helvering v. Horst,* [*supra*], [a court can find that a] purported gift, whether or not technically complete, had made no substantial change in the economic relation of members of the family to the income.

[E]xistence of the family relationship does not create a status which itself determines tax questions, but is simply a warning that things may not be what they seem. It is frequently stated that transactions between members of a family will be carefully scrutinized. But, more particularly, the family relationship often makes it possible for one to shift tax incidence by surface changes of ownership without disturbing in the least his dominion and control over the subject of the gift or the purposes for which the income from the property is used.

The fact that transfers to members of the family group may be mere camouflage does not, however, mean that they invariably are. [O]ne's participation in control and management of the business is a circumstance indicating an intent to be a bona fide partner despite the fact that the capital contributed originated elsewhere in the family. If the donee of property who then invests it in the family partnership exercises dominion and control over that property—and through that control influences the conduct of the partnership and the disposition of its income—he may well be a true partner. Whether he is free to, and does, enjoy the fruits of the partnership is strongly indicative of the reality of his participation in the enterprise.

The cause must therefore be remanded to the Tax Court for a decision as to which, if any, of respondent's sons were partners with him during 1940 and 1941. As to which of them, in other words, was there a bona fide intent that they be partners in the conduct of the cattle business, either because of services to be performed during those years, or because of contributions of capital of which they were the true owners? No question as to the allocation of income between capital and services is presented in this case, and we intimate no opinion on that subject.

C. THE 1951 LEGISLATION

READ: Code § 704(e)

Congress entered the family partnership fray in 1951 by enacting what is now Section 704(e). The Senate Finance Committee Report explained Congress' concerns as follows:

THE REVENUE ACT OF 1951
Senate Finance Committee Report No. 82–781.
pp. 38–40 (September 15, 1951).

[Section 704(e)] is intended to harmonize the rules governing interests in the so-called family partnership with those generally applicable to other forms of property or business. Two principles governing attribution of income have long been accepted as basic: (1) income from property is attributable to the owner of the property; (2) income from personal services is attributable to the person rendering the services. There is no reason for applying different principles to partnership income. If an individual makes a bona fide gift of real estate, or of a share of corporate stock, the rent or dividend income is taxable to the donee. Your committee's amendment makes it clear that, however the owner of a partnership interest may have acquired such interest, the income is taxable to the owner, if he is the real owner. If the ownership is real, it does not matter what motivated the transfer to him or whether the business benefitted from the entrance of the new partner.

Although there is no basis under existing statutes for any different treatment of partnership interests, some decisions in this field have ignored the principle that income from property is to be taxed to the owner of the property. Many court decisions since the decision of the Supreme Court in *Culbertson* [*supra*] have held invalid for tax purposes family partnerships which arose by virtue of a gift of a partnership interest from one member of a family to another, where the donee performed no vital services for the partnership. Some of those cases apparently proceed upon the theory that a partnership cannot be valid for tax purposes unless the intrafamily gift of capital is motivated by a desire to benefit the partnership business. Others seem to assume that a gift of a partnership interest is not complete because the donor contemplates the continued participation in the business of the donated capital. However, the frequency with which the Tax Court, since the *Culbertson* decision, has held invalid family partnerships based upon donations of capital, would seem to indicate that, although the opinions often refer to "intention," "business purpose," "reality," and "control," they have in practical effect reached results which suggest that an intrafamily gift of a partnership interest, where the donee performs no substantial services, will not usually be the basis of a valid partnership for tax purposes. We are informed that the settlement of many cases in the field is being held up the reliance of field offices of the [IRS] upon some such theory. Whether [*Culbertson* and an earlier Supreme Court case] afford any justification for the confusion is not material—the confusion exists.

[Section 704(e)] leaves the Commissioner and the courts free to inquire in any case whether the donee or purchaser actually owns the interest in the partnership which the transferor purports to have given or sold to him. Cases will arise where the gift or sale is a mere sham. Other cases will arise where the transferor retains so many of the incidents of ownership that he will continue to be recognized as a substantial owner of the interest which he purports to have given away. The same standards apply in determining the bona fides of alleged family partnerships as in determining the bona fides of other transactions between family members. Transactions between persons in a close family group, whether or not involving partnership interests, afford such opportunity for deception and should be subject to close scrutiny. All the facts and circumstances at the time of the purported gift and during the periods preceding and following it may be taken into consideration in determining the bona fides or lack of bona fides of a purported gift or sale.

Not every restriction upon the complete and unfettered control by the donee of the property donated will be indicative of sham in the transaction. Contractual restrictions may be of the character incident to the normal relationships among partners. Substantial powers may be retained by the transferor as a managing partner or in any other fiduciary capacity which, when considered in light of all the circumstances, will not indicate any lack of true ownership in the transferee. In weighing the effect of a retention of any power upon the bona fides of a purported gift or dale, a power exercisable for the benefit of others must be distinguished from a power vested in the transferor for his own benefit.

Since legislation is now necessary to make clear the fundamental principle that, where there is a real transfer of ownership, a gift of a family partnership interest is to be respected for tax purposes without regard to the motives which actuated the transfer, it is considered appropriate at the same time to provide specific safeguards—whether or not such safeguards may be inherent in the general rule—against the use of the partnership device to accomplish the deflection of income from the real owner.

Therefore, [Section 704(e)] provides that in the case of any partnership interest created by gift the allocation of income, according to the terms of the partnership agreement, shall be controlling for income tax purposes except when the shares are allocated without proper allowance of reasonable compensation for services rendered to the partnership by the donor, and except to the extent that the allocation to the donated capital is proportionately greater than that attributable to the donor's capital. In such cases a reasonable allowance will be made for the services rendered by the partners, and the balance of the income will be allocated according to the amount of capital which the several partners have invested.

Note that Section 704(e) does 2 things: First, Section 704(e)(1) provides a safe harbor. If capital is a material income-producing factor to a partnership,[3] the mere fact that a state-law partner acquired a capital interest[4] in the partnership by gift or purchase does not of itself prevent that person from being treated as a partner for tax purposes. A partner not within the scope of the safe harbor, including a partner in a service partnership (a partnership where capital is not a material income-producing factor), is treated as a partner for tax purposes only if she satisfies the requirements of *Culbertson* and the other general rules of tax ownership.

Second, Section 704(e)(2) provides special income allocation rules for partnerships that have either (i) a donee partner or, (ii) under Section 704(e)(3), a partner who purchased her interest from a family member.[5] These rules apply regardless of whether such a transferee partner can avail herself of the Section 704(e)(1) safe harbor. If the transferor partner in such circumstances provides services to the partnership, she must be allocated an allowance for reasonable compensation for such services before any partnership income is allocated to the transferee partner. Similarly, such a transferor partner must receive no smaller a proportionate share of the return on the partnership's capital than the transferee. For purposes of Section 704(e)(2), a person's family consists of her ancestors, spouse, and lineal defendants (and related trusts).

REVIEW: Code § 704(e)

D.   THE CURRENT REGULATIONS

READ: Reg. § 1.704–1(e)

Section 1.704–1(e) of the regulations interprets Section 704(e). In Section 1.704–1(e)(2), the regulation addresses what is required in order for a transferee to be treated as the owner of a partnership interest so as to qualify under Section 704(e)(1) if the other requirements—capital interest and capital a material income-producing factor—are satisfied. As suggested by the 1951 legislative history excerpted above, all the facts

3. Section 1.704–1(e)(1)(iv) of the regulations discusses when capital is a material income-producing factor in a partnership.

4. Section 1.704–1(e)(1)(v) of the regulations defines capital interest so broadly that it includes any interest other than an interest in future profits only.

5. The regulations have rules to prevent avoidance of this rule by having the transferor loan money to the family member (on non-arm's-length terms) who then uses the loan proceeds to acquire a partnership interest from the partnership or a third party. Treas. Reg. §§ 1.704–1(e)(3)(ii)(*b*), (4).

and circumstances are relevant to this determination.[6] Certain factors are identified as being particularly important, however. The most prominent factor is whether the transferor has retained, including through the terms of the underlying partnership agreement, such control over the enjoyment of the purportedly transferred interest that there really has been no transfer.[7] For example, the transferee should not have limitations on her ability to sell or liquidate her interest.[8] The regulations look askance if the transferor is the managing partner and has powers not customary in arms'-length arrangements.[9] It is particularly troubling if the transferor managing partner can retain partnership cash without regard to the reasonable needs of the business.[10] Conversely, if the transferee has real participation in the management of the partnership, that suggests a bona fide transfer.[11] Operating the partnership as if it were an arm's-length business arrangement also is important under the regulations.[12] Finally, notwithstanding the language in the legislative history excerpted above, the regulations indicate that a transfer without a tax avoidance motive is more likely to be respected.[13]

Section 1.704–1(e)(3) of the regulations provides rules for assuring that transferor partners are allocated appropriate compensation for their services and capital when such allocations are required by Section 704(e)(2). The regulation provides only for the allocation of income away from the transferee and to the transferor.[14] No rules are provided for allocations when a family partnership has losses rather than profits.

Under these regulations, one first determines the reasonable compensation for the services of the transferor and transferee in light of what would be paid for comparable services to a third party.[15] For this purpose, reasonable compensation reflects compensation for managerial responsibilities and risk taking.[16] In light of this determination, the transferor must be allocated reasonable compensation for services. Then, any remaining profits of the transferor and transferee after a reduction for reasonable compensation for the services of both the transferor and the transferee is treated as the return to capital and must be allocated between the transferor and transferee proportionately to their respective interests in partnership capital.[17] How these interests are to be determined in a partnership with complex special allocations is not clear.

REVIEW: Reg. § 1.704–1(e)

Problem Set X.D

A wealthy, high-tax-bracket client of your law firm has heard about the family partnership at the health club. She wants to form an invest-

---

6. Treas. Reg. § 1.704–1(e)(2)(i).

7. Treas. Reg. § 1.704–1(e)(2)(ii).

8. Treas. Reg. § 1.704–1(e)(2)(ii)(*b*).

9. Treas. Reg. § 1.704–1(e)(2)(ii)(*d*).

10. Treas. Reg. § 1.704–1(e)(2)(ii)(*a*).

11. Treas. Reg. § 1.704–1(e)(2)(iv).

12. Treas. Reg. § 1.704–1(e)(2)(vi).

13. Treas. Reg. § 1.704–1(e)(2)(x).

14. Treas. Reg. § 1.704–1(e)(3)(i)(*b*).

15. *Id*.

16. Treas. Reg. §§ 1.704–1(e)(3)(i)(*c*), (ii)(*c*).

17. Treas. Reg. § 1.704–1(e)(3)(i)(*b*)

ment partnership with her low-tax-bracket adult son. He will put up $10,000 that she will give him. She will put up $10 million. Profits will be allocated proportionately to capital. Each year, she will give him some of her share of the partnership. She will have exclusive power to manage the partnership, including controlling distributions. She plans on distributing just enough cash to cover their respective income taxes on partnership income. If the son marries a nice girl, your client will have the partnership distribute all profits (not including capital gains). If the son marries and then divorces, your client will have the partnership stop making any cash distributions. Your client is certain that her tennis partner has just such a family partnership and wants you to set one up.

1.   What do you tell her about the income tax consequences?

2.   Are there ways to change the basic structure so that it is more advantageous from an income tax point of view?

Chapter XI

THE ANTI–ABUSE REGULATIONS

A. INTRODUCTION

SKIM: Reg. § 1.701–2

This final chapter of the partnership discussion in this text examines regulations that potentially apply to any partnership transaction, the Anti–Abuse Regulations of Section 1.701–2, adopted in 1994. Interestingly, these regulations bring us back full circle to the basic analysis of the tension between the aggregate and entity approaches that was discussed in Chapter I. As noted there, long ago Mark Johnson and other experts recognized that the aggregate approach more closely conforms to the underlying economics, while the entity approach has admirable simplification advantages. At the heart of the Anti-Abuse Regulations is the continuing struggle between capturing the economics and achieving acceptable levels of simplicity. Thus, for example, Section 1.701–2(e) provides that the IRS can treat a partnership as an aggregate whenever appropriate unless Congress clearly indicated otherwise. Similarly, Section 1.701–2(b) authorizes the IRS to treat partnership assets as owned directly by the partners when appropriate. From a legal point of view (as compared to these policy concerns), however, the Anti–Abuse Regulations are best understood by examining them in the broad context of the general problem of how courts interpret the income tax statute in light of both the variety and complexity of business transactions and the very real impact of tax planning in the structuring of transactions.

B. THE TAX "COMMON LAW"

The question of how courts should interpret the income tax statute when applied to complicated, tax-planned transactions was first faced in the context of tax-free corporate reorganizations. Over 50 years ago, Professor Stanley Surrey of the Harvard Law School, one of the key players in the 1954 ALI report (discussed in Chapter I of this text), and one of the most thoughtful commentators on tax matters in the United States, observed in an often-quoted passage that:

> These [corporate] reorganization sections are written against the background of normal business transactions. They are stated in

terms of specific rules which chart a tax-free corridor through which may flow the corporate transactions intended to be so favored. But the very breadth of the transactions to which the rules could extend and the mechanical terms in which they are written combine to make such corridor a tempting avenue of tax avoidance to persons who were not intended to be the recipients of such a safe-conduct pass. This is especially true in the case of closely-held family corporations where the corporation may be readily maneuvered by the shareholders. From the very beginning the courts, prompted by the Commissioner, have undertaken the task of policing this tax-free corridor. Their guarding has been vigorous and diligent, and many a corporation or shareholder who presented a pass carefully prepared to match the literal language of the sections has nevertheless been denied entrance. As a consequence, the literal language of the sections cannot be relied upon, and safe passage depends upon knowledge of the rules of the judicial gendarmerie. An attorney who reads [Section 368(a)(1)(A)] and believes that a statutory merger always constitutes a reorganization may be mistaken—his particular statutory merger may be on the judicially proscribed list if it fails to possess the necessary "continuity of interest" . . . Some of these judicial rules have been incorporated in the statute; part of the flavor is in the Regulations. But most of them still remain as they originated—judicial safeguards devised to protect the underlying statutory policy. Nor is the role of the judiciary confined to enforcing rules previously announced. Anyone applying for passage through the corridor runs the risk of the judicial policeman inventing a new rule on the spot if he thinks such action is demanded. It must be remembered that most of the taxpayers who thus prompt judicial ingenuity have no real business in the corridor. But when such trespassers are in the throng, the barriers designed to separate them may catch an innocent, or may force the innocent to take added precautions to identify himself. These rules may also produce some uncertainty and confusion where the innocent too closely resembles a trespasser. Some have criticized the judicial vigilance on this score. Others believe that any effort to prescribe statutory rules covering all of the everyday transactions of the business world is bound to fail unless courts and administrators are able to cope with transactions that would otherwise involve a distorted application of such rules.[1]

Compare Professor Surrey's analysis with the approach of the Anti–Abuse Regulations, as indicated in the following language in Section 1.701–2(a):

Subchapter K is intended to permit taxpayers to conduct joint business (including investment) activities through a flexible economic arrangement without incurring an entity-level tax. Implicit in the intent of subchapter K are the following requirements—

1. Stanley S. Surrey & William C. Warren, *Federal Income Taxation—Cases and* *Materials* 1023–24 (1950) (footnotes omitted).

(1) The partnership must be bona fide and each partnership transaction or series of related transactions (individually or collectively, the transaction) must be entered into for a substantial business purpose.

(2) The form of each partnership transaction must be respected under substance over form principles.

(3) Except as otherwise provided in this paragraph (a)(3), the tax consequences under subchapter K to each partner of partnership operations and of transactions between the partner and the partnership must accurately reflect the partners' economic agreement and clearly reflect the partner's income (collectively, *proper reflection of income*). However, certain provisions of subchapter K and the regulations thereunder were adopted to promote administrative convenience and other policy objectives, with the recognition that the application of these provisions to a transaction could, in some circumstances, produce tax results that do not properly reflect income. Thus, the proper reflection of income requirement of this paragraph (a)(3) is treated as satisfied with respect to a transaction that satisfies paragraphs (a)(1) and (2) of this section to the extent that the application of such a provision to the transaction and the ultimate tax results, taking into account all the relevant facts and circumstances, are clearly contemplated by that provision.

The student reading this quotation from the Anti–Abuse Regulations for the first time probably finds it innocuous. After all, nobody can argue with the proposition that taxpayers should not be allowed tax results that were not intended by Congress in transactions without a business purpose, right? Nevertheless, practitioners howled as the Anti–Abuse Regulations were promulgated. Many in the Subchapter K bar believe that the judicial doctrines first developed in Subchapter C (although applied later throughout the Code) have no role in interpreting Subchapter K. After all, judicial opinions like the Tax Court's in *Foxman*, set out in Chapter VIII, above, suggest that Congress intended that Subchapter K provide taxpayers, in addition to flexibility in structuring the underlying economic arrangements, flexibility in choosing the tax treatment (electivity in tax treatment), unlike Subchapter C.

A more powerful critique of the Anti–Abuse Regulations is that they draw a line between intended and unintended results in Subchapter K that is not articulated expressly in the regulations and, perhaps, cannot be drawn. (A line can be inferred, however, from the regulations' examples, as discussed below.) Finally, some practitioners believe that the Anti–Abuse Regulations are invalid under the general rules of administrative law.[2]

---

2. For a thorough critique of the legality of the Anti–Abuse Regulations, see William S. McKee, William F. Nelson & Robert L. Whitmire, *Federal Taxation of Partnerships and Partners* ¶ 1.05[5] (3d Ed. 1996 & 2001 Supp.) (hereinafter McKee).

C. THE ABUSE OF SUBCHAPTER K RULE

READ: Reg. §§ 1.701–2(b), (c), and (d)

The Anti–Abuse Regulations contain 2 substantive rules: (i) the abuse of Subchapter K rule of Section 1.701–2(b) and (ii) the abuse of entity rule of Section 1.701–2(e). This section of this text reviews the abuse of Subchapter K rule. Then, the abuse of entity rule is discussed in Section XI.D.

Section 1.701–2(b) sanctions the use of a tax partnership "in connection with a transaction a principal purpose of which is to reduce substantially the present value of the partners' aggregate federal tax liability in a manner that is inconsistent with the intent of subchapter K."[3] This test resembles a broad-brush application of the test of substantial economic effect in Section 1.704–1(b)(2)(iii)(*a*), which disregards allocations that reduce taxes more than they impact the pre-tax economics.[4]

Such a tax reduction transaction that is inconsistent with the intent of Subchapter K is to be taxed so as to "achieve tax results that are consistent with the intent of subchapter K." The transaction may be taxed (i) by applying an aggregate approach method, (ii) by treating one or more state-law partners as other than partners for tax purposes, (iii) by using a different tax accounting method, (iv) by reallocating tax items, and (v) by making any other appropriate change in the tax treatment of the partners.[5]

Unfortunately, the abuse of Subchapter K rule gives little direct guidance on how to determine if a favorable tax result is inconsistent with the intent of Subchapter K. Section 1.701–2(c) suggests factors to be used in evaluating a transaction, but the factors are not particularly helpful. The examples contained in Section 1.701–2(d) are of some assistance, however. Some general principles can be inferred from these examples—particularly from comparing and contrasting Examples 8 through 11—even though the examples themselves contain little explicit analysis that can be applied to other situations.[6]

In Example 8, a partnership is formed for the purpose of gaming Section 732(b): One partner contributes property with a built-in loss. Later, this partner is liquidated in exchange for other property. The contributing partner gets a high basis in the distributed property under Section 732(b). No Section 754 election is made. Thus, the partnership keeps its high basis in the property originally contributed by the now-departed partners under Section 734(a).[7] Then, the former partner sells

---

3. The Anti–Abuse Regulations apply only for income tax purposes. IRS Announcement 95–8, 1995–7 I.R.B. 56.

4. Thus, it is not surprising that an allocation that has substantial economic effect, per se, does not pose problems under the abuse of Subchapter K rule. Treas. Reg. § 1.701–2(d)(Examples 5, 6). A valid special allocation alone does not protect a transac-

tion that overall presents problems, however. Treas. Reg. § 1.701–2(d)(Example 7).

5. Treas. Reg. § 1.701–2(b).

6. The instant analysis of the regulation's examples draws heavily on McKee, *supra* note 2, at ¶ 1.05[2][b].

7. Remember the discussion in Sections VII.F and VIII.F of this text regarding how Section 732 preserves the total outside basis

the distributed asset and recognizes a loss. (The loss built into the contributed asset was moved to the partner's partnership interest by Section 722, then to the distributed asset by Section 732(b), and finally recognized.) Also, in the example, the partnership recognizes the same loss, the loss originally built into the contributed property, by selling the contributed property (which had a transferred basis under Section 723). Of course, the partnership's loss reduces the remaining partners' outside bases, so that associated future gain (or reduced loss) is assured, but that gain (or reduced loss) will be recognized at the earliest when the interests of the remaining partners are sold or liquidated, which may not be for some time. Example 8 concludes that this transaction is to be recharacterized under Section 1.701–2(b) (but does not say how): The transaction is so tainted by tax planning that it is questionable. Moreover, there is no evidence to suggest that Congress intended for Sections 732(b) and 734(a) to be used to create 2 tax losses out of one economic loss. Thus, much as lauded in the Surrey quotation at the beginning of this Chapter, the tax administrator must step in so that a literal application of the tax statute not have an apparently unintended effect (a duplicated loss).

Matters are different in Example 9. There, an historical partner in a long-standing partnership was planning to leave the firm. Property with a basis well below both its value and the withdrawing partner's outside basis is distributed in liquidation. No Section 754 election is in force. Thus, under Section 732(b), the basis in the distributed property is stepped up at no tax cost to the partnership under Section 734(a). The distribution was planned with these tax benefits in mind. Nevertheless, the example concludes that Congress intended this result: Sections 732(b) and 734(a) are not drafted to be a one-sided win for the Government. The facts in the example present as sympathetic a case as possible for taxpayer benefits under Section 734(a), except for the tax planning. Apparently, the Treasury realized that trying to eliminate all tax planning here would be unreasonable and impractical. The transaction is not recharacterized under Section 1.701–2(b).

How does one reconcile Examples 8 and 9? In one case, it is not acceptable to game Section 734(a), but, in the other, it is. The most relevant difference apparently is that, in Example 8, the partners form a partnership to get the troubling tax advantage, while, in Example 9, the partnership was formed for acceptable purposes (conducting a business with one level of tax) although later the partners intentionally arranged matters so as to get particularly good tax treatment. Further insight can be gained from the last 2 examples.

Unfortunately, Examples 10 and 11 involve a problem under an old version of Section 732(c). (The current version is analyzed in Section VIII.F of this text.) Congress saw fit to solve this problem by amending

(in partnership interests and in assets now owned directly by the partners) without, in the absence of a Section 754 election, a corresponding adjustment in the basis of assets still owned by the partnership so as to maintain the total basis (inside and outside the partnership) in assets other than partnership interests.

Subchapter K. Nevertheless, it is possible to discern a general point in the examples. In Example 11, a new partner is admitted to an existing partnership in order to exploit old Section 732(c). The transaction is recharacterized under Section 1.701–2(b). In Example 10, the historical partners of a long-standing partnership take advantage of prior law. Section 1.701–2(b) does not apply.

Thus, while not articulated, there seems to be a theme in the examples interpreting Section 1.701–2(b). As long as all partners become so to conduct business and investment activities while being subject to only one level of tax, all the benefits of Subchapter K follow.[8] In contrast, entering Subchapter K (either by forming a partnership or by admitting a new partner to an existing partnership) to take advantage of features of Subchapter K other than one level of tax is subject to attack. Under this analysis, the abuse of Subchapter K rule ultimately looks to the reasons that the taxpayers became partners—an intent test. It is important to remember, however, that the instant analysis is based on inferences drawn from examples. The actual language of Section 1.701–2(b) can be read to go much further in overriding the express language of Subchapter K.

The specific consequences of running afoul of Section 1.701–2(b) are not spelled out. As already noted, the regulations give the Commissioner broad powers to adjust the tax treatment however "appropriate to achieve tax results that are consistent with the intent of subchapter K, in light of the applicable statutory and regulatory provisions and the pertinent facts and circumstances."[9] Apparently, Treasury expects that the principal impact of the Anti–Abuse Regulations will be to deter troubling transactions rather than to recharacterize them.

REVIEW: Reg. §§ 1.701–2(b), (c), and (d)

D. THE ABUSE OF ENTITY RULE

READ: Reg. § 1.701–2(e) and (f)

Section 1.701–2(e) of the regulations provides the abuse of entity rule: A partnership is taxed as an aggregate of its partners when necessary to carry out the intent of a non-Subchapter K rule unless entity treatment is "clearly contemplated" by a relevant provision of the Code or Regulations. There is no express guidance (i) on when aggregate treatment is necessary to effect the intent of a provision or (ii) on how one decides if entity treatment is "clearly contemplated."

Fortunately, it is possible to make some sense of the general rule by looking at the examples contained in Section 1.701–2(f). Read Example 1. The underlying non-Subchapter K provision is Section 163(e)(5). It was

---

8. Example 2 respects a partnership formed to void the 75 shareholder rule in Subchapter S's Section 1361(b)(1)(A), which is discussed below in Section XII.B.1.

9. Treas. Reg. § 1.701–2(b).

enacted in 1989 to disallow excessive interest deductions for corporations that issue equity-like high-yield original discount obligations. The question arises as to the treatment of a corporate partner in a partnership that issues an obligation that would run afoul of Section 163(e)(5) if the obligation were issued by the corporate partner. Section 703 provides that a partnership generally computes its taxable income as if the partnership were an individual. Example 1, however, concludes that a corporate partner should apply Section 163(e)(5) to its share of the partnership's interest deduction with regard to the debt: Section 163(e)(5) does not contemplate partnership-level characterization. Allowing corporations to issue such debt through partnerships would gut the effectiveness of Section 163(e)(5).

The other 2 examples of the application of the abuse of entity rule in Section 1.701–2(e) are similar: aggregate treatment is required with regard to the application of a Code provision (i) that applies to special taxpayers and (ii) that is silent on the treatment of partners (Example 2), but not otherwise (Example 3). Thus, one concludes that the abuse of entity rule is a safety net against legislative sloppiness: If Congress forgot to think about partnerships in drafting a rule, aggregate treatment will apply to bail the fisc out. While one can be troubled that such a rule is necessary, it seems reasonable. It should be noted that Section 1.701–2(e), as so interpreted, is not much different from the cases interpreting non-Subchapter K Code Sections in the partnership context prior to these regulations, like *Coggin Automotive*, excerpted above in Section III.B of this text.

REVIEW: Reg. § 1.701–2(e) and (f)

Problem Set XI.D

Sally owns 100% of the stock of The CLOSE Corporation, which is her only significant investment outside her pension plan. She retired from the business a long time ago and has been looking to diversify. An accounting firm comes up with a plan: CLOSE will form a partnership with CONGLOMERATE, Inc. CLOSE will contribute all of its assets to the partnership. CONGLOMERATE will contribute CONGLOMERATE stock of equal value. All future profits of the contributed business will be allocated 95% to CONGLOMERATE and 5% to CLOSE. All future partnership profits on the CONGLOMERATE stock will be allocated 95% to CLOSE and 5% to CONGLOMERATE. How will the partnership formation and operation be taxed?

Chapter XII

SUBCHAPTER S

A. INTRODUCTION

This final chapter of this text reviews Subchapter S of the Code. It provides a hybrid regime for taxing certain closely-held corporations that is similar, but not identical, to Subchapter K. This regime was adopted in 1958 and substantially amended in 1982 to more closely resemble Subchapter K. The historical purpose of Subchapter S was to give businesses desiring limited liability for its equity investors under state law the option of a simple set of tax rules that require only one level of tax. Now that LLCs are taxed under Subchapter K unless they check the box to be taxed under Subchapter C, Subchapter S is not needed to fulfill its historical purpose.[1] This has not relegated Subchapter S to the scrap heap of tax history, however. Many old Subchapter S corporations will continue for some time, since it is not possible to reorganize a pre-check-the-box Subchapter S corporation into an LLC taxed as a partnership without triggering a tax on any unrealized gain in the corporation's assets, including goodwill.[2] Also, occasionally there are tax reasons to form a new business as a corporation that elects to taxed under Subchapter S.[3]

---

1. Subchapter S's simpler rules alone do not make it more attractive than Subchapter S. As to be discussed below, in the situations where Subchapter S is simpler than Subchapter K, the simplicity is achieved at the cost of less favorable tax treatment. The principal exception is that Subchapter S has nothing analogous to Section 704(c)(1)(B) or reverse Section 704(c) allocations, as to be discussed below.

2. I.R.C. §§ 336, 1371(a)

3. For example, a Subchapter S corporation can use the tax-free reorganization provisions of Subchapter C, while a tax part-nership cannot. Thus, venturers forming a new enterprise with the goal of selling out tax-free to an acquiring corporation may start as an S corporation to set the stage for the hoped-for future tax-free disposition. Also, taxpayers frequently try to use a one-shareholder services Subchapter S corporation to convert compensation that should be subject to Social Security and other payroll taxes into a profit share and distribution not so taxed. *See Joseph Radtke, S.C. v. U.S.,* 895 F.2d 1196 (7th Cir.1990) ("Dividends" treated as remuneration for services.).

B. QUALIFICATION

READ: Code §§ 1361(a), (b), (c)(1), and (3) through (6), 1362(a), (b), and (c), and 1363(a)

The heart of Subchapter S, Section 1363(a), applies only to "S corporations." These corporations are described in Section 1361(a)(1) as (i) small business corporations (ii) for which a Section 1362(a) election is in effect.

1. Small Business Corporation

Section 1362(b) provides the basic requirements to qualify as a small business corporation. Read it. The corporation must have 75 or fewer shareholders.[4] For this purpose, Section 1361(c)(1) provides that spouses and their estates count as only one shareholder. Only individuals, estates, certain trusts, and certain exempt organizations[5] are permitted shareholders.[6] Thus, an S corporation cannot have a C corporation, a partnership, or a non-qualified trust as a shareholder. Nonresident aliens also cannot be shareholders of an S corporation.[7] Financial institutions, insurance companies, certain possessions corporations, DISCs, and former DISCs cannot be small business corporations.

A small business corporation can have only one class of stock. Section 1361(c)(4) provides that differences in voting rights are ignored for this purpose.[8] Also, Section 1361(c)(5) provides that certain non-contingent debt is not treated as stock for this purpose even though the debt may treated as stock under general tax principles.

An S corporation may own stock of another corporation.[9] If an S corporation owns 100% of the stock of another corporation, the parent S corporation can elect to treat the subsidiary as a "qualified subchapter S subsidiary" under Section 1361(b)(3). When this election is in effect, the

---

4. Interestingly, the partnership Anti-Abuse Regulations bless organizing a business as a partnership of 2 S corporations to avoid the 75 or fewer shareholder rule. Treas. Reg. § 1.701–2(d)(Example 2). Of course, this structure is not interesting in a post-check-the-box world.

5. I.R.C. § 1361(c)(6).

6. An estate of an individual in bankruptcy qualifies as an estate for this purpose. I.R.C. § 1361(c)(3).

7. The principal purpose of Subchapter S is to eliminate double taxation, not all taxation. A nonresident alien that is not actively involved in a US business generally is subject to US tax only on US-sourced fixed income, like interest and dividends. Being a shareholder of an S corporation by itself probably would not subject an alien to taxation on her share of the corporation's income. Hence, allowing a nonresident alien to be a shareholder in an S corporation usually would mean exemption from all US

tax for her share of the S corporation's income, not just one level of US taxation, and therefore was not allowed by Congress. Incidently, this problem is solved differently for US partnerships. As to a partnership, the veil is pierced so that a partner is treated as being engaged in the partnership's activities so as to be taxed thereon. Then, Section 1446 imposes a partnership-level withholding tax on a nonresident partner's share of taxable US income.

8. Section 1.1361–1(l) of the Regulations indicates that, for there to be just one class of stock, every share must have identical proportionate rights to distributions and liquidation proceeds. Note that the purpose of the one class of stock requirement is to avoid needing a mechanism like Section 704(b) for S corporations. Thus, focusing on rights to cash flow makes perfect sense.

9. Prior to 1997, an S corporation could not own 80% or more of the stock of another corporation. I.R.C. § 1361(b)(2)(A) (1996)

subsidiary's separate identity is ignored for tax purposes. All of the subsidiary's tax items are treated as belonging to the parent corporation.

2. Election

A qualified small business corporation must elect to be taxed under Subchapter S. Section 1361(a)(2) requires that all shareholders at such time consent to the election.

Under Section 1362(b), an election takes effect at the beginning of a tax year of the small business corporation. The election continues in effect until revoked or until the corporation ceases to qualify for Subchapter S treatment under Section 1362(c). No new consents are required when stock changes hands. In order to be effective for a corporate tax year, the election must be filed within the first 2–1/2 months of that year. The election also can be filed in the preceding corporate tax year. Section 1362(b)(5) gives the IRS authority to accept late elections if there was reasonable cause for the delay.

> REVIEW: Code §§ 1361(a), (b), (c)(1), and (3) through (5),
> 1362(a), (b), and (c), and 1363(a) and Reg.
> § 1.1361–1(*l*)(1)

C. REVOCATION AND CESSATION

READ: Code §§ 1362(d) through (g)

An S corporation can revoke its status under Section 1362(d)(1). Read it. Shareholders representing over 1/2 of the shares (voting or nonvoting) must consent to the revocation. The revocation becomes effective (i) in the corporate tax year made, if filed within 2–1/2 months of the beginning of the year, and, (ii) otherwise, at the beginning of the succeeding corporate tax year.

Status as an S corporation also terminates when the corporation cease to qualify as a small business corporation under Section 1362(d)(2). Read it. For example, if a corporation becomes a minority shareholder of an S corporation, the S corporation no longer qualifies to be a small business corporation so that Subchapter S no longer applies. Similarly, an S election terminates if the corporation has more than 75 shareholders at any point in time.[10] Termination by cessation takes effect on the day of cessation.[11]

Finally, an S corporation that once was a C corporation can lose its S corporation status if it has too much passive income under Section 1362(d)(3). This is analyzed in more detail below in Section XII.G.

---

10. The no more than 75 shareholders rule applies at any particular time and not over any period of time. Rev. Rul. 78–390, 1978–2 C.B. 220.

11. Under Section 1362(e), this creates a short tax year in which the corporation is an S corporation, followed by a short tax year in which the corporation is a C corporation.

If an election terminates, Section 1362(g) provides that no new election may be made for 5 tax years unless the IRS consents to an earlier reelection.

Section 1362(f) grants the IRS authority to ignore inadvertent terminations (other than by revocation). For example, if some stock in an S corporation is sold to a corporation without the S corporation's knowledge and the S corporation redeems out the corporate shareholder the minute the new shareholder is discovered, the IRS may ignore the inadvertent termination.[12]

REVIEW: Code §§ 1362(d) through (g)

Problem Set XII.C

1. SBC, Inc. is incorporated and commences business on March 17, 2002. It properly adopts the calendar year as its tax year. SBC files an S election that is signed by all of the original shareholders (individuals who are US citizens) on June 1, 2002. What is SBC's tax status for 2002?

2. How would your analysis of Problem 1 change if it was later discovered that one of the original shareholders gave his shares to his daughter on May 15, 2002 and so informed the corporate secretary immediately?

3. The facts are the same as in Problem 2. SBC's accountants first discover the transfer in January of 2003. They immediately get the daughter to consent to S status and file an election with the IRS claiming a retroactive election back to March 14, 2002. What is SBC's status for 2002 and 2003?

4. On January 12, 2004, one shareholders sells her stock to a US citizen. The next day, the new shareholder contacts the IRS and indicates that she does not consent to the Subchapter S election and will not pay tax on income that she does not receive. What is SBC's status for 2004?

5. Another shareholder moves to Spain, a community property jurisdiction. In December 2005, he gets married there to a woman who is neither a citizen of nor resident in the United States. What is SBC's status for 2005? (Note Treas. Reg. § 1.1361–1(g).)

6. On January 23, 2006, one shareholder transfers her shares of SBC to her wholly-owned corporation. The minute SBC finds out, its management talks this former shareholder into having her wholly-owned corporation transfer the SBC stock back to her. What is SBC's status for 2006?

7. On April 4, 2007, shareholders of SBC representing 66% of the shares file a revocation of SBC's S election with the IRS. What is SBC's status for 2007 and 2008?

8. In any case above where SBC's S status terminated, how soon afterwards can SBC re-elect S status?

---

12. *See* Treas. Reg. § 1.1362–4(b).

D.   TAXATION OF S CORPORATION OPERATIONS

READ: Code §§ 1363(a) through (c), 1366(a) through (e), 1367, 1377(a), and 1378

This section of this text discusses the taxation of S corporations that never were C corporations. Special problems presented by former C corporations are discussed in Section XII.G, below.

The basic rules regarding the taxation of S corporation operations resemble the analogous provisions of Subchapter K, discussed in Chapter III of this text, quite closely. No tax is imposed on the respective entities under Sections 701 and 1363(a). Sections 703(a) and (b) and 1363(b) and (c) provide entity-level determinations (as if the entity were an individual) and entity-level elections. Section 1378 provides S corporations simpler rules regarding permitted tax years than Section 706(b) affords partnerships, however. Basically, an S corporation must use the calendar year[13] unless there is a business purpose for a different tax year. The rules for evaluating a business purpose for a tax year here are the same as under Section 706(b)(1)(C). Sections 444 and 7519 apply the same to tax partnerships and S corporations.

The incomes of tax partnerships and S corporations pass through with the appropriate character under Sections 702(a) through (c) and Sections 1366(a) through (c), respectively. Since S corporations have only one class of stock, nothing similar to Section 704(b) is needed for S corporations. Each shareholder is taxed on her pro-rata share of the corporation's tax items under Section 1366(a). Section 1366(e) provides rules for family S corporations like those for family partnerships in Section 704(e).

As to timing, tax partnerships' and Subchapter S corporations' incomes are included in the owners' tax years that include the end of the entities' tax years under Sections 706(a) and 1366(a). When a new shareholder joins an S corporation during a corporate tax year (by acquiring an interest from the entity or a former owner), that shareholder's share of the corporation's tax items for the year is determined by pro-ration under Section 1377(a)(1).[14] In contrast, Section 706(d)(1) allows an actual allocation to the period that a new partner is in the firm. When a shareholder disposes of stock, Section 1377(a)(1) again generally requires pro-ration, but, if the shareholder disposes of all of her stock, actual allocation also is allowed by Section 1377(a)(2). A Section 1377(a)(2) allocation does not change the timing of the disposing shareholder's income, however, as would be the case with a partner

---

13. After all, the owners of S corporations are almost always individuals, who almost always use the calendar year, so that rules that look to the tax years of the owners similar to those in Section 706(b)(1)(B) would serve little purpose if applied to S corporations.

14. This proration so reduces the need for an S corporation rule analogous to Section 706(d)(2) that there is none.

disposing of her entire interest in a partnership under Section 706(c)(2)(A).[15]

The rules in Section 1367(a) controlling the basis of an S corporation shareholder in her stock—her outside basis—work much like those for partnerships in Sections 705(a) and 732(a)(1). Income allocations increase outside basis. Distributions and loss allocations, to be discussed shortly, reduce outside basis.

Section 1366(d) serves the same loss limitation function for S corporations that Section 704(d) serves for tax partnerships: The total amount of an S corporation's losses passed through to a shareholder that are allowed as a deduction cannot exceed her outside (stock) basis, with any disallowed loss carried forward indefinitely to be used at such time, if any, that the owner gets outside basis (from future income allocations or subsequent capital contributions). There is an important practical difference in how losses pass through S corporations and partnerships, however. Subchapter S contains nothing that is analogous to Section 752. Since, under state law, S corporations shield their members from liability on corporate obligations, there is no reason to allow corporate debt to be treated as shareholder debt for tax purposes. Consequently, the Section 1366(d) limitation applies with regard to an outside basis that does not include entity debt, even when that debt is guaranteed by the shareholders.[16] Debt-financed losses do not flow through S corporations. Section 1366(d)(1)(B) softens this, however, by allowing losses in excess of a shareholder's remaining stock basis when the shareholder lends money to her S corporation. The Section 1366(d)(1) loss limitation is the sum of the shareholder's remaining basis in her stock of the S corporation plus her adjusted basis in any loans made to the S corporation.[17] As a consequence of Section 1366(d)(1)(B), tax results similar to those with partnerships can be achieved with an S corporation by having its shareholders borrow money pro-rata and then relend the borrowed funds to the S corporation.

The PAL rules of Section 469 and the At–Risk Rules of Section 465 apply to shareholder of S corporations as to members of LLCs taxed as partnerships.

REVIEW: Code §§ 444, 1363(a) through (c), 1366(a) through (e), 1367, 1377(a), 1378, and 7519 and Reg. § 1.1377–1(b)(3)(iii)

Problem Set XII.D

1.   Redo Problem Set III.B by assuming that A and B form an S corporation that they own 50–50.

---

15.   Treas. Reg. § 1.1377–1(b)(3)(iii).

16.   *See, e.g., Jackson v. Commissioner,* T.C. Memo 2001–61; T.C.M. (RIA) 54274 (2001) (Halpern, J.).

17   Losses so allowed in excess of stock basis reduce the basis of the debt without impacting stock basis. Future income allocations reverse this debt basis reduction prior to increasing stock basis. I.R.C. § 1367(b)(2).

2. Sam and Dave form a corporation that timely elects S status. They own its stock 50–50. Each works full time for the S corporation. Each paid $50,000 cash for their stock so that their initial outside bases were $50,000. The corporation loses $66,000 in its first year. In order to get more cash, the corporation borrows $50,000 in the 2d year. The lending bank requires the joint and several guarantee of Sam and Dave. The corporation loses another $66,0000 in the 2d year. Sam borrows $50,000 from a bank. The proceeds of this borrowing are lent to the corporation in the 3d year for a 10–year term with market-rate interest only to be paid until maturity. The partnership loses another $66,000 in the 3d year. Describe the tax consequences in all 3 years to Sam and Dave.

3. Redo Problem 5 in Problem Set IV.B on the assumption that FUEL is in an S corporation.

3. Redo Problem 6 in Problem Set IV.B on the assumption that Larry, Moe, and Curly were equal shareholders in an S corporation.

E. DISTRIBUTIONS

READ: Code §§ 1368(a), (b), and (d) and 1371(a)

SKIM: Code §§ 301(a) through (d), 302, 311(b), 316, 317(b), 331, 334(a), and 336

The basic tax rules applicable to an S shareholder who receives a distribution from her S corporation, which are contained in Section 1368(b), work much like the partnership rules in Section 731(a). Cash distributions first reduce outside basis before triggering gain.[18] The timing rules are different in the 2 contexts, however. As to an S corporation, the second sentence of Section 1368(d) increases stock basis for income during the year prior to determining the tax consequences of distributions. This only happens with a partnership if the distribution is treated as a draw by Section 1.731–1(a)(1)(ii) of the regulations. In contrast, when an S corporation has a loss for a tax year, distributions during the year are taken into account before applying the loss limit (Section 1366(d)), which also is the partnership rule.[19]

Subchapter S, because it includes relevant provisions of Subchapter C under Section 1371(a), has involved rules for determining which distributions are subject to the rules just described. For partnerships, there are just 2 kinds of distributions, those in liquidation of the entire interest of a partner and all others. For corporations, at first pass, there are 3 kinds of distributions: (i) Section 301 distributions, (ii) stock redemptions, and (iii) distributions in complete liquidation of the corporation. Section 301, by its terms, applies to distributions "by a corporation to a a shareholder with respect to its stock." As to a shareholder of

---

18. With S corporations, since outside basis does not include entity borrowings, distributions of borrowed funds, say borrowing against unrealized appreciation in entity assets, is more likely to trigger gain.

19. Treas. Reg. § 1.704–1(d)(2).

an S corporation, Section 301 distributions are taxed under Section 1368(b), as just described. Section 317(b) provides that a redemption is any purchase by a corporation of its own stock. Those redemptions described in Section 302(b) are taxed as if the corporation purchased the stock from the shareholder. Section 302(b) redemptions consist of (i) redemptions that significantly reduce the shareholder's proportionate interest in the corporation, usually taking stock owned by related persons into account (Sections 302(b)(1) through (3)), and (ii) distributions in partial liquidation of the corporation (Section 302(b)(4)). All redemption distributions not described in Section 302(b) are treated as Section 301 distributions by Section 302(d). Distributions in complete liquidation of the entire corporation are treated as if the shareholders sold their stock back to the corporation by Section 331.

As to the distributing entity, distributions of non-cash property are taxed much differently with regard to S corporations than with regard to partnerships. With a partnership, a distribution of non-cash property has no immediate tax consequences to the partnership, under Section 731(b), and usually has no consequences to the partner under Section 731(a). In contrast, when an S corporation distributes property, (i) in the case of nonliquidating distributions (Sections 301 and 302 distributions), Section 311(b) triggers unrealized gain, and, (ii) in the case of liquidating distributions, Section 366 generally triggers gain and loss. This gain or loss is taxed to the shareholders pro-rata, with the appropriate adjustments to their stock bases. The distribution then is taxed to the shareholders using the property's value, and the property gets a new fair market value basis under Section 301(d) or 334(a).

Note the remarkable simplification achieved by taxing in-kind property distributions: Subchapter S needs nothing analogous to Sections 704(c)(1)(B), 731(c), 732(c), 734(b)(and related aspects of Sections 754 and 755), 737, or 751(b)!

REVIEW: Code §§ 1368(a), (b), and (d) and 1371(a)

Problem Set XII.E

1. Redo Problem Set III.C by assuming that Sally and Ann form an S corporation whose stock is owned 50–50.

2. Redo Problem Set VII.B on the assumption that the partnerships are S corporations.

3. Redo Problem 1 in Problem Set VII.C on the assumption that Bunker and Lamar form a 50–50 S corporation.

4. Redo the Olive and Paula example in Section VII.E of this text on the assumption that they start as 45—55 owners of the stock of an S corporation.

5. Redo Problem 2 in Problem Set VII.G on the assumption that Ellen, Liz, and Eric form a Subchapter S corporation.

F. CONTRIBUTIONS

SKIM: Code §§ 351(a), 358(a)(1), 362(a), and 1032 and Reg. § 1.1032–1(a)(last sentence)

As one moves further away from the day-to-day taxation of the business, the rules in Subchapters K and S resemble each other less and less. This was seen already with regard to the taxation of in-kind property distributions, as just discussed. The same is true with in-kind property contributions: Partnerships can receive property from partners without a tax to the partner or the partnership under Section 721(a). Matters are different in Subchapter S. Section 1032 does allow a corporation to acquire anything, property or services, with its stock without the issuing corporation being subject to tax.[20] But, an exchange of property for stock generally is taxable. After all, a corporation is an entity, so swapping property for stock is not a mere change in form, but a real exchange of different properties that should be taxable. The only relevant exception to the general rule of taxation of swaps of property for corporate stock is contained in Section 351(a). There, if a group of shareholders who end up with 80% or more of a corporation transfer property to the corporation for its stock, the exchange is viewed as a mere change in form that is not taxed.[21] The transferred properties get transferred bases under Section 362(a). Under Section 358(a)(1), the shareholders increase their outside bases by the basis of their respective transferred properties, rather than by the property's value, as in a taxable exchange.

Note that, perhaps because the opportunities for property contributions are more limited with S corporations than with partnerships, Subchapter S contains nothing that is analogous to Sections 704(c) or 737 or the reverse Section 704(c) rules in the Section 704(b) regulations.

Problem Set XII.F

Mork and Mindy form a new corporation that elects S status. Mork puts up $1 million of cash. Mindy puts up 10 parcels of real estate with a total basis of $500,000 and a total value of $1 million. They each get 1/2 of the company's stock. The partnership sells one of the parcels, which has a basis of $10,000, for $120,000. What are the tax results? In this light, was the deal structured fairly to Mork?

G. SHIFTING BETWEEN C AND S

READ: Code §§ 1362(d)(3), 1368(c) and (e), 1371(b) and (e), 1374, 1375, and 1377(b)

The tax discussion thus far has assumed that any S corporation never was and never will be a C corporation. Special rules apply to corporations that change status.

---

20. Treas. Reg. § 1.1032–1(a)(last sentence).

21. The application of Section 351 in incorporating a partnership was discussed above in Chapter IX of this text.

Matters are fairly simple when an S corporation becomes a C corporation. Section 1371(e) gives the former S corporation time after it loses S status to make tax-free Section 1368(b) distributions of earnings that were earned while the corporation was an S corporation and, thus, were already taxed to the shareholders. Otherwise, as a C corporation, distributions would be ordinary income dividends under Section 301 to the extent of C undistributed earnings.[22] The usual period for making such distributions is one year from the loss of S status. If the IRS determines that a corporation no longer qualifies as an S corporation or that a former S corporation had more S income than reported, however, the corporation also has 120 days from the determination to distribute S earnings before C earnings.

Matters are more involved when a C corporation elects S status. First, as when an S corporation becomes a C corporation, special rules for distributions are needed: Section 1368(c) lets the corporation distributes S earnings before old C earnings. Also, a net operating loss carryforward from a C year cannot be used in an S year under Section 1371(b). After all, there is no entity tax to use the C entity's loss against.

Special policy problems are presented by a C corporation that elects S status. First, such an election can be used to avoid the double tax on gain on a C corporation's assets. Without some sanction, closely-held C corporations about to sell highly appreciated assets could elect S status and turn 2 ordinary income taxes into one capital gains tax.[23] This problem is not present when a C corporation converts to a tax partnership, because, as discussed in Chapter IX of this text, the required liquidation of the C corporation triggers a double tax under Sections 331 and 336. In contrast, there is no tax, per se, on converting from C to S status. To prevent abuse, however, Section 1374 imposes a deferred Section 11 corporate tax on certain gains of an S corporation that was a C corporation in the preceding 10 years.[24] Any gain in the 10–year period is so taxed unless the corporation establishes either (i) that the gain was not built into the sold asset when the corporation elected S status[25] or (ii) that the total gain already taxed under Section 1374 equaled the overall net built-in gain in the corporation's assets at the time that it elected S status.[26] Built-in C losses and corporate NOL carryforwards apply to reduce the Section 1375 tax.[27]

Another potential abuse when a C corporation elects S status also drew Congress' attention: A C corporation could sell its assets and,

---

22. Under Section 1371(c), S earnings do not create earnings and profits that result in a dividend when distributed under Section 301. But, Section 301(c)(1) treats C corporation distributions as coming first out of C earnings and profits, so that, if the former S corporation is profitable, distributions would be taxable but for Section 1371(e).

23. Otherwise, the corporation might have retained C status, preferring a lower current corporate tax under Section 11 than

a higher current tax on its shareholders as an S corporation under Section 1.

24. The taxes under Section 1374 and 1375, discussed below, reduce the income passed through to the shareholders under Section 1366(a). I.R.C. §§ 1366(f)(2), (3).

25. I.R.C. § 1374(d)(3).

26. I.R.C. § 1374(c)(2).

27. I.R.C. §§ 1374(b)(2), (d)(2).

rather than liquidate, elect S status and continue by holding investments (presumably avoiding the personal holding company tax in Section 541). The Section 331 tax would be deferred (by not liquidating) and the corporate tax on the income from the investments would be avoided permanently (by electing S status). Further, if a shareholder then were to die, the Section 1014 basis step-up would eliminate the Section 331 tax permanently. Congress found the possibility of such transactions troubling. It enacted Sections 1362(d)(3) and 1375 in response. Section 1375 imposes a Section 11 tax on the excess net passive income of an S corporation that still has retained C earnings. Excess net passive income is passive income (i) in excess of 25% of gross receipts (ii) reduced by a pro-rata share of the corporation's deductible expenses directly connected to the production of the passive income.[28] Then, if the corporation continues to have retained C earnings and passive income in excess of 25% of gross receipts for 3 consecutive years, the corporation loses its S status by operation of Section 1362(d)(3). Fortunately, Section 1378(e)(3) makes it easier for an S corporation to avoid Sections 1362(d)(3) and 1375 by allowing it to distribute C earnings (taxable dividends) before S earnings.[29]

REVIEW: Code §§ 1362(d)(3), 1368(c) and (e), 1371(b) and (e), 1374, 1375, and 1377(b)

Problem Set XII.G

The MUNI Corporation is a C corporation with the calendar year as its tax year that actively trades municipal bonds. Faye buys 10% of the stock in 2001 for $150,000 (which basis stays the same for the rest of 2001). By the end of 2001, MUNI has $500,000 of accumulated earnings and profits. The corporation properly elects S status for 2002. That status is properly revoked for 2004. In each of 2002, 2003, and 2004, the corporation has $200,000 of exempt Section 103 interest and $200,000 of capital gains. During 2002, MUNI pays total dividends of $400,000 in cash, 10% of which go to Faye. No dividends are paid in 2003. As in 2002, $400,000 of total dividends are paid in 2004. How is Faye taxed with regard to her MUNI stock for 2002 through 2004?

H.   SALE OF STOCK

SKIM: Code §§ 338(a) and (d), 341(a), (b), and (e) and Reg. §§ 1.338(h)(10)–1(a), (b), (c), and (d)(1) through (5)

The sale of stock in an S corporation generally is treated the same as any other sale of stock. Thus, generally, capital gain results. There is nothing in Subchapter S similar to Section 751(a) that recharacterizes gain on the sale of stock in an S corporation that holds ordinary income

---

28. I.R.C. §§ 1375(b)(1)(A), (2).

29. Sections 1362(f) and 1375(d) allow the IRS to waive the tax or termination if the corporation tried to distribute its C earnings in good faith but made a mistake that was corrected in a reasonable period after discovery.

assets as ordinary income. The collapsible corporation rules of Section 341 can trigger ordinary income on the sale of stock of a corporation used to convert ordinary income to capital gain by incorporating ordinary income assets, but a Section 341(f) election avoids the tax and costs little.

There is nothing in Subchapter S that is directly analogous to the adjustment of the inside basis of partnership assets upon a disposition of a partnership interest that is provided by Section 743(b). The closest provision that is applicable to Subchapter S is a Section 338(h)(10) election, which provides an election to treat the sale of 80% of the stock of an S corporation to a buyer corporation as a sale of the S corporation's assets so that the buyer adjusts asset basis.

Index

References are to Pages

225

†